LAOS

LAOS

Buffer State or Battleground

HUGH TOYE

London
OXFORD UNIVERSITY PRESS
NEW YORK   TORONTO   KUALA LUMPUR
1968

Oxford University Press, Ely House, London W.1

GLASGOW NEW YORK TORONTO MELBOURNE WELLINGTON
CAPE TOWN SALISBURY IBADAN NAIROBI LUSAKA ADDIS ABABA
BOMBAY CALCUTTA MADRAS KARACHI LAHORE DACCA
KUALA LUMPUR HONG KONG TOKYO

PRINTED IN GREAT BRITAIN BY
HAZELL WATSON AND VINEY LTD
AYLESBURY, BUCKS

PREFACE

THIS attempt to relate the current problem of Laos to its historical sources originated in the period 1960–2, when I had the good fortune to spend nearly two years there. During this period, perhaps the most critical in recent Laotian history, I was able to observe political and military developments at close quarters, and to make the acquaintance of some of the national leaders. I returned to Europe with a great affection for this lovely land and for its charming people, affection which provided the impetus for a prolonged historical study. Part of the result is set out in the present volume, which was started in the leisure moments of a two-year appointment in Paris and carved into shape during my tenure of the Gwilym Gibbon Research Fellowship at Nuffield College, Oxford, in 1964–5.

My debt to the scholars of Indo-Chinese history, in particular to M. Georges Coedès, Professor D. G. E. Hall, and Mr. Donald Lancaster, will be obvious to those who know their works, even where it is not acknowledged in footnotes. I have been fortunate in the number of friends who have helped me with advice, information, patience, by lending me documents or finding me books, and in the Canadian, British, French, Indian, and Thai colleagues whose knowledge of Laos and sympathetic interest in its people have been a constant encouragement. In particular I thank Mr. John Shattock for the idea of writing about Laos, Dr. Saul Rose and Mr. G. F. Hudson for penetrating criticism and sound counsel, Mr. Stuart Simmonds for his generosity, his expert knowledge, and for allowing me to forget that I can read neither Lao nor Thai, Mr. Tej Bunnag and Mr. Patrick Tuck for contributions from their own research, Mr. Guy Wint and Major General R. E. Lloyd for encouragement, sponsorship, and much forbearance, Mr. J. M. Addis, Major General F. J. C. Piggott, Mr. F. A. Warner, Mr. A. S. B. Olver, Brigadier C. I. V. Jones, Sir Anthony Rumbold, and Mr. W. A. R. Wood for reading and commenting on the typescript in one of its several stages, and my wife for doing so at every stage. I am also most grateful to Miss Julie Savage for doing most of the hard work on the Index.

Translations from the French are my own except where otherwise stated. The spelling of place names follows the pre-war map
Burma, Malaya and Indo-China, published by John Bartholemew,
which is still the best general map available, except where a
different spelling is in current use. Here, and also in dealing with
historical and personal names, my aim has been simplicity and
ease of understanding rather than scrupulous adherence to a system of transliteration. I apologise to Thai and Indo-Chinese
scholars if this has sometimes led me to take liberties with their
history and languages.

Wheatley, Oxon.   HUGH TOYE
    August 1966.

CONTENTS

LIST OF ILLUSTRATIONS

MAPS

ACKNOWLEDGEMENTS

The author acknowledges with thanks the permission he has received to quote extracts from A. J. Dommen, *Conflict in Laos* (Pall Mall Press, London, 1964), W. J. Lederer, *A Nation of Sheep* (Cassell, London, 1961), and Arthur J. Schlesinger, Jnr., *A Thousand Days* (André Deutsch Ltd., London, 1965); and to reproduce photographs from British Army Public Relations Service, GHQ FARELF (Crown Copyright), the Associated Press Ltd., and Éditions Arthaud, Paris.

ABBREVIATIONS

C.D.N.I.	Committee for the Defence of National Interests
C.I.A.	The United States Central Intelligence Agency
D.R.V.N.	Democratic Republic of Vietnam
H.M.S.O.	Her Majesty's Stationery Office
N.L.H.S.	Neo Lao Hak Sat; Laotian left-wing political party
P.E.O.	Programs Evaluation Office; the military section of the United States Operations Mission in Laos from 1958 onwards.
R.I.I.A.	Royal Institute of International Affairs
S.E.A.T.O.	South East Asia Treaty Organization
U.S.I.S.	United States Information Service

Note: British Command Papers are referred to by their Cmd. or Cmnd. numbers after their first appearance.

TO BETTY

INTRODUCTION

FOR over a thousand years the Indo-Chinese peninsula has been the scene of a conflict between the Indian-influenced kingdoms to the south and west of the Annamitic Chain, and the Chinese-influenced Vietnamese, pressing southwards with their colonists from the over-crowded delta of the Red River. It is not so much a matter of cultural differences, manners, and ways of thought, although after a millenium the yawning gulf that lies between the austere and self-contained civilization of China and the tolerant earthiness of Hindu cultures, adds an inevitable measure of mutual dislike to the antique fears and ambitions of thirty generations. It is a matter of land; the need for living space on the one hand and the fear of conquest and extermination on the other.

The historical role of this conflict has long been recognized. Less clearly has it been seen that the ancient quarrel also underlies many of the modern problems of Indo-China. Amongst the most difficult of these problems is that of Laos, a country which has been cast in modern times for the role of neutral buffer state between Siam and the Vietnamese, the old protagonists who are now backed by the two sides in the Cold War. This study of Laos in its contemporary role shows how essential elements of the modern confrontation represent a renewal of the ancient conflict, and how the geographical and ethnic anomalies of Laos as formed under French rule, together with the traditional fears and ambitions of its neighbours, have prevented its establishment as a stable buffer state.

The book is divided into two parts: Part One outlines in two chapters the historical antecedents; Part Two deals with the development of the Laotian question from 1940 to 1964 in six chapters, the last of which considers in conclusion the conflicting interests which will have to be reconciled in a future Laotian settlement.

The long process of Vietnamese expansion southwards from the Red River delta to that of the River Mekong had resulted by the nineteenth century in a confrontation between Siam and the Vietnamese across a neutral buffer zone which stretched along the Annamitic Chain from Dien Bien Phu in the north to Cambodia

in the south. Cambodia paid tribute to both the Siamese king and
the Vietnamese emperor. In the north traditionally neutral hill-
states likewise acknowledged a dual suzerainty. In between lay the
belt of territory bounded by the River Mekong and the Annamitic
mountains; this was partly inhabited by hill peoples whom neither
side had ever been able to subdue and had in part been depopulated as a defensive measure by Siam.

In the second half of the nineteenth century France extended
her empire over Vietnam and, in spite of Siamese opposition, over
the whole of the neutral zone. She based her imperial prosperity
upon the vigour of the Vietnamese who were seven times as
numerous as her Laotian and Cambodian subjects, and it was
naturally in populous Vietnam that the main economic development took place. The logic of geography and population caused
France to see her imperial problems from the Vietnamese point
of view and to rule as a Vietnamese ruler might have done. She
tried to solve the problem of over-population in the Vietnamese
way, encouraged migration from Tongking into the less populous
lands, subordinated the interests of Cambodian and Lao, and took
what France and Vietnam wanted from the Siamese. In consequence the traditional fears, hatreds, and enmities of the Indo-
Chinese peninsula were intensified and the circumstances in which
Laos would one day be called upon to act as a buffer state wer e
prepared.

The second part of the book opens with the French capitulation
to Germany in 1940. Vietnamese nationalists already saw themselves as the natural heirs to French power and Siam was well
aware of the danger which this Vietnamese ambition represented.
The Siamese tried, with Japanese favour, to push their eastern
frontier back to the former neutral zone. Laos gained, as a result
of strong Siamese pressure, the beginnings of a national consciousness which gave rise to an anti-French independence movement
after the Japanese defeat in 1945. It was however a Lao national
consciousness and a Lao independence movement. The hill
peoples of Laos, who made up more than half of its population,
were still kept at arm's length. In 1949 the Independence leaders
chose modified independence under the French rather than co-
operation with the Vietnamese in continued resistance to them.

The Vietnamese rebellion against the French had by this time
turned into the Indo-China War. The Communist leadership of

the rebels, the aid they received after 1949 from the Communist Chinese, and the intervention of Communist China in the Korean War, brought American help to the French in Indo-China and also to Siam, whose fear of a revival of Vietnamese power now began to appear in anti-Communist terms. The settlement of the Indo-China War at Geneva in 1954 and the establishment of a Communist state in North Vietnam led to the formation of S.E.A.T.O., by which the United States and its allies sought to base a firm anti-Communist position on Siam. The old struggle between Siam and the Vietnamese, now coinciding with the world ideological conflict, thus took its place in the Cold War.

Fundamental to the Geneva settlement of 1954 was the concept of a neutral Laos separating pro-Western Siam and the Communist world of North Vietnam and China, on the analogy of the nineteenth-century buffer zone. China exerted pressure on the North Vietnamese to withdraw their troops from Laos on condition that the Americans did not attempt to establish military influence there. Laos undertook to integrate the Pathet Lao movement, which the North Vietnamese had sponsored during the war, into the life of the country and to preserve strict neutrality.

But Laos as formed by the French was not a national entity. Nor was it either geographically or ethnically the same as the nineteenth-century buffer zone. Firstly, the dominant Lao people, while forming less than half of the population in Laos itself, were far out-numbered by the Lao in north-eastern Siam with whom they shared their history, language, and customs. Secondly, the frontier with North Vietnam ran through the territory of the formerly neutral hill peoples. On the Vietnamese side of the border these peoples had been largely conciliated by the subtler racial policies of the Communists; this affected their kinsmen on the Laotian side who resented Lao domination as they had always done. The peoples of Laos were thus much more likely to take the part of one or other of their two neighbours than to unite against them. Unless this tendency to division could be overcome —and it had already been exploited by the Vietnamese in the formation of the predominantly tribal Pathet Lao—Laos could not function satisfactorily as a buffer state.

Everything thus depended on the integration of the Pathet Lao into the Laotian national structure. This was partially achieved in 1957. Amid many misgivings and open Siamese and American disapproval the Pathet Lao was admitted to a government of national union. When, however, it appeared at partial elections in 1958 that the process of integration had already allowed the Pathet Lao to obtain strong political influence throughout the country, the growing apprehensions of Siam and the United States caused the abandonment of the policy of reconciliation. The Pathet Lao resumed their rebellion. By the end of 1959 the United States was hardly less committed on the one side than was North Vietnam on the other. Laos had become a theatre of the Cold War.

As the issue was joined, Siam needed strong friends in Laos, the United States needed anti-Communist ones. With Marshal Sarit master of Siam, who could be more suitable for both roles than Sarit's kinsman Phoumi Nosavan? With General Phoumi rising to power, Siamese interests seemed secure against Vietnam, as well as those of the United States against Communism. Early in 1960 the General rigged the elections and emerged as virtual dictator of Laos.

There followed the neutralist *coup d'état* of August 1960. A month later Prince Souvannaphouma, who had negotiated the agreement with the Pathet Lao in 1957, began another attempt to create national unity. If the Siamese had been nervous in 1958, they were now thoroughly alarmed. Phoumi overthrew the prince's government with Siamese and American help. Russia came to the aid of the Neutralists. In the ensuing civil war the Neutralists, in alliance with the Pathet Lao who were more strongly backed than ever by the North Vietnamese, took control of most of the Laotian hill country. Phoumi's forces appeared incapable of stopping them. A cease-fire was arranged and a new Geneva Conference was convened in May 1961.

The attempt to achieve a settlement of the Laotian question by international agreement in 1961–2 appeared at first to have some hope of success. When the newly elected President Kennedy met Mr. Khrushchev at Vienna in June 1961, the two statesmen agreed that Laos should be neutral ground between them; none of the great powers wanted to fight a war over Laos. The acceptance of Laotian neutralism by the United States, however, redoubled the fears of Siam, who saw a neutral Laos as no barrier to the approach of Vietnamese power. In spite of all American diplomacy could do, it was not until June 1962, when S.E.A.T.O.

forces had been deployed on the Mekong as the ultimate reassurance for the Siamese, that General Phoumi could be induced to accept a neutralist régime. By this time the development of the Sino-Soviet dispute and of the war in South Vietnam had gravely prejudiced the prospects of the international settlement which had for months only awaited formal and unanimous Laotian assent.

The essentials of the Geneva bargain of 1962 were not dissimilar from those of the 1954 agreement in so far as they concerned Laos. Externally, the condition was that American and Vietnamese troops should be removed from the country. Internally the three factions needed to be kept in careful balance as they progressed towards integration. Neither of these conditions could be kept. On the one hand the North Vietnamese involvement in the South Vietnamese war had now reached a point where Laotian territory held by the Pathet Lao was constantly used for the passage of reinforcements from North to South Vietnam. This traffic was excluded by the 1962 settlement and its continuance was quite unacceptable to the United States. On the other hand the Soviet Union, in the stress of the dispute with the Chinese, terminated the airlift to the Neutralist forces which had enabled them to remain independent of the two extremes. Under the competitive pressures of left and right the Neutralist position crumbled. The coalition broke up. Partition by altitude, along much the same contour line of ethnic division that had limited direct Siamese authority before the coming of the French, was an accomplished fact in 1964 as in 1961.

The problem of Laos is for the moment overshadowed by the war in Vietnam. When that war is ended it seems likely that another attempt at a Laotian solution will be necessary. The book concludes with tentative definitions of the Siamese and Vietnamese interests which will have to be reconciled if a lasting settlement is to be achieved.

PART ONE

THE HISTORICAL ANTECEDENTS

CHAPTER I

Vietnam and the Indian-influenced States of Indo-China

When the Geneva Conference of 1954 sought to end the war in French Indo-China, one of the basic assumptions made was that Laos would become a neutral buffer between non-Communist Thailand and Communist North Vietnam, and so help to prevent the clash between the Western world and the Communist bloc which appeared imminent. In the following seven years it proved impossible to secure the internal stability in Laos which was essential for its role as a buffer state. At the end of 1960 a civil war broke out in which factions in the country were favoured by Thailand and North Vietnam, backed respectively by the United States and the Soviet bloc. There followed a second Geneva Conference, which tried to establish the neutrality of Laos by international guarantee. This attempt also failed and Laos lapsed into a *de facto* partition between two groups supported on each side by the world power blocs.

The failure of Laos to act as a buffer state arose partly from divisions among its own people. Partly it sprang from political developments in the Indo-Chinese peninsula under French rule and during its decline. But before these matters can properly be examined it is relevant to ask why there should be a buffer state in this area at all. The answer to this question is not to be found simply in the modern ideological conflict. The roots of the problem lie in a deep mistrust between the Thai and Vietnamese peoples which has ancient historical origins.

The Ancient Quarrel[1]

Two thousand years ago Chinese imperial power extended
southwards along the Indo-Chinese coast well beyond the seventeenth parallel. In 111 B.C. China had annexed the independent
kingdom of Vietnam, then centred in the lower valley of the Red
River, where it was cut off from the River Mekong valley to the
south-west by the formidable mountains of the Annamitic Chain.
South of the Chinese borders were the Chams. The Mekong
delta was inhabited by the Khmers, the Menam valley and lower
Burma by their close relatives, the Mons. These non-Chinese
peoples possessed a common civilization which they shared with
the coastal and valley communities of Malaya and Indonesia.

In the early centuries of our era Indian influences, customs, and
culture flooded into this little world. The reasons for and the
manner of their arrival are a matter of debate, but that they did
arrive is beyond dispute. Throughout the region, in what is now
Indonesia, Burma, Malaya, Thailand, and the states of Indo-
China, kingdoms arose which practised Indian religion, arts, and
customs and whose sacred language was Sanskrit.

The earliest of these states of which we know emerged some-
where about A.D. 100 in the Mekong delta. The Chinese called it
Funan. At its zenith Funan stretched from the Kra Isthmus in
the west to Camranh Bay in the east. Beside it on the coast to the
north grew up the kingdom of Champa, founded in A.D. 192 when
a local official rebelled against his Chinese masters in what was
then the southernmost province of the empire of China.

The virile, aggressive Chams eventually spread as far south as
the Mekong delta and westwards into the middle Mekong valley.
From the first, however, they were at odds with the Vietnamese,
their even more vigorous neighbours to the north, whose sophisti-
cated Chinese culture must have contrasted sharply with their
own Indian manners.[2] In A.D. 939 the Vietnamese threw off the
yoke of China and took up the conflict with the Chams on their
own account. For Vietnam it was a matter of land, of population

---

[1] The principal authorities used for the early history of Indo-China are:
D. G. E. Hall, *A History of South-East Asia* (London, 2nd edn., 1964),
G. Coedès, *Les états hindouisés d'Indochine et d'Indonésie* (Paris, new edn.,
1964), and L. P. Briggs, *The Ancient Khmer Empire* (Philadelphia, 1951).

[2] The struggle 'in its cultural aspect represented a struggle between
Chinese and Indian influence'. Hall, op. cit. (1st edn.), p. 186.

pressure from Chinese immigration and from her own fecundity.[3] The struggle went on for five more centuries up and down the narrow plain between the Annamitic Chain and the sea. Bit by bit the Chams were ousted or absorbed and their lands settled by the teeming Vietnamese.

Far back in the sixth century, meanwhile, Funan had given place to the kingdom which the Chinese called Chen La, from whose ruins there emerged three hundred years later the Indianized Khmer kingdom of Cambodia. The Khmer empire and its great capital of Angkor reached their zenith in the twelfth century when the Cambodians ruled not only the coastal provinces of Funan but also the hinterland, the Menam and Mekong valleys as far to the north and east as the Annamitic Chain. Early in the thirteenth century, however, Khmer power began to give way to that of the Thai peoples who, pushed in their turn by Chinese pressure, were now moving into this area from the north and north-west.

The Thais had hitherto figured in Champa and at Angkor as prisoners of war, slaves, or barbarian allies from the outer fringes of civilization. Syams, they were called, the name of the Thai group which was settling in the north of the Menam basin. The great bas-reliefs at Angkor Wat show a detachment of them in the Khmer army, their curious dress and unmilitary appearance contrasting sharply with that of the business-like Khmer legionaries. The Chinese had known this ancient people as early as the sixth century B.C. Chinese records often refer to them as the barbarian folk south of the Yangtse River. They were to be found near Lake Tali in Yunnan, across that great upland where the Red River, the Mekong, the Salween, and even the Irrawaddy, flowing close by on neighbouring courses, gave easy access for their raiders to the rich deltas of Burma and Indo-China.

The Thais came under Chinese suzerainty early in the Christian era but made many attempts to assert their independence and never received the stamp of Chinese civilization that so marked the Vietnamese. In the ninth century they twice raided China by way of the Yangtse valley, raged down the Red River to sack Hanoi, and even conquered parts of the Irrawaddy delta. As time went on small groups of them settled among the Khmers, Mons, and

[3] Charles Robequain, *The Economic Development of French Indo-China* (London, 1944), pp. 34–35.

Burmese. At the end of the eleventh century the Thai-Syam state of P'ayao appeared between the Mekong and Menam rivers in the far north of modern Thailand. While raiders still ranged far and wide, other Thai settlements to the south and west of Lake Tali began to form themselves into new independent states, among them the twelve Thai-Lu states known as the Sipsong Panna.

Unlike the southward drive of the Vietnamese, the spread of Thai rule did not involve large movements of population any more than did the Norman invasion of England or the growth of the Khmer empire. What happened was that, after a certain amount of Thai settlement, a Thai ruling class seized power in the centres concerned and a restricted Thai middle class followed. The original inhabitants adopted the language and some of the customs of the new rulers; intermarriage blunted still further the edges of racial difference and gave the new states ethnic as well as political reality. The further south conquest and assimilation went, the larger were the indigenous populations encountered, and the weaker the Thai ethnic element in the resultant mixture. Hence, in part, the difference today between the Thai of Bangkok, the Lao of Laos and north-east Siam, and the hill-Thai of the Laos-Vietnam border.

The process was not always peaceful, but few battles are recorded. In its story of the origins of the Sipsong Panna, the chronicle of the pagoda of Chom Yong in the eastern Shan States gives an example of the sort of thing that may have occurred.[4] It tells of Phya Ngam, chief king of a group of seven non-Thai kingdoms on the upper Mekong. There were Thai communities in several of these kingdoms but they were subject to the non-Thai rulers whom they called Khas. One day the ruler of the Thai state of Xieng Hong who was also subject to the Khas, called together his four sons. 'The Khas are our masters', he said, 'it is shameful for us to suffer their yoke.' Sonanta, his second son, replied, 'Give me five hundred men and I will deliver you.' Sonanta took the five hundred men and with them offered his services to Phya Ngam. He was welcomed and allowed to build a fortified settlement of his own where, from time to time, Phya Ngam would visit him. At length he invited the king and his suite to a great dinner. Three sorts of wine were served, the first one good, the second strong, the third poisoned. 'The whole country

4 F. Garnier, *Voyage d'exploration en Indochine* (Paris, 1885), p. 400.

was subdued', says the chronicler. The ruler of Xieng Hong sent his other three sons to govern neighbouring princedoms.

Early in the thirteenth century the Mongols began their conquest of China. A great surge southwards of Thai migration followed. In the Menam valley two Thai-Syam chiefs combined to defeat the Khmer regional commander and established the kingdom of Sukhothai. Fresh impetus came from the Mongol annexation of Tali in 1255. Thai-Shan princedoms took over much of the territory of the Pagan kingdom of Burma, overthrown by Kublai Khan in 1287. Thai-Lao princes came southwards to Luang Prabang[5] in the Mekong valley. The Thai prince of Xieng Sen pushed steadily against the Mons on the upper Menam and in 1297 founded Chiengmai.

Meanwhile Sukhothai, which had absorbed much Khmer territory to the south and east, began to decline. In the middle of the fourteenth century power passed to two new kingdoms, the Thai-Syam kingdom of Ayuthia on the lower Menam, and the Thai-Lao kingdom centred at Luang Prabang, forerunners of the modern states of Thailand and Laos.[6]

The Thais have been called the world's best diplomats. Certainly they are marvellous assimilators, for they have the graceful gift of making the manners or culture they borrow appear to arise out of their own genius. At Sukhothai they had had easy access to the capitals of their neighbours, the Mons and the Khmers, and it was here between A.D. 1250 and 1350 that the characteristics of Siamese civilization had been elaborated. From Cambodia, says Coedès:[7]

The Siamese assimilated political organisation, way of life, writing and a great many words. Siamese artists learnt what the Khmer artists had to teach them and transformed it according to their own genius, under the strong influence of their western neighbours, the Mons and the

[5] The modern name, which dates only from the sixteenth century, is here used to avoid complication. For a discussion of the town's various names see: G. Coedès: 'A propos des anciens noms de Luang Prabang', in *Bulletin de l'école française d'extrême orient*, XVIII (1918), pp. 9–11.

[6] Again, although the ancient kingdom was called Lan Xang, the modern word Laos is used throughout. To avoid confusion with the generic sense of the word *Thai*, *Siamese* and *Siam* are used for the Thai people of the lower Menam valley and for their country, which is now called Thailand.

[7] Op. cit., pp. 402–3.

Burmese. From the latter the Siamese took their legal traditions, of Indian origin, and also Ceylonese [Theravada] Buddhism together with its artistic traditions.

Meanwhile, of course, other Thai peoples continued to inhabit the upland regions of Yunnan and Tongking from which the Siamese had come, their character being moulded somewhat differently over the centuries by the influence of their Chinese and Vietnamese neighbours.[8]

As they learnt so the Siamese fought. From Ayuthia their pressure on the Khmers continued until the great walled city of Angkor Thom was besieged and sacked in 1431. As soon as the Siamese had departed the Khmer crown prince procured the assassination of the Siamese governor and was crowned in the ruined capital. Angkor was however no longer considered a safe centre for the kingdom; it was evacuated in 1432, the Khmer court moving eventually in 1434 to Phnom Penh which is again the Cambodian capital today.

Over the next hundred years peace between Siam and Cambodia never lasted long. The Siamese raided a passive Cambodia at intervals until 1540. During most of the four decades which followed Siam was fighting for her life against the Burmese conqueror, Bayinnaung. Cambodia took her revenge, carrying the war again and again deep into Siam. The Siamese recovered after the death of their Burmese oppressor in 1580 and from 1594 there was a Siamese garrison in the Cambodian capital. The weakening of Siam in the early seventeenth century led the Cambodians to reassert themselves and fight off a Siamese invasion in 1622. Siam nevertheless continued to look to the borders of Cambodia for booty, and for slaves to satisfy the continued demand for labour in her vast under-populated lands. Unlike the Vietnamese, the Siamese did not colonize: they never had the people to spare.

The Vietnamese, having long ago extinguished all but the name of freedom in Champa, were by now also encroaching upon Cambodia, using the methods of forceful colonization they had employed against the Chams:

Exiles, deserters and other vagabonds infiltrated into the country. In time their numbers enabled them to form colonies, the inevitable

[8] See L. P. Briggs 'The Appearance and Historical Usage of the terms Tai, Thai, Siamese and Lao', in *Journal of the American Oriental Society*, 1949, p. 61.

prelude to annexation. Thus in 1658 the provincial governor of Tran-bien occupied the colony of Moi-Xui under the pretext that the King of Cambodia had violated the Vietnamese frontier. When King Ang Chan resorted to arms he was defeated and captured and sent in a cage to Hué. There, on paying homage as a vassal, he was liberated and escorted back to his capital. His two brothers, however, refused to accept the situation and set themselves up as joint kings. In 1673 the inevitable succession dispute gave the Vietnamese an opportunity to intervene effectively and install two tributary rulers, one as king at Udong [the latest Cambodian capital], and the other as second king at Saigon.[9]

Before the end of the seventeenth century Cambodia was once more under Vietnamese suzerainty after a brief reassertion of Siamese influence, but in 1714 a further succession dispute brought the Siamese back again. Thus, in the ancient conflict of Chinese-influenced Vietnam with the Indianized peoples, the first clash had occurred with Siam.

There had been a clash of equal moment a little earlier in the kingdom of Laos. In 1700 a pretender who had promised homage to the Vietnamese was placed by Vietnamese arms on the Laotian throne. Although the kingdom now broke into three, the portion which remained under Vietnamese suzerainty far outflanked the Siamese in Cambodia. The power of Vietnam had crossed the Annamitic Chain and reached the Siamese frontier.

The Kingdom of Laos

To understand how the situation had arisen and the nature of the conflict that now existed in Laos, it is necessary to trace in outline the history of the Laotian kingdom from the time when it emerged from legend as a confederation of Thai-Lao states in the fourteenth century.[10] Tradition says that the Lao people origin-ated in the valley of Dien Bien Phu, whence part of them migrated to Luang Prabang, driving the earlier inhabitants, who came to be

[9] Hall, op. cit. (2nd edn.), p. 399. Robequain, op. cit., p. 65, also discusses what is known of the process of Vietnamese colonization.

[10] The only existing history of Laos is: P. Le Boulanger, *Histoire du Laos français* (Paris, 1931), which is based on Laotian annals, some of which are available in *Mission Pavie, études diverses*, vol. II (Paris, 1898). Mahasila Viravong's *History of Laos* (U.S. Joint Publications Research Service, 1958) is a collection of documentary material but not a systematic history.

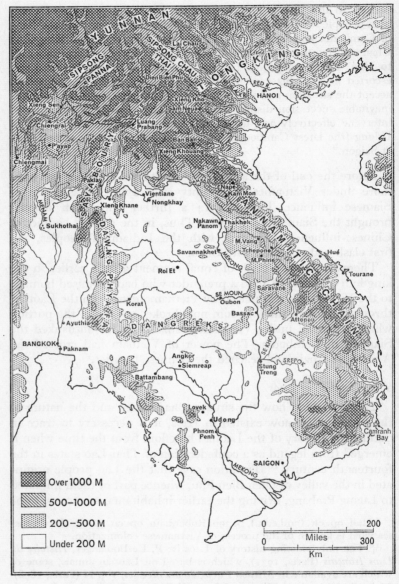

Indo-China, Relief and History.

known as Khas,[11] into the hills. This movement was probably historical and it could well have taken place in the eleventh century or perhaps earlier. The Lao princes of Luang Prabang became vassals of Cambodia and their state part of the Indianized civilization of the Khmers. Before the fourteenth century began their allegiance had been transferred to Sukhothai. When, however, the power of Sukhothai was fading, the Lao prince Fa Ngum, who was in exile at Angkor, obtained from the Cambodians the military backing he needed to displace his grandfather as king of Luang Prabang. This he did in 1353,[12] forming a wide confederation of Lao states in the Mekong valley and temporarily restoring Cambodian influence there. With him there came from Cambodia Theravada Buddhism, which had already been adopted by the Siamese, and the Prabang, a sacred golden Buddha of reputed Ceylonese origin, which, in the sixteenth century gave the Laotian capital its modern name, and which became the palladium of the kingdom.

The authority of King Fa Ngum extended over the Sipsong Panna[13] on the upper Mekong, the Sipsong Chau Thai[14] on the Black River, the mountain state of Xieng Khouang, Muong Phoueun as it was called, and thence southwards to the borders of Cambodia. His frontier with the Vietnamese to the east ran along the watershed of the Annamitic Chain down to the high plateaux in the south, whose unconquered Kha tribesmen effectively insulated him from the Chams. He took possession of the Korat Plateau, perhaps originally to help the Khmers repulse an expedi-

[11] *Kha* is a Lao term applied to these peoples but not used by them. It means *slave* and is used here for convenience only. The same people are known in South Vietnam as *Moi*. A modern term recently introduced by the Lao is *Lao Theung* or *Lao of the mountains and forests*. While socially less opprobrious this is ethnically misleading.

[12] Coedès, op. cit., p. 405 points out that the details of Fa Ngum's conquests are based only on the Laotian annals which cannot be accepted without reserve. However, this date is supported by a Sukhothai inscription, which cannot be dated earlier than 1359, mentioning Fa Ngum as Sukhothai's neighbour on the Mekong (ibid., p. 407).

[13] Sometimes translated 'land of the twelve thousand ricefields', *sipsong* meaning *twelve*, and *pan na* a unit of measurement for ricefields. In fact, however, *panna* is generally interpreted as *cantons* and the Sipsong Panna did consist of twelve cantons.

[14] The twelve Thai cantons, an area centred on the Black River valley.

tion from Siam; Chiengmai to the west was his vassal; even
Ayuthia may have sent him tribute.

The successors of Fa Ngum up to the middle of the sixteenth
century were men of peace and the full extent of Laotian power
was not maintained. Chiengmai was quickly lost, while Xieng
Khouang and the Sipsong Chau Thai soon came to owe a partial
allegiance to Vietnam. For the most part, however, the greater
powers of Indo-China—Siam, Cambodia, Champa, and Vietnam—
were sufficiently embroiled among themselves. Laos was remote,
comparatively poor, and fraught with perils for the stranger.
The one occasion when its tranquillity was seriously disturbed
from outside, by the Vietnamese in 1479, is the more worth
studying.

In 1400 a usurper had seized the throne of Vietnam and the
deposed dynasty had appealed to China. The Chinese occupied
the Vietnamese capital, Hanoi, and ousted the interloper; but they
soon made it clear that they intended to stay, attempting for instance to force their language on the country. The Vietnamese
found this oppressive and in 1418 began to resist. Three years
later Luang Prabang offered to help, but hardly had the substantial Laotian force arrived than it changed sides and joined the
Chinese. The Vietnamese nevertheless won their war and a new
dynasty was founded by the victorious leader.

It was not until their decisive victory over Champa in 1471 that
the Vietnamese chose to recall the treachery of the Laotians—so
at least runs the story. By 1478 they appear to have been waiting
for an excuse to attack. The occasion for their expedition of the
following year is said to have been an unsatisfied request to the
Laotians for a white elephant.[15] The invaders had to travel some
three hundred miles, much of it across the broadest part of the
Annamitic Chain, difficult country and short of supplies. Perhaps
for this reason they came by three routes, assembling in Xieng
Khouang, at Xieng Kho on the borders of modern Sam Neua,
and in the Sipsong Chau Thai. When all was ready they converged
on Luang Prabang along the same valleys that the Viet Minh
invaders of Laos used in 1953 and 1954. A bitter fight ensued;

[15] For the significance of the white elephant in the Indianized states see
Guy Wint, *The British in Asia* (London, 1947), p. 92. The Vietnamese,
however, had no traditional regard for white elephants; if mentioned, it
was a mere excuse.

the Laotians were beaten and the king fled down-river with the debris of his army.[16]

According to the Laotian annals the king's son rallied the fugitives and drove the enemy from the Mekong valley, but it seems more probable that the Vietnamese withdrew of their own accord after sacking Luang Prabang. This was until recently one of the most malarial places in Indo-China[17] and it could not have been easy to maintain an army there. Malaria too may account partly for the Laotian tradition of heavy Vietnamese casualties on the way home. The speedy restoration of relations with Vietnam and the swift Laotian recovery from total defeat argue that the expedition had been essentially punitive, possibly originating in some frontier or trading dispute and designed to inspire respect.

However that may be, no action at all would have been possible for Vietnam without the connivance or coercion of states like Xieng Khouang and the Sipsong Chau Thai, whose neutrality between their two more powerful neighbours was now becoming traditional. Their rulers married princesses from both sides of the mountains. Sometimes they paid tribute in one direction, usually in both. This is understandable from all three points of view. Firstly, the mountain states depended on their neighbours for basic necessities such as salt. Secondly, to the Vietnamese in the plains of Tongking, the mountains of Xieng Khouang and the Sipsong Chau Thai could be seen as the dominating heights to the south-west and west, the natural refuge of bandits preying on the prosperous plainsmen and their trade. To the land-bound kingdom of Laos, on the other hand, the passes through these same hills were the trade-routes to Vietnam and the sea, and the gateway to the kingdom for an invader. Furthermore, he who controlled Xieng Khouang could menace trade and communications on the Mekong, which was the central highway of the whole Laotian country.

Both Laos and Vietnam therefore had legitimate interests in the neutrality and co-operation of the mountain states, who in turn

---

[16] Le Boulanger, op. cit., p. 66 and *Mission Pavie, études diverses*, II, pp. 50–51 are clear as to the fall of Luang Prabang after a bitter battle.

[17] In 1941, before the introduction of anti-malarial prophylactic drugs, French troops in Luang Prabang had an annual hospitalization rate from malaria of 317 per cent.

needed both their neighbours. The highland princes made the most of their position. Considering themselves too weak to maintain absolute independence, they established themselves by alliances and marriages in a balancing position between the two, so preserving their individuality and prerogatives of government.

The damage done by the Vietnamese attack on Luang Prabang was soon restored and the city quickly recovered its influence over the upper Mekong states. The episode had however been a most unpleasant experience and it undoubtedly played its part in the renewal of close relations between Laos and Siam that now took place. The long reign of the great Siamese King Trilok[18] (1448–88) was drawing to a close. Trilok had created for his kingdom a strong, centralized social and administrative organization which was to last unchanged into the nineteenth century. The development could not but have its effect on other states of common origin, including Laos, whose attention was in any case turning southwards because of the demands of European traders, now arriving on the coasts, for the gumlac and benzoin it produced. The king began to spend part of each year in Vientiane. Then in 1558 the Burmese conqueror, Bayinnaung, occupied Chiengmai, thus threatening both Luang Prabang and Ayuthia. The Laotian warrior king, Setthathirat, having failed to dislodge him, thereupon entered into an alliance with Siam and in 1563 transferred his capital to Vientiane where he would be safer from Burmese attack.

Bayinnaung moved against Ayuthia in 1564. The city surrendered and the Burmese army returned north to chastise Chiengmai for its attitude after the Burmese had left it earlier in the campaign. The ruler of Chiengmai fled to Vientiane and the Burmese followed. Setthathirat's new capital was not yet fortified. The Laotian king slipped away to the east, raised the countryside against the invaders and so harassed them that in 1565, at the height of the rains, they made for home. The Siamese immediately tried, with Setthathirat's help, to recover their independence, but Bayinnaung returned in 1568, sacked Ayuthia, demolished its walls, and deported its population. The Burmese punitive expedition against Vientiane nevertheless failed, and in 1571 Setthathirat marched southwards against Cambodia, who had been taking her

---

[18] Boromo Trailokanat. See Hall, op. cit., pp. 168–9, for a summary of his reforms.

From B. P. Groslier, *Angkor, hommes et pierres* (Arthaud, Paris, 1956)

Angkor Wat: 'Syams' in the army of King Suryavarman II

From F. Garnier, *Voyage d'exploration en Indochine*, Paris, 1885

The passage of a rapid

From F. Garnier, *Voyage d'exploration en Indochine*, Paris, 1885

The Nam Khane at Luang Prabang in 1867

revenge for past humiliations by raiding his prostrate ally, Siam.[19].

This campaign was Setthathirat's last. He seems to have made little impression on the Cambodians and on his way home he mysteriously disappeared, possibly in the course of a foray against the still unconquered Khas of the southern highlands.[20] Laos went through a period of Burmese domination and anarchy which lasted until the accession of Setthathirat's son, permitted by the failing power of Burma in 1592.

The seventeenth century saw the golden age of Laos under King Souligna Vongsa, whose court was visited by Dutch traders and Portuguese missionaries between 1641 and 1647. Vientiane was a proud city, Souligna Vongsa a stern king who made his name respected at home and abroad. Perhaps for this reason his relations with his neighbours in his early years were not always harmonious. The European accounts speak of a Siamese embassy received with great suspicion, of a rupture of relations with Vietnam, and of rumours of war with Cambodia. The king acknowledged no superior: 'there is not a monarch in existence, however powerful, that he does not consider to be beneath him'.[21]

As time went on Souligna Vongsa's relations with his neighbours improved and he was able to re-define his frontiers with Siam and Vietnam. South of the Sipsong Chau Thai and Xieng Khouang, which continued to pay tribute to both Vietnam and Laos, the frontier with Vietnam still followed the Annamitic Chain as far as the broad central highlands which neither side could penetrate. In doubtful areas where the watershed was hard to distinguish,

[19] G. Maspéro, *L'Indochine* (Paris, 1929), vol. I, p. 116, mentions this expedition and says that it was beaten off by the Cambodians. B. P. Groslier, *Angkor et le Cambodge au XVIème siècle* (Paris, 1958), pp. 15–16, finds support in the Cambodian annals but wrongly quotes Le Boulanger as saying that the Laotian annals confirm.

[20] Le Boulanger, op. cit., p. 90 says that he disappeared after having decided to abandon an unsuccessful campaign against the Khas.

[21] P. Levy, 'Two accounts of travels in Laos in the seventeenth century', in De Berval (ed.), *Kingdom of Laos* (Saigon, 1959), pp. 66–67. The Manchus were ousting the Mings in China at this time. It may therefore have been true, as the missionaries assert, that the king did not acknowledge Chinese suzerainty for the moment. This was not normal. Both Vietnam and Luang Prabang held seals bestowed on them by China as a token of authority. The camel seal of Luang Prabang, received from the Manchus in exchange for that held from the Mings, can still be seen in the royal palace today.

it was agreed that people who built their houses on stilts and with verandahs were to be considered Laotian and the rest subjects of Vietnam. The distinction might have been drawn in other ways, for the difference is one of culture rather than of race. Those who ate long-grained rice with chop-sticks and ornamented their houses with dragons belonged to the Chinese-influenced civilization of Vietnam although their language might be closely akin to Lao; those who ate glutinous rice with their fingers, and decorated their houses with serpents, were part of the Indian-influenced civilization of Laos, Cambodia, and Siam.

The frontier agreed by Setthathirat with Siam in 1560 was re-affirmed by Souligna Vongsa. From the northernmost limits of Siamese power in the Menam valley, it ran north and south along the Dawng Phya Fa hills between the Menam and Mekong basins, perhaps as far south as Korat. In the south the provinces of Bassac, Attopeu, and Saravane were already Laotian and the boundary with Cambodia was at the waterfalls of Khone[22] where it remains today.

The end of Souligna Vongsa's reign was marred by tragedy. The crown prince, the king's only son, seduced the wife of the chief of the palace pages. The king insisted on his trial and execution according to law.[23] In 1694, therefore, when Souligna Vongsa died, there was no crown prince and the king's two grandsons were too young to succeed him. There followed a period of disorder which in 1700 permitted the dead king's nephew, the son of a brother who had taken refuge at the Vietnamese court, to seize the throne with the help of a Vietnamese army. This brought Laos under the suzerainty of Vietnam. Souligna Vongsa's grandsons had, however, escaped to Luang Prabang where in 1707 they proclaimed their independence; the new king in Vientiane was never able to dispute this and Luang Prabang thus evaded Vietnamese dominance. Six years later the princedom of Bassac also broke away, to pass thereafter more and more under the influence of Siam. What remained was the kingdom of Vientiane, the great expanse of middle Laos from the Annamitic Chain to the Dawng Phya Fa hills. The richest and most populous part of the country, including the great plain that is today north-eastern Siam, now owed allegiance to Vietnam.

[22] Noted by Van Wusthoff: P. Levy, loc. cit.
[23] Le Boulanger, op. cit., p. 129.

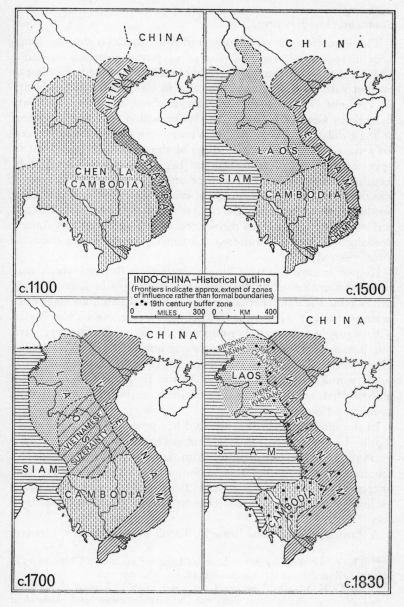

INDO-CHINA – Historical Outline
(Frontiers indicate approx. extent of zones of influence rather than formal boundaries)
••• 19th century buffer zone
MILES   300   0   KM   400

Siam and the Vietnamese

The extension of Vietnamese influence to the Vientiane kingdom materially altered the pattern of power relations in Indo-
China. At the very time when Siamese interests were beginning to
conflict with those of the Vietnamese in Cambodia, the authority
of Vietnam had reached the Siamese frontier. The immediate
struggle in Cambodia, where the reimposition of Siamese control
in 1714 did not halt the tide of Vietnamese colonization, masked
for a time the significance to Siam of the change in Laos. But in
1753 another Burmese conqueror began to make himself felt.
Ayuthia was again under Burmese attack in 1760 and in 1767 it
was destroyed. Instead of helping Siam as Setthathirat had done
two hundred years earlier, the ruler of Vientiane sided with Burma,
and when in 1771 he was threatened with punishment by Luang
Prabang who had also suffered a Burmese occupation, a Burmese
force rescued him.

Helped meanwhile by Chinese attacks on Burma, which may
have been prompted by the Burmese campaigns in Laos,[24] Siam
had regained her independence under Phya Taksin, and was once
more embroiled with the encroaching Vietnamese in Cambodia.
This struggle was again coming to a climax when, in 1773, civil
war broke out in Vietnam. It was not until after the Vietnamese
Prince Nguyen Anh had, with French assistance, reconquered the
country and established himself as the Emperor Gia Long of a
unified Vietnam in 1802, that Siamese authority in Cambodia
could be seriously challenged.

In the interval Siam consolidated her power. Having decisively
repulsed a new series of Burmese invasions, she occupied Vientiane
in 1778 and exacted tribute from Luang Prabang. Whatever
the immediate cause of this action, and on this there is some
uncertainty, the plain fact was that Siam could not afford
to leave the Laotian states free to co-operate with her major
enemies.[25]

A domestic revolt now brought Siam's leading soldier, General

[24] The renewal of regular tribute by Luang Prabang to China in 1734
is recorded in the annals: Le Boulanger, op. cit., pp. 190–1.
[25] See D. K. Wyatt, 'Siam and Laos, 1767–1827' in *Journal of Southeast
Asian History*, September 1963, an admirably clear and consistent
reconciliation of the available material on this complicated period.

Chakri,[26] founder of the present royal dynasty, to the throne. The reign of King Rama I, as he was called, was to see another great struggle with Burma and the annexation by Siam of much of western Cambodia. By the time Rama I died in 1809 the foundations of Siamese strength were firmly laid.

To the east, however, the power of Vietnam had revived. Cambodia, her territory greatly reduced, was already paying tribute to both her neighbours, and in 1806 the Laotian Prince Anou, whose family King Rama had restored to rule Vientiane in 1782, formally renewed his kingdom's homage to Vietnam. There had been an embassy to Hué with a letter which read somewhat as follows:

Vientiane has long been the vassal of Vietnam and used to pay tribute every three years. The revolt of the Tayson [i.e. the Vietnamese civil war] forced it into submission to the Siamese who are illtreating its people. Today the prince of Vientiane, seeing the power and fame of the Emperor Gia Long, asks to be allowed once more to be the servant of Vietnam and to pay tribute as in the past.[27]

Gia Long showed great interest, acknowledged Vientiane formally as a vassal, agreed to a triennial tribute, and sent back the embassy loaded with presents.

This curious transaction was not necessarily detrimental to Siamese suzerainty over Vientiane. It was accepted that the rulers of small states placed between powerful neighbours might pay tribute in more than one direction, although a suzerain would make his authority predominate if he could. The Siamese would refer to a vassal owing a dual allegiance as a 'bird with two heads';[28] similarly the towns of the neutral Sipsong Chau Thai were sometimes called 'the towns on the two sides of the sky'.[29] Siam's influence over Vientiane was, however, still stronger than that of Vietnam and she made no particular issue of Prince Anou's action.

In 1812, after a few years in which the power of Siam and Vietnam had been precariously balanced in Cambodia, Siam intervened to support a pretender to the Cambodian throne and the king

[26] He was Taksin's *chakri*, i.e. military commander, and turned the title into the name of a dynasty.

[27] Le Boulanger, op. cit., p. 161.

[28] This phrase and the general view of Siamese policy as pragmatic and defence-orientated, I owe to Mr. E. H. S. Simmonds' reading of Siamese records of the period.

[29] See Prince Damrong Rachanuphap, *A Collection of Chronicles* (Prachum Pongsawadan), Part XXIV (Bangkok, 1924), p. 2.

fled to Saigon. Vietnam reinstated him in the following year with a Vietnamese garrison. Siam then seized a broad band of Cambodian territory south of the Dangrek mountains, which included the province of Stung Treng east of the Mekong. This, together with the existing vassal state of Bassac, constituted a thick wedge of Siamese territory between the ruler of Vientiane and his Vietnamese allies in Cambodia.

Prince Anou appears in fact to have been cherishing ideas of independence. In 1819 his services in stifling a Kha revolt in the south won from the Siamese the governorship of Bassac for his son. At Anou's instigation the son proceeded to fortify Oubon, which lies fifty miles from Bassac in the direction of Bangkok,[30] and to raise troops there. Anou claimed that this would help in the defence of Siam, but the Siamese who saw no danger in this particular area can hardly have believed him. The prince also sent emissaries to Luang Prabang proposing a secret alliance against Siam. He himself maintained a considerable court and Vientiane recovered something of its former glory. At length in 1827, perhaps believing a rumour that the British, after their victory in the first Burma War, were about to attack Siam, Anou marched on Bangkok from Oubon and Vientiane.[31] The Siamese gathered their forces, defeated the rebel and once more occupied his capital.

Prince Anou escaped and, when his efforts to drum up support from his Laotian allies had failed, he took refuge at the court of Vietnam. The king of Siam had just written to the emperor pointing out that Anou owed allegiance to them both and threatening invasion if Vietnam supported him. However, a suzerain had certain obligations to his vassal. The emperor solved the difficulty by giving Anou two companies of soldiers for the journey only. They were to return after installing him in Vientiane.[32]

In these circumstances Anou's cause was hopeless. After another defeat near Vientiane in 1829 he was intercepted by Prince Noi of Xieng Khouang when on his way to China, and handed over to Siam. He died in Bangkok a few years later. For having delivered

[30] The new capital of Siam since the accession of Rama I.
[31] So Prince Phanuphantuvongswardja in *Répression de la révolte de Vientiane* (Bangkok, 1926), whose account is supported by the Vietnamese annals: Bui Quang Tung, 'Chao Anou, roi de Vientiane', in *Bulletin de la société des études indochinoises*, XXXIII (1958), pp. 401–6.
[32] Bui Quang Tung, loc. cit.

Anou to the Siamese and for other acts of insubordination, the emperor of Vietnam executed Prince Noi and annexed his princedom.

Vientiane was devastated. Not only did the Siamese loot and burn the city itself, carrying off the sacred Prabang, its most precious statues and other booty; they also depopulated much of the trans-Mekong area. The river towns were moved to the Siamese bank. Nongkhay was built eleven miles down-stream to replace Vientiane, Xieng Khane was rebuilt south of the Mekong. The people of Kam Mon were removed across the river almost as far as Roi Et; those of Vientiane itself were transported even deeper into Siam.

This was of course far more than mere retribution for Anou's rebellion or the traditional enslavement of a conquered people. It was a defensive measure directed against Vietnam. By emptying the country beyond the Mekong, Siam secured the river as a possible defence line for herself, denied it to Laotian rebels of the future and made the return of Vietnamese influence more difficult. The despatch of an army in 1831 to restore Siamese authority in Cambodia was part of the same struggle. The British intervention in lower Burma had reduced the danger to Siam from the west. She could now afford to look resolutely once more towards the east.[33]

The Siamese invasion of Cambodia started well. The Cambodians were defeated, the Siamese occupied most of southern Cambodia, and the king fled to Vietnam. Then resistance began to stiffen. Irregulars harried Siamese detachments, the eastern provinces prepared to fight, and finally Vietnam sent an army. In front of this the Siamese withdrew, and the king of Cambodia was restored to his throne. When he died in 1834, however, the Vietnamese proceeded to integrate his country into their own. In 1841 the Cambodians rebelled, murdered every Vietnamese they could find, appealed to Siam for help and offered the crown to a prince who was living under Siamese protection. But the Vietnamese were too strongly entrenched for such a manoeuvre to succeed. After four years of effort Siam could achieve no more than a resumption of dual suzerainty. King Ang Duong, great-great-grandfather of Prince Sihanouk, accordingly received his crown jointly from the two. A wise and pious monarch with no illusions

---

[33] Walter F. Vella has an extensive account of Siamese dealings with Laos and Cambodia at this time in *Siam under Rama III* (New York, 1957), pp. 78–114.

about the jealous intentions of his neighbours, he gave neither of them any excuse to resume their quarrels at his expense.

In Xieng Khouang also the traditional dual relationship was eventually restored. At first Siam had acquiesced in the annexation of the mountain state by Vietnam. The removal of Vietnamese influence from the Mekong valley, however, had restored the significance of the mountain barrier. Siam was now the Mekong valley power and it was not long before she had adopted the traditional Laotian interest in the hills. At length a rebellion took place with her encouragement in Xieng Khouang, and in 1855 the Vietnamese found it prudent to reinstate a member of the old ruling family.[34] The new ruler paid tribute to his neighbours on both sides of the mountains as his forbears had done.

Thus for the moment equilibrium had been restored in what was now Siam's conflict with the Vietnamese, a conflict which she had inherited from the Chams and Cambodians and in which Cambodia was the prize. It was an equilibrium established by buffers. The two peoples were separated in the south by Cambodia, in the north by Xieng Khouang and the Sipsong Chau Thai, states who showed their neutrality by paying tribute to both sides. In the centre there was the long depopulated zone between the Mekong and the Annamitic Chain, and the Kha and Moi tribesmen in their highlands, unsubdued by either side. Siam stood in awe of her thrusting and dynamic rival and her mood was defensive. The teeming Vietnamese, secure in the knowledge of their past achievements, their hardihood and vigour, looked to the empty Mekong valley and beyond as the natural sphere of their future action. Each found the civilization, religion, language, and manners of the other alien if not barbaric. There was no reason for liking or trust between them; a succession dispute in Cambodia or Xieng Khouang could well again have led to war.

History had thus provided some reason for the attempt to establish a buffer zone between Siam and Vietnam. A century later when the French empire in Indo-China had come and gone, that reason had been immeasurably reinforced.

[34] Le Boulanger, op. cit., pp. 234–5. James McCarthy, *Surveying and Exploring in Siam* (London, 1900), p. 38, has a substantial account of the rebellion, which Le Boulanger does not appear to have seen. McCarthy was in Xieng Khouang with the Siamese in 1884–5 and probably heard first-hand evidence.

CHAPTER II
The Consequences of French Rule

THE French formed their Indo-Chinese empire between 1858 and 1907. From the first they were in conflict with Siam across the neutral zone, which they eventually absorbed. Their first move was in the south. Having annexed part of southern Vietnam, they proceeded in 1867 to replace the joint suzerainty over Cambodia hitherto shared by Vietnam and the Siamese, with exclusive French protection. Twenty years later, masters of all Vietnam and the conscious heirs of the Vietnamese expansionist tradition, they began to penetrate the north and centre of the former buffer zone. The greater part of what is now Laos was surrendered to them by Siam in 1893; the rest, together with the Cambodian provinces Siam had managed to keep, was French by 1907. These acquisitions, and the area of influence in Siam which France obtained as a result of her agreement with Britain in 1896, brought her well beyond the furthest limits ever attained by Vietnamese authority.

This advanced position was not fully maintained. Except in Cambodia, France did not confirm her influence over the western half of the middle Mekong basin. But the rest was organized as a unity, Cambodia and Laos becoming the up-country regions of what was in effect a French empire of Vietnam. Vietnamese efforts in the nineteenth century to integrate border territories into Vietnam had failed. Those of France succeeded; over the appearance of local autonomies there was imposed an administration of which the lower officials and technicians were predominantly Vietnamese, and which adopted some of the traditional Vietnamese points of view.

The defeat of France by Germany in 1940 started the disintegration of French power in the east. Siam, fearful that the whole of French Indo-China would become Vietnamese as and

when French power departed, tried to reassert herself in Cambodia and Laos. The old rifts reopened. By the time the French
empire was finally dissolved in the Geneva settlement of 1954 they
had become a great chasm, widened and deepened by the tensions
of the Cold War in which Siam and North Vietnam were on
opposite sides, and in which a resurgent China supported North
Vietnam. There was thus urgent reason for the attempt to turn the
kingdom of Laos, whose territory had once insulated the two
peoples in the north, into a neutral buffer state.

But could this be done? The kingdom of Laos as formed by
France did indeed contain much of the territory which had
separated Siam and Vietnam in the nineteenth century. The zone
Siam had depopulated was, however, no longer empty. Its Lao
people had returned from across the Mekong. The population of
Laos was now composed of two traditionally hostile groups,
approximately equal in strength, each backed in its internal
quarrel by close ethnic kindred in Siam and North Vietnam. This
was bound to make stability difficult, and without stability 'a
buffer state loses its purpose'.[1]

*   *   *

The potential instability of Laos had resulted from the circumstances in which the French colonial empire was created. France
moved into Indo-China after the Opium Wars in the 1840s and
1850s had demonstrated China's inability to resist Western pressure.[2] The first phase of her conquest she owed to her missionaries
and admirals; the second to her explorers, in particular to a young
naval officer of genius, Francis Garnier, whose courage and enterprise were to prepare the way for the French conquest of Tongking,
and to Auguste Pavie, whose winning of Laotian hearts proved
remarkably useful to the colonial party in Paris.

In 1858 the duties of France to her missionaries in Vietnam
happened to coincide with her desire for a naval base in the Far
East.[3] After several forceful attempts to secure freedom from

[1] Professor H. Trevor Roper in his introduction to Prince Chula
Chakrabongse, *Lords of Life* (London, 1960).

[2] The best general account of the French conquest of Indo-China is in
D. Lancaster, *The Emancipation of French Indo-China* (London, 1961), to
which I am greatly indebted.

[3] See Pierre Renouvin, *La question d'extrême orient* (Paris, 1946), p. 66.
Vietnamese persecution of the missionaries was in fact done more for

persecution for her missionaries, she seized Tourane.[4] In 1859, having still failed to obtain satisfaction from the Vietnamese emperor, she occupied Saigon. This led to the cession of about half of southern Vietnam to France in 1862. As the country was pacified French influence spread across the Mekong into Cambodia, which the weakening of Vietnamese power had left under the domination of Siam.

France was already acting very much as, given the power, the Vietnamese themselves might have done. As early as 1861 an officer had been sent to inform the king of Cambodia that France intended to occupy southern Vietnam and was anxious to help him maintain his country's independence. The king, who only in the previous year had owed his throne to Siamese help against a rebellion, replied coldly. France nevertheless continued to court him and in April 1863 sent a sloop under the command of Lieutenant Doudart de Lagrée with orders to make a geographical survey of the country and to establish close contact with the king. He succeeded: 'the [king's] children eat out of my hand', he wrote, 'and climb on my shoulders'.[5] French missionaries in Cambodia were also at work. The king was eventually persuaded that his only hope of avoiding absorption by Siam lay in accepting the protection of France. In September 1863 he agreed to a treaty transforming into a protectorate the suzerain rights over his kingdom which France claimed as heir to the power of Vietnam in the south.

Siam, supported by the British whose commercial interests in that country were already substantial, protested that the treaty ignored her title as joint suzerain over Cambodia, and then insisted that the Cambodian king go to Bangkok to receive his crown, thus acknowledging Siamese overlordship in the accepted fashion. But France was not to be diverted. As soon as the monarch left his capital on 3 March 1864, Doudart de Lagrée landed a naval party and hoisted the French flag. The king, hearing from afar the guns with which the flag was saluted and fearing a revolution, changed

political than religious reasons. The emperors saw them as agents of the encroaching French: P. Devillers, *Histoire du Vietnam de 1940 à 1952* (Paris, 1952), p. 185.

[4] Now Da Nang, one of the main United States bases in South Vietnam.

[5] R. Vercel, *Francis Garnier* (Paris, 1952), p. 27.

his mind; he formally accepted the treaty with France on 17 April. The Siamese ended by acquiescing in what they could not alter. In 1867 their claims to suzerainty over Cambodia were exchanged for French recognition of their possession of the formerly Cambodian provinces of Battambang and Siemreap. France had meanwhile annexed the remainder of southern Vietnam. The foundations of her empire in the East had been laid. Her eager young men burned to extend it.

For by now French eyes were being drawn to the supposedly rich possibilities of trade with Yunnan which, even before the British annexation of Rangoon and lower Burma in 1852, had long assumed great importance in British eyes. In 1863 Francis Garnier, a young naval officer who had already distinguished himself in the conquest of southern Vietnam, had conceived the idea of a voyage up the River Mekong, known hitherto only by the accounts of the Dutch and Portuguese visitors in the seventeenth century, and by that of the explorer Henri Mouhot who had died near Luang Prabang in 1861.[6] Like several of his naval contemporaries Garnier dreamed of giving France possessions in the Far East as vast and flourishing as the British empire in India. The central artery would be the Mekong, whose fertile delta was already in French hands. The first essential was exploration, to determine the possibilities of the river as a means of access to Yunnan.

By June 1863 Garnier was urging the idea of a Mekong expedition upon his superiors in Saigon and his friends at home, with all the enthusiasm and eloquence of which this intense young man was capable. At length, says a fellow-officer,[7] 'his letters, his representations and those of his friends to Count Chasseloup-Laubat, then Minister for the Navy, won confidence in and finally acceptance for his project'. The Minister authorized the expedition in 1865; as Garnier was still only twenty-six, Doudart de Lagrée was chosen to command it.

The expedition left Saigon on 5 June 1866. It returned there two years and fourteen days later, having voyaged up the Mekong,

[6] H. Mouhot, *Voyages dans les royaumes de Siam, de Cambodge, de Laos*, F. de Lanoye (ed.), (Paris, 4th edn., 1883).
[7] Capitaine de Vaisseau Trève, 'Notice sur Francis Garnier' in *Revue maritime et coloniale*, 1874, quoted in F. Garnier, *Voyage d'exploration en Indochine* (Paris, 1885), p. iv.

marched through the chaos of the Panthay[8] rebellion in Yunnan and sailed down the Yangtse-kiang to Shanghai. The journey cost the life of Doudart de Lagrée who died three months before it ended. For Garnier, whose work as deputy had been of outstanding importance and who wrote the excellent official account,[9] it won wide public acclaim. The findings were clear. The Mekong was not, after all, a navigable highway to Yunnan, access to which should rather be obtained by the Red River from Hanoi, a relatively easy and very much shorter route. The Mekong valley was nevertheless a desirable acquisition for France. There was gold, silver, and other minerals. The people were amenable and would prosper when freed from their present evils, the scourge of the slave trade which created insecurity and terror in the south,[10] and the oppressive hand of Siam. However the country was thinly populated and could not be exploited without labour from overpopulated Vietnam. 'At the sight of a naturally fertile soil', said one of the explorers, 'only half-inhabited and only half-cultivated . . . one cannot help thinking of the Vietnamese.'[11] When the Vietnamese crossed the mountains into the Mekong valley, they would transform the country by their industry and healthful example.

Thus from the first the French view coincided with Vietnamese ambitions as to their future role on the Mekong. The defensive measures taken by Siam in 1830 had, however, been effective; the zone between the river and the Annamitic Chain was still largely free from Vietnamese influence. Even in 1877, ten years

[8] The Thai Muslim rebellion against Chinese rule in Yunnan began in 1855 and lasted until 1873 when it was put down with the help of arms from the French.

[9] F. Garnier, *Voyage d'exploration en Indochine*, two vols. (Paris, 1873), and one volume (Paris, 1885). References are to the later edition. Among Garnier's honours was a gold medal awarded to him jointly with David Livingstone by the first international geographical conference at Brussels in 1871, and the patron's medal of the Royal Geographical Society.

[10] On the slave trade in southern Laos, see Aymonier, *Voyage dans le Laos* (Paris, 1895), vol. I, p. 122, *Mission Pavie, géographie et voyages*, vol. IV, pp. 156, 184, 207, and Garnier, op. cit., pp. 85–86.

[11] L. de Carné, *Voyage en l'Indochine et dans l'empire chinois* (Paris, 1872), pp. 96–97. When Dr. Harmand visited Laos in 1877 he said that the climate was so bad that France would have to colonize the country with Vietnamese and send few Europeans: E. Lefèvre, *Un voyage au Laos* (Paris, 1898), p. 164.

after the Mekong expedition, Vietnamese authority extended only
over Tchepone, Muong Vang, and Muong Phine,[12] and even so
Siamese influence was present as well. Except at Nakawn Panom,
from which runs the shortest route between Vietnam and the
Mekong, where there had been Vietnamese traders since the
seventeenth century and where there was now a regular Vietnamese
colony, the Vietnamese were as far away from the Mekong as ever.

Having started their voyage with the promise 'to do better than
the English', the explorers were plagued throughout it by the fear
that their rivals would forestall them. At one time they heard of a
great British expedition coming down the river towards them. They
quickly put their records in order so that they could prove their
exploration as far as it had gone. But their immediate, obsessive
reaction was anxiety for the prestige of France. What sort of
comparison, said Garnier, would the Laotians make between the
modest French undertaking, neglected by its authorities, run on
the cheap, and a fat British mission of forty Anglo-Saxons lavishly
equipped by an imaginative government.[13] The incident ended in
laughter, for the rumoured English turned out to be a solitary
Dutch geographer in Siamese employ, equally apprehensive of the
vast, heavily armed French expedition which report had led him to
expect. But the moral remained. Again and again the explorers
found evidence of English enterprise, British textiles specially
designed for Laotian markets, British Indian currency in circ-
ulation alongside the local cowrie shells, while the only signs
they could see of France were bottles of liquor in the Phnom Penh
shops.[14]

By the time Garnier led the expedition back to Saigon in June
1868 a British reconnaissance party had in fact already entered
Yunnan from Burma.[15] The explorer's message was the more
urgent and he argued it with his usual one-pointed force. The best
way into Yunnan was by the Red River from Hanoi. To gain the
riches she sought, France had only to control the river. It was not
long before proof was provided. At Hankow the mission had en-

[12] Garnier, op. cit., pp. 223–8, note, quoting Dr. Harmand.

[13] Garnier, op. cit., p. 268. The total budget allotted for the mission
over the two years was 20,000 francs: Vercel, op. cit., p. 51.

[14] Vercel, op. cit., p. 47.

[15] Hall, op. cit., p. 594. It was followed by numerous British journeys
overland between China and Burma in the next ten years.

countered Jean Dupuis, the French trader and adventurer, then on his way to Yunnan. Garnier had told him of his views about the Red River and had urged him to use this route on his way back. The stalwart Dupuis, who had had a similar idea himself, found that the river was navigable without undue difficulty and in 1873 delivered a cargo by this route to Yunnan.

The Franco-Prussian War had meanwhile diverted France and Garnier from oriental ambitions. Garnier was the first to recover. By the middle of 1871 he was urging his countrymen that the moment of national disaster they were experiencing was also the moment to resume their expansion and restore their prestige in the East. France was depressed and her response discouraging.[16] Garnier therefore obtained the long leave he required for a further exploration of the upper Yangtse and Yunnan on his own account. From this adventure he was recalled to Saigon in August 1873 by the governor of the colony, Admiral Dupré.

The voyage of Dupuis up the Red River had been made against the wishes of the Vietnamese authorities in Hanoi. When he reappeared there in April 1873 with a load of Yunnanese tin and copper, and announced that he meant to go back with a cargo of salt, trade in which was a government monopoly, he met sharp Vietnamese opposition. The authorities refused him the salt and did whatever else they could to thwart and harass him. Dupuis was accompanied by 150 well-armed Yunnanese, lent to him as an escort by the Chinese authorities in Yunnan. With these he now occupied part of Hanoi, calling meanwhile for help to the French in Saigon who had hitherto supported him. The Vietnamese also appealed to Saigon, asking that Dupuis be removed.

Admiral Dupré had recommended to his government in the strongest terms that France should follow up the initiative of Dupuis in opening the Red River to trade, by establishing a protectorate over Tongking.[17] The answer from Paris had been firm:

[16] French reluctance to acquire colonies at this time, and the contrast with the brief colonialist spell later on, is clearly shown in S. H. Roberts, *The History of French Colonial Policy 1870–1925* (London, 2nd edn., 1963), pp. 424–8. It may be compared with British reluctance to exploit the opportunities gained by Raffles in South-East Asia earlier: S. Rose, *Britain and South-East Asia* (London, 1962), pp. 29–36.

[17] Northern Vietnam. The three divisions of imperial Vietnam were Tongking in the north, Annam in the centre, and Cochin China in the south.

'à aucun prix il ne faut engager la France au Tonkin'.[18] Dupré argued that the Vietnamese request, which he heard was being supplemented by an appeal to the English, had created a new situation. 'Let me act on my own', he said, 'I take full responsibility. If the results are not what I have led you to expect you can disavow me.'[19]

While Paris was slowly accustoming itself to the idea of an inexpensive protectorate,[20] the admiral recalled Garnier from his exploration and gave him command of a force of two hundred men —he had only asked for sixty—to go to Hanoi. Garnier's orders, which he drafted himself,[21] were concerned with composing the Dupuis affair and opening the Red River to navigation. The real object was, however, to present France with a protectorate over Tongking which she could accept as a *fait accompli*.

Garnier reached Hanoi on 5 November 1873. On 20 November he seized the citadel by surprise assault. With his own men and those of Dupuis, together with additional volunteers he was able to enrol, he then proceeded within a month to capture the five key towns of the Red River delta. On 21 December, just as talks with representatives from the Vietnamese imperial court were beginning, he was killed leading a handful of men in a sortie against bands of Chinese irregulars who were helping the Vietnamese.

Paris could no longer pretend not to know what was afoot. Garnier's bold action was disowned and his conquests handed back. In exchange the Vietnamese emperor recognized French conquests in the south, admitted French trade to his major ports, opened the Red River to French commerce, and again promised toleration for the Christians.

There were other concessions and at first the French were quite pleased with their bargain. But they had lost face. As soon as French troops were removed the Vietnamese began to harass the Christians and all those who had helped Garnier and Dupuis. Increasingly unsettled conditions in the country soon ended any possibility of free navigation on the Red River. By 1879 the treaty

---

[18] P. Lehault, *La France et l'Angleterre en Asie*, vol. I (Paris, 1892), introduction, p. xix, and p. 689, note 2.

[19] J. Ferry, *Le Tonkin et la mère-patrie* (Paris, 1890), p. 86.

[20] Ferry, op. cit., p. 86: 'Enfin le ministre finit par céder: il consent à l'établissement éventuel d'un protectorât au Tonkin.'

[21] Garnier, op. cit., introduction, p. x.

From G. Maspéro, *L'Indochine*, Paris, 1929

King Sisavang Vong in 1928

The Plain of Jars

was virtually a dead letter and in 1880 China publicly reasserted her suzerainty over Vietnam.

France now had the clear choice between annexing Tongking and abandoning her interests there. She decided on annexation. In 1882 Hanoi and part of the Red River delta were seized, but again the leader of the French expedition was killed by Chinese irregulars in Vietnamese employ. The French realized that they could never control Tongking unless they had mastered the emperor. This final step was taken in 1883. Over the following two years its consequences were forced upon China. By the Treaty of Tientsin in 1885, China accepted the French presence in Tongking. The whole of modern Vietnam thus came under French rule.

The French Mekong expedition of 1866–8 had attracted little attention in Siam, whose hand still rested comparatively lightly on her far-flung Laotian territories. If the Siamese were concerned at all it was in relation to Cambodia, whose loss they were still reluctant to accept. The establishment of French authority in northern Vietnam, however, contained a possible threat to Siamese security which depended, in Xieng Khouang and the Sipsong Chau Thai, on joint suzerainty of the sort that had been abruptly ended in Cambodia.

This was already in the minds of the Siamese when in 1884 they despatched an expedition to deal with Chinese outlaw bands who had been preying on northern Laos at intervals for twelve years. These bands, closely related to those responsible for the death of Garnier in 1873, consisted of soldiers who had fled from China after the final defeat of the T'ai P'ing army there in 1864.[22] Known by the colour of the pennants they flew as Black, Yellow, or Red Flags, they had spilled over the border into Tongking and upper Laos. In 1872 two thousand Red Flags, ousted from the Black River valley by Yellow Flags at the end of 1871, moved south and installed themselves at Ban Ban in eastern Xieng Khouang, a strategic point even today on the main route into Vietnam. They were still there, having ravaged the country as far as Vientiane and the Mekong, in 1884.

The Siamese had tried and failed to remove the interlopers in 1872–3. In 1884 a stronger force laid siege to Ban Ban but was

[22] See Lady Flavia Anderson, *The Rebel Emperor* (London, 1960), for an account of the T'ai P'ing rebellion.

eventually forced, by malaria and the rains, to withdraw.[23] Following this failure Siam decided to occupy all the high country north and east of Luang Prabang, including the Sipsong Chau Thai. Two forces were raised for this purpose. The first, assembled at Nongkhay in 1885 to deal with the Red Flags in Xieng Khouang, found that the outlaws had retired further north. A second force of a thousand Siamese and Laotian troops under Colonel Wai Woranat,[24] reached Luang Prabang in October 1885. It was intended for the Sipsong Chau Thai and for Sam Neua, a formerly autonomous hill state annexed by Vietnam after the Siamese conquest of Vientiane. Woranat appointed two commissioners to supervise the administration of the country at the side of the king, and set off on a cautious campaign in the hills.

The French representative in Bangkok did not hear of the new Siamese expedition until after it had left the capital. According to Le Boulanger, it had been kept secret from the French at the instance of British advisers to the king of Siam, who were hoping that it might limit French penetration of Tongking, considered dangerous to British commercial plans and interests in Yunnan.[25]

It is certainly true that by 1885, when they signed their treaty with the Chinese, the ambitions of the French were sharply in conflict with British interests in South-East Asia. This had been most marked in Burma. King Mindon had long realized the possibilities of playing off other European powers against the British, who had occupied the southern part of his country in 1852. In 1872 he negotiated a commercial treaty with France and in the following year he received a French envoy who, after giving soothing assurances to the British, made damaging secret agreements with Mindon, which included an undertaking to provide French officers to train his army.

Like Garnier's action in Tongking a year later these agreements were quickly disavowed by the French government in the ⸱aftermath of the Franco-Prussian War. But the years when France was

[23] James McCarthy, op. cit., pp. 86–91 has an eye-witness account of part of this siege.

[24] Properly, the Chaomoen Wai Woranat, the title by which he was generally known. His name was Jerm Sangchuto. The Sangchuto family is related to the Bunnag family of Siam, and it is to Mr. Tej Bunnag of St. Antony's College, Oxford, that I owe this detail.

[25] Le Boulanger, op. cit., pp. 251–2.

recovering her morale and strength after defeat in Europe, also saw a dramatic deterioration in British relations with Burma. After the accession of King Thibaw in 1879 matters began to move towards a crisis. In May 1883 Thibaw sent a mission to Europe which installed itself in Paris and at once asked France for arms. In spite of repeated French reassurances to England, the Franco-Burmese treaty signed at the beginning of 1885 was accompanied by a guarded French promise that as soon as Tongking was pacified, arms and military stores would be sent to Burma from there.

This secret promise did not leak out until August 1885, when it became one of the inner causes of the British annexation of upper Burma.[26] But the British had reason to think that France had designs on Siam as well as on Burma. A pre-emptive move to forestall the French in upper Laos was thus as much a British as it was a Siamese interest.

By October 1885, when Colonel Wai Woranat reached Luang Prabang, France was heavily involved in operations in Tongking and her expansionist government had fallen. British annexation of upper Burma was imminent. Confronted with the evidence of her secret dealings, France had withdrawn her consul from Mandalay. The Siamese expedition into upper Laos appeared, however, to aim at territory to which she could reasonably lay claim now that Tongking was French. Sam Neua, the Sipsong Chau Thai, and Xieng Khouang had all owed allegiance to Vietnam as well as to Luang Prabang; their position was arguable. Luang Prabang itself had invoked the protection of Vietnam by volunteering tribute in 1831. Although no protection had been granted and Siamese predominance had not been challenged, the court of Hué thus had a possible claim even here, and the claims of Hué were now the rights of France.

In order to settle these matters in their favour without becoming embroiled with the English, the French asked Siam for a joint

[26] The occasion for the annexation was, of course, Thibaw's case against the Bombay Burma Trading Corporation. J. G. Scott, *Burma, from the earliest times to the present day* (London, 1924), p. 320, calls this 'a reckless step which warranted active intervention by the British Government without the undesirable development of friction with France'. For the kind of policy that was being recommended to Paris, see Deloncle's report dated 19 July 1889 at Appendix I, which quotes despatches he wrote in 1884. J. G. Scott, *France and Tongking* (London, 1885), pp. 369–81 shows that the British were fully aware of French ambitions in Siam.

commission on the boundaries of Luang Prabang and Tongking. In May 1886 laboured negotiations resulted in a provisional agreement which regulated French commerce in Luang Prabang and gave France the right to open a vice-consulate there, but which left the question of a boundary commission unsettled. To the post of vice-consul was appointed Auguste Pavie. His immediate instructions were to find a practicable route between the upper Mekong and Tongking, and to hold himself in readiness to join an eventual boundary commission.

Auguste Pavie, then in his fortieth year, had already made a name for himself in Cambodia where he had been a member of the Postal Service since 1871. His explorer's interest in the country, his knowledge of the language, and his evident gift for friendship with its people came to official notice and he was given the task of constructing the telegraph line from Phnom Penh to Bangkok. Having turned this undertaking into a first class piece of exploration, Pavie was sent to Paris in 1885 with thirteen young Cambodians whom he planned to have educated so that they could help France in the pacification of their country. His idea was approved and the eventual result was the foundation of the École Coloniale in Paris. Who could be better fitted for the new post at Luang Prabang?

Pavie reached Bangkok as vice-consul designate in March 1886, impatient to begin. But the Franco-Siamese agreement was still provisional and the Siamese were able to prevent Pavie from reaching Luang Prabang until their military expedition had had time to achieve its aims. On 12 March 1887, a month after the Frenchman had at last reached his post, Colonel Woranat returned in triumph from his campaign in the north and very agreeably showed Pavie his maps, which marked all the cantons of the Sipsong Chau Thai and Sam Neua as dependencies of Luang Prabang. In spite of himself Pavie was impressed with the alert, self-assured, and polished young officer, but he knew quite well how these results had been obtained. Hostages had been taken from most of the chiefs as a guarantee of their good behaviour, good behaviour which was naturally to include the right answers to any questions about suzerainty posed by France. The colonel had a large number of hostages with him, and four young princes taken in the north had already been sent down the Mekong chained and trussed up in pig baskets. These, it transpired, were the three

sons and a son-in-law of the powerful chief of Lai Chau, Prince
Cam Sinh. They had been seized by Colonel Woranat when visiting
him at Dien Bien Phu on behalf of their father.[27]

The reasons for this action, which was to cost Siam any claim
she might have had to the Sipsong Chau Thai, are still obscure,
although both on this occasion and on an earlier visit to Dien
Bien Phu in 1884, the Siamese had been accompanied by a British
geographer in Siamese government employ, James McCarthy.
McCarthy, who was making a map with which the Siamese hoped
to establish their frontier claims, says that in 1884 satisfactory
assurances had been received from Lai Chau. At the end of 1886,
however, he had arrived in Dien Bien Phu a few days after the
colonel to find the Lai Chau princes already under arrest. It would
appear that the Siamese commander was not satisfied with the
deputation of princes from Lai Chau and hoped to induce Prince
Cam Sinh to come to Dien Bien Phu himself. McCarthy thought
that so far from achieving this result the arrests would lead to endless complications unless Cam Sinh could be appeased. He urged
Woranat without success to release the men.[28]

The explanation may lie in the internal politics of the Sipsong
Chau Thai or in an underlying resentment on the part of Lai Chau
at Siamese interference. An over-forceful demand for hostages might
well have caused the princes to point out that, since the French
treaty with China in 1885, they were in a position to invoke the
protection of France if they chose.[29] This was not of course what
Woranat wanted to hear. The account given by the princes themselves to Pavie after their release, that they had been arrested for
saying that Lai Chau would recognize French rather than Siamese
authority, was probably an adaptation of the truth composed to
please their liberator.

However that may be, soon after the Siamese had left Dien Bien
Phu, Cam Sinh sent an expedition southwards under his eldest
son Cam Oum—better known by his Vietnamese name, Deo-van-

[27] *Mission Pavie, géographie et voyages*, vol. VII, p. 96.

[28] McCarthy, op. cit., pp. 108–9. The French and Siamese versions of
the affair are not easy to reconcile. Prince Damrong, *A Collection of Chronicles* (Prachum Pongsawadan), Part IX (Bangkok, 1918), pp. 76–111,
attributes the incident to the internal politics of the Sipsong Chau Thai;
Pavie, loc. cit., says that Lai Chau preferred French to Siamese suzerainty.

[29] Hall, op. cit., p. 649 comes close to this explanation.

Tri—to rescue his sons. By the time Deo-van-Tri reached Luang Prabang, the Siamese army had left for Bangkok. Prince Souvannaphouma, the 'second king' or viceroy of Luang Prabang, was killed in the subsequent fighting and it fell to Pavie's party to rescue the aged King Oun Kham, regally determined not to leave his palace, and to accompany him on his flight down-river. Few Europeans in the Orient can have had such an opportunity. Pavie made the most of it. His patient goodwill and kindness in time of disaster won him the hearts of the king and his people, and undermined the position of the Siamese. Pavie also took the initiative in the release of the Lai Chau princes, an act which helped him at the end of 1888 to secure the Sipsong Chau Thai for France without serious opposition from Siam.

Nothing had happened yet to change the dependence of Luang Prabang on Siam, though Pavie, already a bitter enemy of the Siamese, had conceived a great longing to make Laos French, as he put it, by the consent of its people. France had, however, already given evidence of her ambitions in central Laos. As early as 1884 French defence posts had been set up along the watershed of the Annamitic Chain, from which vantage point the French 'were able to appreciate the strategic importance and potential economic interest of the western slopes...to the middle Mekong'.[30] This was the zone which Siam had depopulated after the sack of Vientiane in 1828. Much of its population had now returned.[31]

At the end of 1887 the French began to revive Vietnamese claims to the area as part of the former kingdom of Vientiane, once a Vietnamese vassal. The Siamese reacted by moving small garrisons towards the Annamitic Chain which they considered to be the eastern frontier of their territory. They firmly rejected French claims on behalf of Vietnam but in September 1888 agreed to evacuate the post they had established at Kam Mon pending a joint delimitation of the frontier.[32]

[30] Lancaster, op. cit., p. 50. The reason for French activity in this area was the resistance of the Vietnamese Emperor Ham Nghi, who held out against them in eastern Kam Mon until 1888.

[31] See Professor Pensri Duke, *Relations entre la France et la Thailande* (*Siam*), (Bangkok, 1962), p. 130, quoting a report by Captain Luce dated 15 October 1888 to the French Minister for the Navy.

[32] For Siamese statements of their position and for the exchanges in Bangkok between March and September 1888, see Duke, op. cit., pp. 117 and 127–9.

Early in 1889 Pavie found the Siamese still in possession at Kam Mon, territory which he alleged had until recently been actually under Vietnamese administration. He proceeded to install a French post nearby at Napé, west of the watershed, and returned with all haste to Hanoi whence he was recalled to France for consultations. It was meanwhile agreed with Siam that neither side would advance further pending a frontier settlement which would be negotiated on Pavie's return.

Pavie reached Paris on 13 June 1889. What he had to say was that as far as he could ascertain from his own explorations and researches in Laos, and from those of Captain Luce in the Vietnamese archives, some of the territory which the Siamese had occupied east of the Mekong certainly belonged to Vietnam and therefore to France. Indeed, Siamese rights to any territory at all east of the Mekong were doubtful, even Luang Prabang having at one time paid tribute to Hué. He himself was strongly in favour of a forward policy.

The French government was already under pressure from colonial enthusiasts at home. One of these was M. François Deloncle, a French consular officer who had been involved in the secret negotiations with Burma in 1884–5 and who, on 19 July 1889, presented a remarkable report on French policy in Indo-China.[33] To Deloncle the affair was already a simple case of Siamese aggression promoted by the English into territory that was unquestionably French. France had rights derived from those of Vietnam over the old Vientiane kingdom, even to the west of the Mekong. Siam should be confined as of old to the Menam valley. She was in any case a bad ruler and France was justified in using any means to evict her. Let there be a campaign to put down the crying evil of slavery in the Mekong valley—the English would swallow that one—let the local rulers be given French assistants to help them in the task, and then let the assistants remain as French Residents. Let quiet political penetration proceed everywhere under the guise of scientific, economic, or commercial enterprise. The commercial agents would naturally be remunerated from the colonial budget. As for Luang Prabang, let the clever M. Pavie worm himself even further into the favour of the aged monarch and

---

[33] L. de Reinach, *Le Laos* (Paris, 1901), vol. II, pp. 19–29; a translation is at Appendix I.

seek a chance to have him sign a convention which—'for some object or other such as the repression of slavery'[34]—would place Luang Prabang under French protection.

Amidst pressures such as this, arrangements were made for Pavie's second mission. It was decided, he tells us, to work by a series of border agreements made on the spot, bringing Siam step by step to recognize the boundary as it had existed before her recent moves.[35] The more extensive French claims would be taken up later. To the topographers already assigned to the mission for frontier demarcation purposes were now added scientific, economic, and commercial specialists who could later represent France in the territories they had explored. The newly formed 'French Upper Laos Company' provided fifteen tons of merchandise with which to start the commercial part of the operation. That meant, chuckles de Reinach, that France would now have private commercial interests in the Mekong valley which would increase her right to intervene there.[36]

It was thus in the conscious role of empire-builder that Pavie returned to Indo-China in November 1889. Like any emperor of Vietnam, the French had decided to extend their influence into the Mekong valley. Pavie broke his journey in Bangkok to settle with the Siamese how the border arrangements were to be made. The king, he tells us, wanted all negotiations to take place in the capital.[37] Before this could be done the appropriate reconnaissances had to be made. The Frenchman therefore set off on his new explorations, and nine months were to elapse before any discussion of frontiers could begin. By that time Pavie's numerous teams of explorers and experts were scurrying in all directions across Laos and north-east Siam, and the Siamese were thoroughly alarmed. Pavie was offered much politeness, therefore, in Bangkok; but there were no discussions. Pavie's agents told him, moreover, that Siam was preparing to reinforce her positions across the middle Mekong after the rains, and to extend them to all areas where she claimed sovereignty. The French border posts were told in January 1891 to do all they could to stop Siamese advances without resorting to force, but six months later it was apparent

[34] De Reinach, op. cit., vol. II, p. 25.
[35] *Mission Pavie, géographie et voyages*, vol. I, pp. 326–7.
[36] De Reinach, op. cit., vol. I, p. 13.
[37] *Mission Pavie, géographie et voyages*, vol. II, p. 8.

that serious preparations were being made to defend Siamese claims.

In July 1891, therefore, declining a Siamese offer to talk the matter out, Pavie went once more to Paris to urge a stronger line of action. A major extension of his activities was planned. He himself was appointed resident French minister in Bangkok where he arrived in June 1892, and more French commercial agents were stationed on the Mekong. France was taking up her Vietnamese heritage with a vengeance. 'We are now obliged', wrote Dr. Harmand from Rangoon a few months later:

to extend up to the Mekong not merely our influence but our direct domination. For we have a duty to meet the historic ambitions of the Asians we have brought under our control, as well as their material needs. The Vietnamese nation is older than ours; it is a nation of conquerors and colonists which we stopped in mid-career more than thirty years ago; we have no right to keep it back for ever from the paths of Destiny.

In order to get full value from the empire, he continued, French policy must be associated with the traditional aspirations of Vietnam, must

embrace the ambitions to which more than twenty centuries of history bear witness, and ensure their realisation. . . . It is to the Vietnamese, shut in and stifled as they are between the sea and the mountains . . . that we must open the Mekong valley.[38]

In Siam, however, tempers were beginning to rise, particularly among the European contract officers and advisers, who felt deeply for their country of adoption and were eager champions of its territorial integrity. While negotiations made little progress, incidents began to occur between the Siamese and French agents. Insignificant in themselves the incidents strengthened further the hand of the colonial lobby in France.

On 4 February 1893, Deloncle made an inflammatory speech in the French Chamber:

[38] Report to the Quai d'Orsay dated November 1892. I am indebted to Mr. P. J. N. Tuck of Wadham College, Oxford, for this extract from the archives of the French Foreign Ministry.

We cannot have conquered Cambodia, Tongking and Annam, we cannot have acquired, by solemn treaties freely signed, rights over all Laos on both banks of the Mekong, just to hand over the advantages of our conquest to Siam. For five or six years Siam has made dupes of us: I say 'Enough!'

The question of frontiers between Siam, Cambodia, and Vietnam, he said, interested no country but France. Indeed, Lord Salisbury had publicly voiced England's disinterest. France was therefore free to take what minor military measures were necessary. It was no great task: after all, he concluded, it might surprise the deputies to know that the Siamese invasion of which he was complaining had been carried out with fewer than two hundred soldiers.[39]

France could hardly lose. She decided to use force if necessary. During March, therefore, Pavie in Bangkok demanded compensation for the damage suffered by French subjects in the various incidents. He also made it clear that France was now claiming in the name of Vietnam all territory east of the Mekong from Kam Mon southwards. The Siamese protested, offering to refer doubtful matters to arbitration; but Pavie who now considered that the whole of Siam would eventually come under French protection,[40] insisted on the immediate evacuation of all Siamese posts in central Laos east of the Mekong.

These demands caused concern in Whitehall where the French admitted that they had similar claims to make on the upper Mekong.[41] Since the acquisition of upper Burma in 1885, Britain had been securing the allegiance of the Shan states who had formerly paid homage to the Burmese kings. The allegiance of Keng Tung obtained in 1890 had brought with it suzerain rights over territory to the east of the upper Mekong. Britain had taken up these rights partly to forestall action by France. She did not propose to keep the trans-Mekong area and meant to divide it between Siam and China so that there would be a buffer zone between the French colonial empire and her own; its disposal was, however, a British prerogative and there could be no question of a

---

[39] De Reinach, op. cit., vol. I, pp. 17–20.

[40] See his letters dated 29 Dec. 1892 to M. Ribot and 28 Jun. 1893 to M. Develle in the French Foreign Ministry Archives, quoted by Duke, op. cit., pp. 140 and 152.

[41] Hall, op. cit., pp. 650–7 gives a clear account of conversations on this matter between Britain and France.

surrender to France. For the moment the British attitude was one of 'cautious diplomatic reserve'.[42]

Siam rejected the French demands on 5 May and appealed to Britain for help. The British Foreign Secretary, Lord Rosebery, replied that Britain could not intervene. Siam should settle the matter directly with France and do nothing that might provoke her to war. However, three French columns had already begun to occupy southern Laos. The incidents that occurred became more serious, opinion in France more inflamed, the European advisers in the Siamese capital more indignant. At length fears of civil disturbances in Bangkok caused the British to send two gunboats to the mouth of the Menam below the capital in case it was necessary to protect their nationals. The French affected to see this as encouragement of Siamese resistance to their claims, and on this excuse, though in reality in order to exert pressure on the Siamese court, decided that they also would increase the number of their warships at Bangkok from one to three. Out of this, largely by misunderstanding and accident, ensued the Paknam affair in which two French gunboats were engaged by Siamese ships and shore batteries as they were entering the mouth of the Menam. The French ships replied with telling effect, and sailed up-river to Bangkok.[43]

Whatever might have been said of previous incidents, the French were technically within their rights at Paknam. Siam, provoked, had put herself grievously in the wrong. On 19 July Pavie was authorized to deliver an ultimatum demanding, on pain of naval blockade, compensation for damage, the punishment of those responsible for the various incidents, and the evacuation by Siam of all territory east of the Mekong as far north as her jurisdiction reached.

This extension of the French demands to the upper Mekong directly involved British rights there. The blockade of Bangkok which actually commenced on 29 July, affected British commercial interests in Siam, nine-tenths of whose foreign trade was in British hands. War with France over Siam was nevertheless out of

[42] Hall, op. cit., p. 656.
[43] This affair has never been properly elucidated. The account of Mr. B. S. N. Murti in his thesis, *Anglo-French Relations with Siam 1880–1904* (London University, 1952), is not fully satisfactory, while Professor Duke (op. cit., p. 155) makes no attempt to unravel the incident at all.

the question.[44] Britain was isolated in Europe and she had an empire to defend. The eyes of Russia, ally of France, rested on the frontiers of British India. What Britain wanted was to keep Siam as an independent state between the two colonial empires in the south, just as she wanted a buffer zone between them on the upper Mekong in the north. She now asked for a clear statement of French aims.

The French replied that, while there could be no going back on the ultimatum whose terms had been published, France was not threatening the independence of Siam. Once Siam had accepted the French demands, the way would be open for the establishment of a buffer state between French and British territory further north. On this assurance Britain advised Siam to accept the French terms.

The Siamese have sometimes blamed Britain for failing to support them in their conflict with France. Officially the British had made their position clear at the outset. Rosebery had plainly said that Siam could not expect British intervention in her border disputes with France. The Siamese appear to have been misled— for it is difficult to explain their action otherwise—by the enthusiasm of their foreign contract officers and also by that of the British minister himself, Captain Jones. Recent research has revealed evidence that even after the Paknam incident, in defiance of Rosebery's instructions, Jones was urging the Siamese to resist the French on the assumption of British support.[45]

The new Franco-Siamese treaty was signed on 3 October 1893. On 25 November the establishment of an Anglo-French boundary commission for the upper Mekong was agreed. France now claimed, however, that all the territory east of the Mekong as far north as the Chinese frontier was French. Pavie was unable to agree with his British colleague on the boundary commission as to the limits of the proposed buffer state and negotiations were transferred to Europe. The considerable Anglo-French tension that ensued

[44] See R. R. James, *Rosebery* (London, 1961), p. 288. In a letter to Queen Victoria, after strongly condemning French conduct towards Siam, Rosebery nevertheless concluded: 'If the French cut the throats of half Siam in cold blood we should not be justified in going to war with her.'

[45] India Office Library: Curzon Papers, F111/87, E. H. French to G. N. Curzon, 26 July 1893. W. A. R. Wood, who succeeded French in the Bangkok Legation, strongly supports this reference, supplied by P. J. N. Tuck.

ended with an agreement in January 1896. Britain gave up her claims to the territory east of the Mekong and conceded the special French interest in Siamese territory in the middle Mekong basin, in return for French participation in a joint guarantee of the independence of Siam in the Menam valley, which contained four-fifths of the population and most of the British interests in the country.[46]

The French empire now extended from the coast of Vietnam to the Mekong throughout the whole length of Laos. It was rounded off in 1904 and 1907 when Siam handed over her Cambodian provinces and the Laotian provinces of Bassac and Sayaboury, as part of a general settlement with France. To Siam the whole painful period may well have come to seem merely a phase in the continuing struggle with Vietnam. For in building her empire France had behaved towards Siam much as a powerful Vietnamese emperor might have done and had made the same demands. The next stage of French colonial development was also in the Vietnamese tradition. Already in 1897 France had begun to organize her conquests as an administrative unity. Although the appearance of local autonomy was largely preserved, although the kingdom of Luang Prabang survived as part of the new Laos, the great French proconsul, M. Paul Doumer, had by 1902 turned French Indo-China into what was in effect a new empire of Vietnam, with a common budget and common services, ruled by a French governor-general in Hanoi. Cambodia and Laos became in a sense the Vietnamese hinterland, a result no emperor of Vietnam had been able to achieve.[47]

The most obvious feature of the new unity was the uneven distribution of its population.[48] The Red River delta, cradle of the

---

[46] Hall, op. cit., p. 662. Criticism of the agreement was vocal both in England, where it was regarded as a pusillanimous surrender, and in France where the eventual annexation of Siam was seen by some as essential to the future of French Indo-China. See on the one hand Sir J. G. Scott, *Burma, from the earliest times to the present day* (London, 1924), pp. 359–61, and on the other, Lyautey, *Lettres du Tonkin et de Madagascar* (Paris, 1921), pp. 470–6. Scott was Pavie's opposite number on the boundary commission and the future Marshal Lyautey a major serving in Tongking.

[47] For the subordination of Laotian requirements to those of Vietnam, see P. Doumer, *L'Indochine Française* (Paris, 1905), pp. 291 and 309.

[48] Robequain, op. cit., p. 49 ff. See also *Indo-China*, Naval Intelligence Division Geographical Handbook, December 1943, pp. 213–38.

Vietnamese nation, had population densities as high as 1,500 to the square kilometre, a figure which approached those of the most crowded regions of monsoon Asia. The Vietnamese as a whole accounted for 72 per cent. of the population. Cambodia, with densities ranging from 83 down to 13 to the square kilometre, and Laos whose average density was only 4, were empty in comparison with the relatively small areas occupied by the Vietnamese.

Here indeed was the old problem of Vietnam, the problem which had through the centuries given rise to the pressure southwards of the Vietnamese people, and which had caused their rulers to regard the Mekong delta, and then the Mekong valley, as the natural sphere of Vietnamese expansion. The French explorers and empire-builders had shared this view. The old problem had now fallen to the new rulers, who attempted to solve it in the traditional Vietnamese fashion—by encouraging emigration southwards from Tongking. There were obstacles. Robequain has spoken of the unpredictable importance of malaria, and of the traditional factors which inhibited the Tongkingese peasant from leaving the coasts and river plains.[49] Migration was never the success which the French had hoped and even in 1939 the colonial government's greatest concern was to level out the density of population which was seen as 'an essential step in harmonious economic development'.[50] The Vietnamese themselves, however, realized the trend and assumed that their advantage would be permanent. 'One day', they dreamed, 'Indo-China will no longer be a collection of separate and distinct countries, but a single country fertilised by Vietnamese blood, inspired by Vietnamese dynamism and power of action.'[51]

Under French rule numbers of Vietnamese certainly moved into Cambodia and Laos as well as into the Mekong delta. By 1936 there were 191,000 Vietnamese in Cambodia and by 1945 there were 50,000 in Laos.[52] Vietnamese immigration could no longer be resisted, but it was not popular with the Cambodians and

[49] Op. cit., p. 60.

[50] Robequain, op. cit., p. 53. See also *Indo-China*, Naval Intelligence Division Geographical Handbook, December 1943, p. 240.

[51] *La Patrie Annamite* (1939), quoted by Pierre Gentil, *Remous du Mekong* (Paris, 1950), p. 24, who recalls that the statement was occasioned by French moves to replace Vietnamese officials in Laos by Laotian ones.

[52] Lancaster, op. cit., p. 70.

Laotians, particularly since, because the main French commercial and economic effort was made in populous Vietnam, the immigrants included numbers of technicians, artisans, and petty officials who were liable to be ahead of the local people in general outlook and social development. In Laos, for instance, where the public services were largely staffed from Vietnam and the urban population was predominantly Vietnamese,[53] the effect was that much of the available secondary education was taken up by the children of immigrants. Thus in the whole decade of the thirties only 52 Lao completed an education at the Lycée Pavie in Vientiane, the only secondary school in the country, as against 96 Vietnamese.[54] Even in 1945, two-thirds of the primary and assistant teachers in Laos were Vietnamese.[55] In commenting on the effects of Vietnamese immigration into Laos, Virginia Thompson writes:

The contempt of the industrious and formalistic [Vietnamese] for the . . . carefree Laotian is only matched by the latter's impotent hatred. Yet the evil is without remedy. Rich, unoccupied land will inevitably attract an industrious and prolific people like the [Vietnamese], who are able and willing to do what the Laotians cannot and will not do.[56]

There was of course another means of reducing the unevenness of the population, on which the French laid great stress in the early years of their rule. From time to time large numbers of Laotians and Cambodians had been transported by victorious armies into Siam. In the treaty of 1893 the French had insisted on the right of these people, now termed French subjects, to return to their old homelands. It was not altogether a practical condition. Nevertheless, by the time the clause was abandoned as part of the Franco-Siamese settlement of 1907, some migration had taken place; in particular a number of Lao had moved to the French

---

[53] E. Pietrantoni, 'La population du Laos en 1943 dans son milieu géographique' in *Bulletin de la société des études Indochinoises* XXXII, iii (1957), pp. 223–43, shows 30,300 Vietnamese out of a total population of 51,150 in the six chief towns: Vientiane, Luang Prabang, Thakhek, Savannakhet, Pakse, and Xieng Khouang.

[54] The tribal areas did not figure in the diploma lists at all.

[55] Somlith Pathammavong, 'Compulsory Education in Laos' in *Compulsory Education in Cambodia, Laos and Vietnam* (UNESCO, Paris, 1955), p. 94.

[56] *French Indo-China* (London, 1937), p. 376.

bank of the Mekong, where Vientiane, as the centre of the French administration, resumed some of its old importance, and the new town of Savannakhet was founded in the south.

The Laos that was formed by the French was, however, very different from the old kingdom, the greater part of which was now within the frontiers of Siam. Old Laos had been the land of the Mekong. The great river had been the national highway of trade and the Lao people of its banks had been united by its simple industries and seasons. Now, from Sayaboury in the north to Bassac in the south, the central feature of the old country was the western frontier of the new. The narrow plain between the Mekong and the hills could never absorb a population that would compare numerically with that sustained by the great plain to the west. The mass of the Lao people was, therefore, still to be found on the right bank of the Mekong under Siamese rule. North-east Siam, as far south and west as the limits of the old kingdom, continued, in spite of Siamese efforts at assimilation, to contain a distinctively Lao population six or seven times as numerous as the Lao in Laos. Indeed the Lao in Siam were almost as numerous as the Siamese themselves.[57]

The new demarcation created other anomalies. As if to compensate Laos for the loss of territory in the west, the French colonial administrators added Sam Neua and Xieng Khouang in the east, areas which had never been subject to direct Lao rule. The Sipsong Chau Thai, on the other hand, inhabited by the same hill people as Sam Neua, and like Sam Neua more inclined towards Vietnam than towards Laos because situated on the Vietnamese slope of the Annamitic watershed, eventually came within the boundaries of French Vietnam.[58] In the south-east, where the sharp mountain range merges into the broad mass of uplands and loses much of its significance as a geographical barrier, the watershed was accepted as the administrative boundary between Laos and Vietnam. Here too the frontier ran through an ethnically homogeneous area, for the unconquered Kha tribes in the southern highlands of Laos were one with the unsubdued Moi tribes in the central highlands of Vietnam, just on the other side of the theoretical watershed. Even the French did not succeed in subduing them.

[57] See additional note 1 at end of chapter.
[58] See additional note 2.

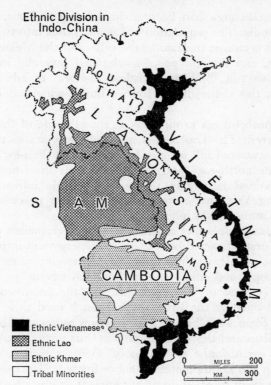

Ethnic Division in
Indo-China

Ethnic Vietnamese
Ethnic Lao
Ethnic Khmer
Tribal Minorities

Data is taken from the *Carte ethnolinguistique d'Indochine*, published in 1949 by the École Française d'Extrême Orient, and supplemented from G. Maspéro (ed.), *Un Empire colonial français; l'Indochine* (2 vols., Paris, 1929).

The new Laos was thus not only not the same as the old kingdom, it was also critically different from the buffer zone which had separated Siam from the Vietnamese in the nineteenth century. The formerly neutral states in the north had been shared out between Vietnam and Laos in a way that left the two most closely akin on opposite sides of the border. In the centre the depopulated tract east of the Mekong was now inhabited by Lao who formed, with the Lao people of Luang Prabang, only two-fifths of the population of Laos, but who could not be separated from the mass of their fellows across the river. Finally, in the south, the Kha and

Moi mountain area had been divided between Laos, Vietnam, and Cambodia. The population of Laos fell thus into two potentially hostile sections: the Lao in the valleys of the Mekong and its tributaries, and the hill peoples who had severally in the past resisted Lao rule.[59] With doubtless the best of administrative intentions, the virtue of the former buffer zone had been destroyed.

In the peaceful era brought by France the life of the Mekong valley revived. The Lao people mingled freely across their great river; the scattered hill peoples hardly noticed the new boundary posts in the north-east, and the Khas astride the frontier in the south remained largely impervious to outside influences. The encroaching Vietnamese communities lived in peace with their Lao and Cambodian neighbours.

The consequences of French rule were nevertheless profound. From the first, attracted by Vietnamese energy and impressed by Vietnamese problems, France had based her empire on the Vietnamese people and ruled it, after her own advantage, to theirs. Siam, the enemy of Vietnam, was also the enemy of France. Restrained only by the British, the French used their power to take from Siam what France and Vietnam required. The balance between Siam and the Vietnamese was thus turned heavily to the east. The expansionist ambitions of Vietnam were encouraged, Cambodian and Laotian interests subordinated, Siam compelled to face a European incarnation of her ancient enemy directly across a land frontier in the Mekong valley. Traditional fears and enmities throughout the Indo-Chinese peninsula were immeasurably increased, the former solution of the buffer zone gravely prejudiced.

ADDITIONAL NOTES TO CHAPTER II

1. This appears to have been true at the beginning of the century, and also in 1929. Lunet de Lajonquière, writing of the situation in 1904 (*Le Siam et les siamois*, Paris, 1906) says Siam contained 1,766,000 Siamese and 1,354,000 Lao. The *Encylopaedia Britannica* (14th edn., 1929) gives 3,800,000 Siamese and 3,600,000 Lao, showing an increase in the proportion of Lao as compared with 1904. As Siamese census figures have not distinguished between Siamese and Lao since 1932, the present situation can only be estimated. Wendell Blanchard (et al.), *Thailand, its People, its Society, its Culture* (New Haven, Conn., 1957) estimates, on a linguistic basis, 5 million Lao for north-east Siam and 2 million for the

[59] See additional note 3 at end of chapter.

north, out of a total 'Thai' population of 18½ million, and an overall total of 22·8 million.

However, the latest census figures show a population of nearly 9 million in north-east Siam and over 5½ million in the north out of a total population of over 26¼ million. This suggests that there may not have been as great a change in ethnic proportions as Blanchard's linguistic estimate implies.

Population figures for Laos are more uncertain as there has been no systematic census since 1941. Joel M. Halpern, *Economy and Society of Laos* (Yale, 1964), pp. 9–13, gives what appears to be a reasonable assessment of the present position. Taking into account a number of hitherto unconsidered factors, he arrives at a figure of 2 million for the total population, the Lao element forming 40 per cent, i.e. 820,000.

Thus, even assuming that Blanchard's figure does not under-estimate the number of Lao in north-east Siam, there are today more than six times as many Lao in this area as there are in Laos itself.

2. The *Carte ethnolinguistique de l'Indochine*, École française d'extrême orient, Saigon, 1949, gives the detailed racial distribution as established by the French, and clearly shows that the eastern frontier of Laos has no ethnic validity: the essentials of this map are reproduced on p. 47. The report Pavie wrote in 1888 for the French Commander-in-Chief in Hanoi is in *Mission Pavie, géographie et voyages*, vol. VII, p. 130 ff. A translation of an extract, showing the situation in north-east Laos and the Sipsong Chau Thai on his arrival is at Appendix II.

3. It is perhaps misleading to say, as Lancaster, op. cit., p. 55, that the Lao accepted French rule with a sense of grievance at the anomaly of the Mekong as a frontier, for the repopulation of the left bank of the river was partly due to the French. Furthermore, one of the reasons for French success in obtaining the co-operation of Laotian officials during their initial occupation of Laos was that the country had been suffering from famine and the Siamese had refused to grant tax reliefs. The real resentment arose much later. It was directed as much at the attachment of Laos to Vietnam, with whom it had no natural ethnic or geographic links, as at the political separation of the two banks of the Mekong. See Katay D. Sasorith, *Le Laos* (Paris, 1953), p. 92.

There are relics even today of popular resentment in north-east Siam at the loss of Laotian territories to France. See, for instance, F. Cripps, *The Far Province* (London, 1965), p. 51, for a popular festival of indignation—a sort of Guy Fawkes Day—against 'Mo Pawi'. This may owe something to the anti-French propaganda campaign mounted by the Siamese in 1940–1, which, according to Mr. W. A. R. Wood, contained similar demonstrations.

PART TWO

THE DEVELOPMENT OF THE PROBLEM, 1940-1964

Introduction

THREE phases can be discerned in the development of the modern problem of Laos as a buffer state. The first, which embraces the Second World War and the war in Indo-China, saw the dissolution of the French empire of Indo-China and the re-emergence of the old conflict between Siam and the Vietnamese in cold war terms. Siam, supported by the West, now faced a Communist North Vietnam backed by the East. One of the principal aims of the Geneva Conference which ended the Indo-China war in 1954 was therefore to establish the kingdom of Laos as a neutral buffer state between them. This phase is covered in Chapters III and IV.

The second phase, lasting from 1954 to 1961, which saw the failure to create a stable neutrality in Laos, is the subject of Chapters V and VI. The inbuilt anomalies of Laos would in any case have made the achievement of internal harmony difficult. The force of the external strains, of the two sides each seeking allies in the country, made it impossible. At the end of 1960 Laos lapsed into a civil war which was ended by international agreement in May 1961, in order that a new Geneva Conference might bring about the stability that was essential. The conference lasted until July 1962. The difficulties it overcame and the continuing divisions in Laos which, even by the end of 1962, were beginning to destroy the settlement it had achieved, constitute a third short phase. This is dealt with in Chapter VII, which also covers in outline the progressive breakdown of the succeeding two years.

In the concluding Chapter VIII an attempt is made to focus attention on the factors which should perhaps be considered in any future Laotian settlement.

CHAPTER III

Laos in the Second World War

SIAM had bowed before the French onslaught, but she remained fully aware of the real nature of the French challenge. When France was defeated in 1940, therefore, Siam was ready with territorial claims on Cambodia and Laos which were chauvinistic in part, but which also marked her realization that the security of her eastern frontier was coming into question. Japan forced France to return the Cambodian and Laotian provinces ceded by Siam in 1904 and 1907. The resulting dissatisfaction in Laos stimulated the French into reforms designed to build up a Laotian national consciousness which would resist Siamese irredentism. From this there grew a Laotian independence movement against the French after the war.

The reconciliation of this movement to France by the grant of limited independence in 1949 left in Laos only a trace of the anti-colonial nationalist resentment which had meanwhile given rise to full-scale war in Vietnam. The trace was however to be important. Prince Souphanouvong, the most ebullient and possibly the ablest member of the Laotian aristocracy, had thrown in his lot with the anti-French rebels in Vietnam, the Viet Minh. His gift for leadership found him allies among the hill peoples of Laos, always more attached to their kinsmen in upland Vietnam than to the Lao whose domination they resented. Siam, deprived once more by the defeat of Japan of the Laotian and Cambodian provinces she claimed, watched anxiously as the Laotian rift brought her old Vietnamese rival towards her borders.

* * *

The escape of Siam from colonialism at the beginning of the century had served her well. The stability that ensued from the establishment of Britain and France as her neighbours brought an era of prosperity to the country. Foreign capital gave her economic strength. Siam took the side of the Allies in the First World

War. Her relations with France became cordial. Once more she assimilated what suited her from the alien, without compromising her independence.

One of the elements Siam had tried was parliamentary democracy; a revolution in 1932 turned her autocratic king into a constitutional monarch. However the parliamentary experiment failed to develop and the country had moved by 1939 to the prevailing fashion of military dictatorship, which intensified the new self-assertive nationalism that revolution had brought. The shadow of Japan was looming southwards through China. Government maps had already been published showing Cambodia, Laos, and part of Vietnam as Siamese territory and the Annamitic Chain as Siam's natural frontier.[1] Never slow to note a changing climate, Siam in 1939 took the new name of Thailand: in advance of the possible arrival of Japan, whose influence upon her had already outstripped that of France, Siam was preparing to claim the leadership of all of Thai race.[2]

The outbreak of the second world war made the new Siamese mood look dangerous. Conscious of her vulnerability on the Mekong, France sought a new non-aggression pact with her neighbour across the river, which was provisionally agreed on 12 June 1940. Siam had, however, on the same day entered into a treaty of friendship with Japan. A few days later France capitulated to Germany and Japan was soon pressing the French for the use of Indo-Chinese territory in her war against China. In August 1940, while Japan bore harder upon the French, the Siamese launched a violent anti-French propaganda campaign along the Mekong, claiming the return of Laos to Siam. The Lao people were reminded of their Thai race, of the fact that overwhelmingly more Lao lived in Siam free from colonialist domination than in the country that

---

[1] When the British and French diplomatic representatives protested at the appearance of this map in schools and public places, the Siamese ruler replied that it was intended only for educational purposes: Sir Josiah Crosby, *Siam: The Crossroads* (London, 1945), p. 114. Sir Josiah Crosby was British minister at Bangkok from 1934–41. See also R. Emerson, L. A. Mills, and V. Thompson, *Government and Nationalism in Southeast Asia* (New York, 1942), p. 219.

[2] The country had been known as 'Muong Thai' or 'Prathet Thai' by the people themselves, and internationally as Siam, the name to which it reverted after the second world war. The name was changed to Thailand again in 1949.

bore their name. 'Your kinsmen', said the leaflets, the radio broadcasts, the agents from across the river, 'live in a free country with free
institutions. They are your own people, separated from you only
by the false frontier of colonialism.'[3] The propaganda had some
effect, particularly in southern Laos where people had always tended
to look across the river to Siam rather than upstream to Vientiane.

The actual Siamese demands were soon made clear. If Japanese
troops were to enter Indo-China, it was argued, a totally new
situation would arise for Siam. Siamese security would demand the
return of part of Cambodia and of the Laotian provinces on the
west bank of the Mekong. Moreover, if French sovereignty over
Indo-China were to end, Siam would not consider herself safe
unless the whole of Laos and Cambodia were returned to her.[4]

This was not the mere treacherous oriental rapacity which some
thought it at the time. The Siamese feared that, with the dis-
appearance of French power, the influence of Vietnam would
reassert itself in the entire area of French control and along the
whole vulnerable eastern frontier of Siam. Japan, though obviously
a force to be conciliated, was unlikely to restrain the Vietnamese.
Siam's object must therefore be, as it had been in 1890, to push
towards the traditional geographical barrier of the Annamitic
Chain. Her claims against France and the attempt to attach to
herself by propaganda the Lao people across the Mekong, were in
the nature of preliminary steps.[5]

The Governor-General of Indo-China, Admiral Decoux, who
had taken office in July 1940 after General Catroux had been recalled by Pétain, who doubted his reliability, did not see the Siamese
point of view. He had formerly been French naval commander in
the Far East and knew only too well that the British could not,

[3] Crosby, op. cit., pp. 111–21 deals with Siamese chauvinism at this
period. See also Admiral Decoux, À la barre de l'Indochine, pp. 123–47,
for a full account of Siamese action against the colony.

[4] See M. Sivaram, Mekong Clash and Far East Crisis (Bangkok, 1941),
p. 7; K. P. Landon, 'Thailand's quarrel with France in perspective' in
Far Eastern Quarterly, I, No. 1 (Nov. 1941), pp. 25–42 has a reasonable
statement of the Siamese case.

[5] The extent to which the continuous nature of the problem was in
Siamese minds can be judged from the fact that, when Siam declared war
on Britain and the U.S. in 1942, one of the complaints against the U.S.
was that she had failed to support Siam against France in 1893: Crosby,
op. cit., p. 137. Admittedly it was a silly complaint, but the fact that it
was made is significant.

and the United States would not, prevent the Japanese having their will of Indo-China. His own forces were too weak to oppose Japan: in September he had been compelled to accept a virtual Japanese occupation of northern Tongking. But France should, he thought, be able to stand up to Siamese pretensions. He therefore reinforced his positions along the Mekong in Laos and prepared to defend western Cambodia where Siam was most likely to attack. Tension sharply increased with the end of the rains. In December the Siamese entered the disputed ground in Laos and began harassing French territory across the river with machine-guns, artillery, and aerial bombardment. The French replied meticulously in kind.

By now eight French or French-led battalions had been concentrated in Cambodia where they confronted a strong Siamese force already on Cambodian soil. The area was however short of water and Decoux was faced with the choice of an advance into Siam or a withdrawal. He chose to advance and on 16 January 1941 his forces attacked. The Siamese, forewarned and in superior numbers, counter-attacked. Some of the French units raised in Indo-China bolted and at the end of the day the French found themselves back where they started; they broke off the action and withdrew to their main position.[6] A naval success in the Gulf of Siam on 17 January provided some consolation for the losers. Three days later, however, the Japanese imposed a suspension of hostilities and finally a settlement, by which France surrendered to Siam the Cambodian province of Battambang, a strip of northern Cambodia extending to the Mekong,[7] the Laotian province of Bassac in the south, and Sayaboury on the western bank of the Mekong opposite Luang Prabang in the north.[8]

[6] Decoux, op. cit., p. 141.

[7] The strip was bounded on the south by the 15th *grade* of latitude, which corresponds in the more familiar measurement to about 13° 30′ N. Lancaster, op. cit., p. 95 calls it misleadingly the 15th *parallel* of latitude, which does not run through Cambodia at all. Decoux, op. cit., p. 144 and fold-out map refer.

[8] Japan's intentions, in case a division of spoils in South-East Asia was made possible by a German victory, are given in W. M. Elsbree, *Japan's role in Southeast Asian Nationalist Movements* (Harvard, 1963), pp. 16–17. Independence movements were to be encouraged and the French forced out of Indo-China. Chiang Kai-Shek was to be offered Tongking and parts of upper Burma; Cambodia was to be presented to Siam.

The prospect of losing Sayaboury with its royal teak forests, and of having the Siamese back on the opposite side of the river, caused consternation in the protected kingdom of Luang Prabang and there was talk of the king's abdication.[9] Only the immediate union of the whole of Laos under the crown of Luang Prabang, it was said, could repair the insult and loss of territory. But the haughty northerners of Luang Prabang were not liked in the south[10] where, furthermore, the arbitrary retirement in 1935 of Prince Nhouy, head of the old royal house of Champassak, who had served as governor of the former kingdom under the French, was still widely resented. Moreover Siamese propaganda had been particularly effective in the south. The union of the whole country was something the French could not yet concede.

Admiral Decoux was, however, able to propose that the kingdom of Luang Prabang, which had hitherto consisted only of Luang Prabang, Sam Neua, Sayaboury, and Phongsaly provinces, should be extended by the incorporation of the provinces of Xieng Khouang, Vientiane, and Nam Tha, to cover the whole of northern Laos. In a state visit to Hanoi, which he made a little later, King Sisavang Vong of Luang Prabang agreed; the new statute was signed on 29 August 1941.

It may be that not since the departure of Auguste Pavie had the French thought so deeply about Laos and the Laotians. When Pavie reached it in 1887 there had been some kind of unity between the land and its people. Laos had seemed to possess a national personality, in spite of its divisions, in spite of subservience to Siam. But now after fifty years of the French peace, there was little more than the indignation of the Laotian aristocracy to set against greater Thai imperialism and to counter the propaganda from across the river.

In fact it was Siam that had changed and grown into assertive modern statehood, while the administrative and social structure of Laos remained much as it had been for centuries. A French and Vietnamese civil service had ruled the country from the ad-

[9] The Siamese had kept Sayaboury by the Franco-Siamese Treaty of 1893 and had surrendered it under the convention of 1904 after repeated representations from the king of Luang Prabang to the French. Le Boulanger, op. cit., p. 343.

[10] See Lancaster, op. cit., p. 71, and Pierre Gentil, *Remous du Mekong* (Paris, 1950), p. 32.

ministrative capital of Vientiane. The kingdom of Luang Prabang had been preserved under French protection, its king having reigned ever since his investiture by the French at the age of nineteen in 1905.[11] The provincial centres had become pleasant French colonial towns. But development had been slight. Laos was still backward, an inaccessible and unprofitable hinterland to the bustling progress of populous Vietnam. Although it represented a third of French Indo-China in area, its population of just over a million in 1941 compared with twenty-two millions in the rest of the country, and its trade amounted to barely one per cent. of the whole.[12]

France might undoubtedly have done more. Laos had always had a favourable balance of trade with the outside world; benzoin and gumlac were still being exported: there was also tin, coffee, and opium. Opium might have made a much greater economic contribution had efforts to control its smuggling proved successful. Tung oil trees, introduced into northern Laos in 1938, also might have led to important development earlier. But there had been no commercial need to exploit the remote resources of Laos, no ambitious urge, no internal pressure that would have created the economic necessity to do so, and in any case too much malaria and too little labour. Thus, when in spite of efforts to improve its navigational possibilities, the Mekong was seen not to be a great highway of commerce, and when the flow of Laotian trade itself proved hardly worth diverting to Saigon, interest had moved away.

The amount that the French administration at Vientiane had been able to accomplish in the way of public works, education, medical, and other services was therefore minimal, and even so it had largely to be financed from the central Indo-Chinese budget.[13] If roads were built, their purpose was to facilitate the movement of troops from Vietnam in case of civil emergency; Luang Prabang, Sam Neua, Savannakhet were connected by simple metalled roads with the road and rail system of Vietnam, but were not linked to each other. Thus Sam Neua could be reached from Hanoi by dry-weather road in a day, but it was still

[11] See additional note 1 at end of chapter.

[12] The figures were: 0·9 per cent. in 1937, 1·3 per cent. in 1938, 0·9 per cent in 1939.

[13] In the period 1896–1917, Laos had covered 56 per cent. of its expenditure from its revenues; in the period 1917–41, only 45 per cent.

several days by mountain trail from Luang Prabang and Vientiane which administered it. Hospitals were built at six of the main centres, but again, although they treated Laotian patients within their capabilities, their *raison d'être* was to serve the few hundreds of French people in Laos.

Education remained for the most part in the hands of the monks. Even by 1940 there were but ninety-two government schools, which catered for less than four and a half per cent. of the children of school age.[14] There was only one secondary school and, as we have already seen, more than half its places were occupied by Vietnamese. The growth of an indigenous middle class had therefore been slow, and its lack, together with the shortage of labour in all spheres, strengthened the existing French inclination to think of the development of the country in terms of its settlement by the surplus population of Vietnam.

The aristocracy, the few families of the Lao *élite*[15]—and it was only the Lao who counted—had found little to regret in a French association which maintained their positions intact in a changing world. They modified their ancient ways a little and played without complaint the parts allotted to them under the colonial régime. Sometimes they did much more. From 1921 onwards Prince Phetsarath, third son and heir of Prince Boun Khong, the viceroy of Luang Prabang when French rule began, took a beneficent and active part in the government of the country on the staff of the French commissioner in Vientiane. He had not inherited the title of viceroy when his father died in 1914, but in the course of his own service he acquired such popularity and authority in Laotian affairs that he was sometimes called 'king of Vientiane'. His younger brother, Prince Souvannaphouma and his youngest half-brother, Prince Souphanouvang, both qualified as civil engineers in France and joined the Public Works Service

[14] Out of an estimated 160,000 children of school age, there were 7,000 pupils in the government schools and 5,600 pupils in the 231 village pagoda schools: see p. 45 above.

[15] For a discussion of the *élite* in Laos, see Joel M. Halpern, *Government, Politics and Social Structure in Laos* (Yale University, 1964). Before the second world war less than a dozen Lao could be said to have received a full college education (p. 6). For French neglect of the hill peoples and their subjection to Lao officials, see Virginia Thompson, *French Indo-China* (London, 1937), p. 369; it should be added that French efforts for the advancement of the minorities were often frustrated by Lao opposition.

in Indo-China. Within the kingdom of Luang Prabang the king's son, Prince Savang, cultured, highly educated in law and political science, won much authority of his own.

But for the rest, for the broad majority of the Laotian people in their ten thousand villages, even for the king and his court, life remained much as it had always been. Needs were simple and satisfied from simple resources, methods were primitive, manners good, communications bad. The hill people were still undisturbed in their mountain fastnesses. Laos remained a Shangri-La, a land of charm and gaiety, of love, fairies, magic spells, cheerful festivals, and the gentle unforgettable music of the khêne.

Now suddenly, in 1941, the Mekong had become a frontier in more than name. There had been a brief, bitter, and terrifying war. The continuing Siamese challenge had to be met. Somehow, in a country which had depended largely on Vietnamese immigrants for its educated class, a sense of positive national unity must be created if its identity was to be maintained. The constitutional statute of August 1941 and the new French policy that went with it, were thus far more than compensation to the king of Luang Prabang for loss of territory and population. France had realized that she might lose all of Laos to the Siamese by default. It was vital to remedy the consequences of past inertia, to rouse the Laotian from his lethargy.

In the time that remained to her France did her best. The Laotian administration was reorganized, salaries were raised and Laotian provincial governors appointed with the title of chao-khoueng. The quality and composition of the European cadre of officials was critically reviewed and strengthened; schemes for further large scale Vietnamese immigration were dropped.[16] Considerably more funds were provided from the central Indo-Chinese budget for projects in Laos. The garrisons along the Mekong were strengthened to discourage Siamese adventures; two Laotian infantry companies were raised. An extensive road-building programme was launched, and the agricultural and forestry services, retrenched in the economic crisis of 1934, were revived. Mobile medical teams were set to work in the mountainous tribal zones of the north, more schools were opened in the rural areas and a

[16] E. Pietrantoni, op. cit., p. 243, mentions plans for bringing 100,000 Vietnamese into the Song Khone valley south of Savannakhet and 50,000 into the Bolovens Plateau.

new emphasis on the production of national leaders was demanded of the School of Laotian Administration in Vientiane. Finally, as a direct reply to Siamese propaganda, an information service was created of which the central figure was M. Charles Rochet, the Director of Laotian Public Education. M. Rochet believed in the Lao, and it was under his inspiration that Katay Don Sasorith and Nhouy Abhay founded the National Renovation Movement which was to provide so many of the independence leaders in 1945 and 1946.[17]

Even now, little if anything was done to correct the balance in development between the Lao and the hill peoples. The Meo, the Kha, even the 'Pou Thai',[18] remained isolated in their mountain fastnesses. This was partly due to difficulty of access, partly to increased reluctance on the part of the Lao to share what few benefits there were with the backward tribal people. Now that political power was coming his way the Lao seemed particularly content that a lack of sophistication should continue in the hills.[19] This was to have unhappy consequences.

The new kingdom of Luang Prabang extended as far south as the Nam Ka Dinh river. The king of Luang Prabang became its ruler under a formal protectorate treaty with the French government—as opposed to an agreement with the Governor-General to which he had owed his former status—and his civil list salary was increased by sixty per cent. For Prince Phetsarath, who had been credited with hopes of a throne, perhaps that of a new kingdom of Vientiane, was revived his father's title of Viceroy. Phetsarath also

[17] Sisouk Na Champassak, *Storm over Laos* (New York, 1961), p. 8. In his moving book, *Pays Lao, le Laos dans la tourmente* (Paris, 1946), which deals chiefly with the period of Japanese violence in Laos just before their defeat, M. Rochet describes the relations between France and Laos at this time. The book shows him as a colonial servant with a rare sympathy for and understanding of his people.

[18] Pavie used the collective term Pou Thai for the Thai folk of Sam Neua and the Sipsong Chau Thai who are now commonly subdivided into Black Thai, White Thai, and Thai Neua. They are essentially the same people and the fact that they straddle the present frontier between Laos and Vietnam is one of the elements of the modern problem. See extract from Pavie's report at Appendix II and map on p. 47.

[19] The French administration had always had difficulty with the Lao leadership over the establishment of schools in minority areas. In 1940 no member of the minority races in Laos had achieved a secondary education.

became prime minister in a modern adaptation of the traditional king's council,[20] with his half-brother Prince Souvannarath as Minister of Economy and the king's brother Prince Settha as Minister of the Interior. The settlement thus also represented a reconciliation between the two branches of the royal family; for the ambitions and influence of Prince Phetsarath and his many able brothers had been viewed with suspicion by the senior line headed by the king.[21]

The new council was to meet under the chairmanship of a high French official, its composition was not far removed from tradition, and its authority was limited. Moreover the changes, territorial and political, were understood only within the small educated circle of Laotians,[22] and the significance of the ceremonies celebrating the transfer of the new provinces to the old kingdom passed the people by. They marked, nevertheless, the beginning of modern national government in Laos. South of the Nam Ka Dinh the country continued to be administered as before, but with some thought of an eventual union of the whole of Laos.

Unhappily, time was fast running out for the French. When she launched herself into war in December 1941 Japan had been prepared to seize French Indo-China, control over which was essential to her operations in Malaya. Admiral Decoux had avoided outright Japanese occupation by agreeing not to oppose Japan's war plans and by putting the economic resources of the country at her disposal. This bargain saved the forty thousand French people in Indo-China from Japanese concentration camps for over three years, and avoided the risk of atrocities upon the twenty-three million Indo-Chinese. It also kept the Japanese to some extent out of sight of the population of the colony as a whole, a fact which, together with Decoux's programme of public works and his success in keeping the economy going, probably slowed down the decline of French prestige in the East. It must be said on the other hand that the passive collaboration of French Indo-China was vital to

[20] The French had 'abolished' the king's council of Luang Prabang, the *Hosanam Luang*, in 1915. Their action had however been disregarded by the ruler and the council had continued to sit.

[21] See additional note 1.

[22] Halpern, op. cit., p. 97, considers that as late as 1959 the Lao *élite* consisted, in terms of political decision making groups, of a few dozen people.

the Japanese; it hastened their conquest of Malaya and delayed Allied victory in the Far East.[23]

After the liberation of France in 1944, Decoux himself assumed full powers in Indo-China in accordance with the standing orders of the Vichy Government. Many of his subordinates, however, had long been in touch with Free France through the French mission in Kunming, and in September one of them, General Mordant, was secretly appointed Delegate-General for Indo-China by General de Gaulle,[24] an arrangement in which the admiral agreed to co-operate when he was informed of it at the end of October. But the circumstances were such—an ebullient, wildly optimistic, ill-co-ordinated and indiscreet resistance movement, increasingly rent by the bitter rivalries of French domestic politics—that the Japanese could not fail to realize that something was afoot. Towards the end of 1944, on the pretext that the reoccupation of the Philippines by the United States in October had made an Allied invasion of Indo-China a serious possibility, they moved in reinforcements and quietly deployed their forces so as to thwart the most probable French course of action.

The French had planned to withdraw their main military units from the towns to areas from which they could retreat freely to the mountains in the event of a Japanese move against French sovereignty. Allied air supply would thereafter enable them to harass Japanese communications and bases. The preparatory steps were being taken when, on 9 March 1945, the Japanese struck. Within twenty-four hours of the rejection of their ultimatum by Admiral Decoux, they were in complete control. Some six thousand French and three thousand Indo-Chinese troops began to fight their way out to China from Tongking. Elsewhere isolated parties of French survivors made their way to the hills, some garrisons fought heroically to the death, but the resistance movement collapsed and co-ordinated action ceased.[25] American forces in

[23] See Decoux's own account, and on the other hand Lancaster, op. cit., p. 96, and P. Devillers, *Histoire du Viet-Nam de 1940 à 1952* (Paris, 1952), pp. 116–17. General de Gaulle makes his own view clear in *Mémoires de guerre, le salut 1944–1946* (Paris, 1959), p. 164.

[24] General de Gaulle had written to General Mordant as far back as 29 February 1944 'pour l'affermir dans les bonnes intentions dont je sais qu'elles sont les siennes'; de Gaulle, *Mémoires de guerre, l'unité 1942–1944* (Paris, 1956), p. 286 and pp. 680–1.

[25] Lancaster, op. cit., pp. 104–6. See also Devillers, op. cit., pp. 121–3.

Yunnan were ordered not to supply the French with the arms and ammunition they needed.[26] The troops who nevertheless escaped were deprived by Chiang Kai-Shek, under whose command they were placed, of any further role in Indo-China.

The Japanese now informed the princely rulers in Vietnam, Cambodia, and Laos that the colonial régime was at an end and that their countries had become independent members of Japan's new order. In Cambodia the position was accepted, in Vietnam the nationalists seized their opportunity, but in Laos, where the Japanese had hardly yet appeared, Crown Prince Savang, in the name of his father, proclaimed the loyalty of the royal court and people of Luang Prabang to France. On 16 March 1945 he ordered a general rising of partisans against the Japanese and severe penalties for anyone who refused to help the French. The Japanese accordingly occupied Luang Prabang early in April, forced the king to declare the independence of his kingdom and obliged the crown prince to promise co-operation. In the meantime, with the full agreement of the king, French and Laotian troops in upper Laos, together with Prince Kindavong,[27] Phoui Sananikone,[28] and many other Laotian leaders, had made their way into China.

Further south the French and Laotian garrisons who could escape took to the jungle, where patriotic organizations fostered by the French since 1941 supported them, helping also the new French resistance groups from India already parachuted into the hills. The young head of the house of Champassak, Prince Boun Oum, led his people against the Japanese in the south.[29] Kou Voravong[30] was with the parachutists in the Paksane area, Leuam Insisiengmay east of Savannakhet.[31] Such was the feeling in the country that most of the French civilians working there who were

[26] See additional note 2 at end of chapter.

[27] Brother of Phetsarath and chaomuong (district governor) of Muong Kassy. He died in 1947.

[28] Chaokhoueng (provincial governor) of Nam Tha, prime minister of Laos in 1950–1 and 1958–9.

[29] See C. H. Duparc, 'Le problème politique Laotien' in *Politique Étrangère* XII (1947), p. 538, and Michel Caply, *Guérilla au Laos* (Paris, 1966), pp. 105–6 for Prince Boun Oum's outstanding leadership at this time.

[30] Later chaokhoueng of Thakhek and Minister of Defence in 1954 when he was assassinated.

[31] Later chaokhoueng of Savannakhet, a strong southerner and conservative, connected by marriage with the Champassak family.

not caught by the initial surprise, succeeded in escaping from the Japanese.

Prince Phetsarath, viceroy and prime minister, behaved with greater circumspection. Realizing, as did the crown prince in Luang Prabang, that the Japanese were now his only protection against the exultant Vietnamese who were already acting as heirs presumptive to French power in Laos, he was careful not to antagonize the new masters. They found his attitude satisfactory and merely appointed 'advisers' to his administration. This gave him a certain freedom. He saw it as an opportunity to prepare Laos for independence and to remove some of the Vietnamese from the Laotian public services. In the north he had some success, but the Vietnamese were tenacious. Caply writes:

Dans les ministères et les services, ils ont, dès le début de l'occupation, tenté de prendre les rênes du pouvoir et de diriger l'administration. Cette dualité de pouvoir, responsables lao dépendant du Premier Ministre où de la Résidence supérieure, cadres annamites prétendant commander avec l'appui nippon, amène, dès le mois d'avril, une stagnation quasi complète des services.[32]

Although the king had limited his declaration of independence strictly to his own domains, Phetsarath and the Japanese ignored sentiment in the south and treated the country henceforth as one. Thanks to the quality of the underground resistance, however, the Japanese writ rarely ran outside the limits of the towns, and many even of the officials appointed by Phetsarath worked secretly with the French.

Elsewhere in Indo-China the best efforts of Free France could do little to save what remained of French prestige in the months that followed. It was a time of cruelty and chaos. The Japanese behaved with their usual sporadic savagery even in Laos. Forty-seven French civilians were murdered in Thakhek. Everywhere the Japanese tried to provoke and sustain anti-French sentiment. Without their French administrators the civil governments were too weak to cope with their problems.

In Vietnam the revolutionary nationalist movement of Ho Chi Minh, nurtured by the Allies for its potential resistance to the Japanese,[33] and now supported by United States secret service

[32] Caply, op. cit., p. 177.

[33] Its actual achievements against the Japanese were minimal. B. B. Fall, *Street Without Joy* (Harrisburg, 1961), p. 24.

missions, consolidated and extended its grip with the connivance of the Japanese, so that when Japan surrendered on 15 August it was in a position to take control of the greater part of Vietnam within a few days. The plan was to disarm the Japanese before the arrival of the Allies, to take over power, and to receive, as the authority in control of the country, the Allied forces coming to demobilize the Japanese.[34] The Viet Minh,[35] as they were henceforth to be called, were effectively masters of Vietnam by 23 August 1945, and were sending armed detachments into Laos and Cambodia.

The armies of the British South-East Asia Command, then poised for an invasion of Malaya, were not prepared for the sudden total victory of the atom bomb, which gave them at a stroke, a vast agglomeration of lands with their hundreds of thousands of internees, prisoners, refugees, and partisans, all in some degree of extremity, and which added, among other things, half of Indo-China to their responsibilities. Military and political considerations had suddenly to give place to human rescue. Everything had to be improvised. Decisions taken for the continuance of war had to be adapted; the only priority was to reach, relieve, and repatriate the prisoners. Information on conditions in the area was scarce, inaccurate, and slow. It took a surprisingly long time even for surrender orders to reach the Japanese in the field, and in the interval there was much local uncertainty from which the Viet Minh profited and the French and French influence in Indo-China suffered.

There were conflicts of Allied policy. Siam had declared war on the Allies in January 1942 and, as a reward from Japan, had received portions of Burma and also the Malayan states she had ceded to Britain in 1909. Britain as well as France was thus inclined to treat Siam strictly as an ex-enemy. The United States, on the other hand, whose interests Siam had not directly damaged, regarded her as an occupied country and sought to moderate French and British attitudes.

Furthermore President Roosevelt had made no secret of his wish to prevent a French return to Indo-China. He had told his Secretary of State, Cordell Hull, in 1944, that 'nothing was to be done

[34] Truong Chinh, *La révolution d'août* (Hanoi, 1962), p. 12.
[35] Viet Nam Doc Lap Dong Minh Hoi, commonly abbreviated to Viet Minh.

in regard to resistance groups or in any other way in relation to Indo-China'.[36] In the face of dogged British resistance he had reluctantly abandoned his plan to place the country under international trusteeship[37] but he was more than ever determined on its independence. Churchill himself was unable to change the president's decision not to supply the French when they were fighting their way out of Tongking, a callous act which served no Allied purpose.[38] It is also certain that had Roosevelt lived he would have tried to prevent their return, as Lord Mountbatten implied in August 1945 when he received General Leclerc in Ceylon.[39]

Official American policy after the Japanese surrender was more friendly to the French. On 22 August 1945 President Truman assured General de Gaulle that his government would not oppose the French return to Indo-China.[40] This was not, however, the feeling in Indo-China itself where American officers attached to the Viet Minh waxed enthusiastic in the anti-colonial cause, while their colleagues assisted from across the Mekong; there were painful incidents in which they treated the French openly as enemies.[41] De Gaulle had few of his own troops in the East and was dependent on his allies for means of transport. He could therefore not have opposed the arrangement made at the Potsdam Conference whereby the Chinese and British were to receive the Japanese surrender in Indo-China, to the north and south of the sixteenth parallel respectively, though he bitterly resented it.

[36] *Memoirs of Cordell Hull* (New York, 1948), vol. ii, p. 1598. Nicol Smith, *Into Siam* (New York, 1945), p. 192 shows that the U.S. State Department was secretly canvassing the views of national leaders in South-East Asia on the return or otherwise of their colonial masters.

[37] See Lord Avon, *The Eden Memoirs, the Reckoning* (London, 1965), pp. 378, 426, and 513 for persistent British opposition to the trusteeship plan of which the 'anti-colonial' Cordell Hull was a supporter. The plan had been dropped by February 1945 as Roosevelt made clear at a press conference after Yalta: see S. I. Rosenman (ed.), *The Public Papers and addresses of Franklin D. Roosevelt: Victory and the Threshold of Peace* (New York, 1950), pp. 562–3.

[38] See additional note 3.

[39] P. Devillers, op. cit., pp. 149–50.

[40] De Gaulle, *Mémoires de guerre, le salut 1944–1946* (Paris, 1959), pp. 213 and 555.

[41] See Lancaster, op. cit., p. 125. Sainteny, *Histoire d'une paix manquée* (Paris, 1953) *passim*, and for a particular instance near Thakhek, P. Kemp, *Alms for Oblivion* (London, 1961), pp. 49–56.

The Chinese also had purposes of their own. In the formal sense, it was from China that France had acquired Tongking in 1885. If there was to be any question of a change in the *status quo*, the Chinese of course expected to benefit.[42] In spite of his assurances to President Roosevelt in 1943 Chiang Kai-Shek had been planning for more than a year to install a puppet régime in Hanoi[43] and was somewhat put out when the Viet Minh forestalled him. While he was friendly and reassuring to de Gaulle, he was determined to extract everything he could from the French predicament.

The result of the conflicting interests of her allies was that, in the face of Viet Minh power, France was left to reconquer Indo-China if she could. The small British force sent to receive the Japanese surrender in the south did more than it at first intended to help the French in Saigon, but its purpose was to save French lives rather than to put down a nationalist rebellion.[44]

The success of Ho Chi Minh in Vietnam was watched with a mixture of admiration and apprehension in Laos. American support of the Viet Minh made it appear doubtful whether the French would be permitted to return. The immediate problem was therefore to protect Laos from the triumphant Vietnamese, which implied a measure of detachment from the remaining French on the part of the Laotian leaders. As early as 20 August Laotian elements of the anti-Japanese guerrillas in Siam, encouraged by their own instructors and by the Viet Minh, were changing direction against France; some hoped to win independence for the Lao people on both banks of the Mekong.[45] Prince Souphanouvong had already been in contact with the Viet Minh for some months; Sithone Khamadam, son of the chief of the Bolovens Kha killed by the French in 1936 after twenty-five years of dissidence, had been released from prison with two of his brothers by the Japanese,

[42] Devillers, op. cit., p. 116. Tongking was already shown as Chinese on one of the maps at the Chinese military school at Cheng Tu.

[43] Ibid., p. 109, Lancaster, op. cit., p. 115. E. R. Stettinius, *Roosevelt and the Russians* (London, 1950), pp. 211–12, quotes Chiang Kai-Shek's assurances to Roosevelt in 1943, during discussions of a possible trusteeship for Indo-China, that he had no designs on the country.

[44] See *Documents relating to British Involvement in the Indo-China Conflict 1945–1965* (Cmnd. 2834) (London, 1965), pp. 6–8.

[45] For the Seri Thai movement and its Lao-pen-Lao (Laos for the Lao) element, see Caply, op. cit., pp. 222–5. This book is an objective and authoritative source for the politics of this period.

and the anti-French Meo leader, Faydang, had sided with the Japanese from the first.[46] When a French military detachment arrived in Vientiane at the end of August, Phetsarath refused to allow the released French commissioner to resume his functions and on 1 September he announced that independence from France had come to stay. In Thakhek the Viet Minh quickly took over from the Japanese who moved south to avoid surrender to the Chinese, harassed such French internees as had escaped massacre, and did their best to wipe out the Franco-Lao irregulars who waited in the jungle. By degrees Xieng Khouang, Sam Neua, Phongsaly passed into Viet Minh control.

On 14 September, however, French troops from the south entered Pakse at the invitation of Prince Boun Oum, and King Sisavang Vong welcomed the French mission parachuted into Luang Prabang, sending loyal greetings to General de Gaulle. The king's decision to resume the kingdom's adherence to France had been telegraphed to Prince Phetsarath on 7 September, but the prince did not reveal this for ten days. By then he was receiving additional support from the Nationalist Chinese who were moving into Laos from the north, and had declared the union of the whole country as the Kingdom of Laos. In Luang Prabang the Chinese brutally harassed the French and behaved as if they had come to stay. In Vientiane the Chinese general invited the formulation of complaints against France,[47] reduced the French detachment to a nucleus, and finally exerted such pressure that the last French elements were compelled to leave.

Phetsarath continued to build up the Independence Movement. Peter Kemp, then a member of the British special force in northeast Siam, who had been trying to help the French against the Viet Minh near Thakhek, visited the prince in the company of a French officer towards the end of September. 'A swarthy, heavily-built man,' he tells us,[48] 'in early middle age, he received us in a cool and comfortable room where the strong morning light filtered faintly through sun-blinds; his beautifully manicured hands and smart white linen suit matched the opulence of his surroundings.

---

[46] For Kha and Meo rebellions against French rule, see Le Boulanger, op. cit., and W. G. Burchett, *Mekong Upstream* (Berlin, 1959). The latter, when its Communist bias is discounted, provides an interesting account of Faydang (pp. 228–33) and the Khamadam family (pp. 209–14).

[47] Gentil, op. cit., p. 30.   [48] P. Kemp, op. cit., p. 47.

He had an unfortunate manner compounded of shiftiness, complacency and arrogance.' The viceroy was contemptuous of the French and made 'exaggerated claims' of the support he enjoyed among his own people.

The extent of popular support for Phetsarath's Independence Movement was indeed doubtful. The prince did of course possess considerable influence among his own people. He was reputed to possess mystic powers,[49] he had been for twenty years the leading Laotian personality in the French administration of Laos, he occupied the principal office of state in the Luang Prabang kingdom and shared the semi-religious popular reverence paid to the king. But there was not sufficient political consciousness in the country for his support to be termed political; there was in Laos none of the deep-rooted popular nationalism that had borne up Ho Chi Minh in Vietnam.

Moreover, Phetsarath was now claiming leadership throughout the whole of Laos, proclaiming a union which the French had regarded as premature only four years earlier. Not only were the king and crown prince against him in the north, but also Prince Boun Oum of Champassak, the foremost personality and traditional leader in the south. The king's opposition had dynastic as well as constitutional elements, for the association with Phetsarath of his brother and half-brother, the Princes Souvannaphouma and Souphanouvong, brought back uneasy memories of their father's hopes of the throne in 1904.[50] For his part, Prince Boun Oum resented the union of Laos under any part of the royal family of Luang Prabang and possessed a southerner's nervousness of Phetsarath's links with the Vietnamese. The viceroy's prestige

[49] Joel M. Halpern, op. cit., pp. 119–25 gives an account of a journey in rural Laos with Prince Phetsarath which illustrates the prince's influence and sheds some light on that of his brothers Souvannaphouma and Souphanouvong today. The popular feeling appears to be that the royal family in general have intermediary powers with the unseen world. If a representative of the family has no personality or natural grace then these powers are thought not to have 'come through' in him. But Phetsarath, Souvannaphouma, and Souphanouvong had and have great personal qualities. However much the two latter may try to discourage popular belief in their powers, it remains an element in their public position.

[50] See additional note 1. See Roger M. Smith in *Governments and Politics of South-East Asia*, G. McT. Kahin (ed.), (2nd edn., Cornell, 1964), p. 534 for the rivalry between Phetsarath and the crown prince.

could never have outweighed these formidable influences on the popular mind. His Independence Movement consisted of a few politically-minded leaders, whose following followed for personal rather than political reasons and whose strength depended on Vietnamese and Chinese backing.

Matters came to a head on 10 October. Fortified by a message from General de Gaulle, the king dismissed Prince Phetsarath both as prime minister and viceroy. Two days later the Independence Committee proclaimed a provisional constitution for a united Laos, formed a provisional National Assembly and a provisional government which included Phetsarath's brother Prince Souvannaphouma and later his half-brother Prince Souphanouvong, who was the most decidedly anti-French of the three. The king was invited to become constitutional monarch of the new state, but he declined, pronouncing the provisional government illegal and against the will of the majority,[51] and summoning the ex-viceroy to Luang Prabang. Phetsarath refused to go and on 20 October his National Assembly passed a motion deposing the king. On 4 November he organized a *coup d'état* in Luang Prabang with the help of the Chinese, who neutralized the French detachment there while the king was forced to surrender.

It now seemed possible that Phetsarath would mount the throne himself. His more extreme supporters urged this course upon him.[52] But substantial French forces had by now arrived in Saigon and it was clearly only a matter of time before they reoccupied Laos. This may have decided him against it. Instead he again invited the king to assume office as constitutional head of the new Laos and to give legitimacy to all that had been done. After long persuasion and with great reluctance King Sisavang Vong agreed and was reinstated with due ceremony on 23 April 1946, two days before the French entry into Vientiane.

The sixteenth parallel, which divided the British and Chinese zones of occupation in Indo-China, cuts the Mekong south of Savannakhet. On 28 February 1946 the signature of a Franco-Chinese agreement, under which the Chinese undertook to withdraw by 31 March, had enabled the French to cross it. Their

[51] Gentil, op. cit., p. 31.

[52] Sisouk Na Champassak, op. cit., p. 13, says that he actually decided on it and changed his mind when he realized the imminence of the French return.

forces at once moved northwards from Pakse and occupied Savannakhet without opposition on 17 March. Six days later Phetsarath offered negotiations, but by then a strong Franco-Lao guerrilla force, together with the advancing French detachments, had routed the Viet Minh and their Free Lao allies under Prince Souphanouvong at Thakhek. Pausing only to clear the road from Thakhek to the Vietnamese coast, which had been Phetsarath's main link with the Viet Minh centre, the French reoccupied Vientiane.[53]

Thus it was that on the day of the king's reinstatement, while Phetsarath and his government participated in the long ceremonies at Luang Prabang, there were scenes of chaos in Vientiane. The Independence partisans, the Viet Minh, and most of the Vietnamese residents[54] of the administrative capital ferried themselves and everything they could carry across the river into Siam.

Only the Chinese remained to oppose the French entry into Vientiane on 25 April, for here as elsewhere in Indo-China the forces of Chiang Kai-Shek did not withdraw until the French had shown that they were prepared to remove them by force. They had already stolen all they could from Laos, and further north still lingered long enough to carry away the opium crop in due season. The French reoccupation of Luang Prabang on 13 May, and the reaffirmation by the king of his links with France, ended the Independence episode in the country itself. The Independence leaders and partisans took refuge in Siam, whose traditional hostility to the French continued in the slender hope of keeping the territory acquired by Japanese favour in 1941. From the Siamese bank of the Mekong, Viet Minh and Lao guerrillas harassed the French as best they could. But the government in exile was soon left behind by the march of events.

[53] It is not true, as Ellen Hammer asserts (*The Struggle for Indo-China* (Stanford, 1954), p. 156), that Independence forces seriously resisted the French return. Such opposition as there was came from the Viet Minh, with a handful of Lao sometimes acting as a front.

[54] The great majority of the Vietnamese residents of Laos left before the return of the French. The Vietnamese population had been estimated at 50,000 in 1940. By 1958 it was only 9,000 (LeBar and Suddard, *Laos, its People, its Society, its Culture* (New Haven, 1960)). Pietrantoni, op. cit., gives the Vietnamese population of Vientiane as 12,400 in 1943, as against 9,570 Laotians. The exodus in April 1946 thus left the place comparatively empty.

Before the monsoon ended in 1946 the French had completed their reoccupation of Laos and repaired the worst of the loot and ruin in Vientiane. At the end of the year international pressure compelled Siam to return her 1941 acquisitions. Meanwhile, on 27 August 1946, the French and Laotians had agreed on a *modus vivendi* which recognized implicitly the unity of the whole of Laos and the autonomy of its provinces. Prince Boun Oum of Champassak, in spite of some southern reluctance, agreed to merge his royal rights into the sovereignty of Laos.

Under the new dispensation the French provincial commissioners became advisers, and the Laotian chaokhouengs ruled their provinces in the king's name. The crown prince took charge of a provisional national government and in January 1947 elections were held to form a Constituent Assembly which proceeded to draw up a constitution. The constitution was promulgated by the king on 11 May and Laos became formally a constitutional monarchy within the French Union. In recognition of his gesture in the cause of national unity, and of his performance as a guerrilla leader in the south, Prince Boun Oum was granted for life the title of Inspector General of the Kingdom with precedence after the king.[55] General elections took place in November; a new government under Prince Souvannarath was formed early in 1948. Phetsarath and the most important of the Independence Movement leaders remained in Bangkok.

Progress towards a final understanding on the international status of Laos was now delayed by events in Vietnam, where after an initial realization that Vietnamese independence was irreversible, France had retreated into a determination to reassert her authority. There had followed the outbreak of hostilities at Hanoi in December 1946. The Viet Minh were not yet ready for war and had withdrawn to long-term bases in the mountains of Tongking.

[55] For the whole problem of political aspirations in southern Laos, see C. H. Duparc, op. cit. The unification of Laos was seen in the south as the absorption of the richer, more populous half of the country by the crown of Luang Prabang. The south had agreed to it on condition of fair southern representation in the government and of consideration of special southern interests. This condition did not appear to have been met. Prince Boun Oum was in France while the Constituent Assembly was meeting, and clearly felt on his return that his position had not been properly safeguarded. The adoption of the flag of Luang Prabang as the national flag was particularly resented in the south.

France assumed that defeating them was only a matter of time and tried to find an alternative Vietnamese political leader who would not demand more independence than she was prepared to give.

Eventually in March 1949 the Emperor Bao Dai of Annam, who had abdicated under pressure from Ho Chi Minh after the defeat of Japan, was persuaded to head the united state of Vietnam which was declared 'independent within the French Union'. This arrangement allowed the French at last to negotiate the association of Laos, Cambodia, and Vietnam in an Indo-Chinese Federation and so preserve some of the advantages of unity; among these was the annual subvention to the kingdom of Laos from the Indo-Chinese general budget. Conventions were signed with Laos and Cambodia, similarly recognizing their independence and establishing its conditions, the principal one being that defence and foreign relations remained French responsibilities.[56]

There were many in Laos who freely acknowledged their debt to France and welcomed as necessary the continuance of some degree of French tutelage. In October 1945, M. Uthong Souvannavong, then Finance Minister in the royal government, had commented thus to Phetsarath on the Chinese invitation to turn against the French:

We are a small people. Few of us are educated. Our country is without great resources and can only live with the support of other countries. We must necessarily choose foreign tutelage. . . . Our interests dictate that among the great powers we should choose France. So we shall preserve the moral and intellectual gains we have made; with another power we should have to go back to school, learn another language. The king has chosen and save for a few fanatics we are attached to France; in the smallest jungle village the Frenchman has been received like a brother. . . .[57]

This was no more than true. In Laos the French had been helped against the Japanese and not betrayed to them as happened so often in Vietnam and Cambodia.[58] Even Phetsarath had prevented

[56] The Laotians signed with the reservation that the frontiers of Laos 'should include the territories which historically depended on the kingdom but which are now attached to neighbouring states for administrative reasons'. Katay D. Sasorith, *Le Laos: son évolution politique, sa place dans l'union française* (Paris, 1953), p. 68.

[57] Gentil, op. cit., pp. 30–31.

[58] The French resistance leader in the Paksane area writes: 'Between March and August 1945, I personally was able to go, alone or with my

the statue of Pavie from being thrown into the Mekong and had at one time protested that he was not anti-French, that he was too old to learn Chinese or English, and that he was only trying to make France understand that times had changed.

When therefore it was clear that real political progress was soon to be made in Laos, the exiled leaders in Bangkok began to reconsider their positions. The retention of defence and foreign affairs in French hands was not the serious limitation upon independence which it seemed in Vietnam, for Laos was short of experienced political leaders and had virtually no military ones. Furthermore Laos could not balance her budget without help from the central exchequer. Much of the reason for nationalist protest had thus departed. At the same time, since the revival of military dictatorship in Siam at the end of 1947,[59] Bangkok no longer welcomed the exiles so warmly. They lived modestly, working as weavers, pamphleteers, or even as hotel dish-washers when funds were low.[60] Prince Souvannaphouma took a post with the Thai Electric Company. Many of his colleagues had already gone home; Nhouy Abhay, for instance, the talented Minister of Education, had returned to Vientiane as long ago as August 1946.

By the beginning of 1948, however, a fundamental conflict had developed among the exiles themselves. Prince Souvannaphouma and Katay Don Sasorith, whose trenchant articles under the pen-name *William Rabbit* had made him the chief spokesman of the movement,[61] were men of moderate views and prepared to trust the French. Prince Souphanouvong, on the other hand, believed that concessions by the French, however far-reaching, were mere colonialist tricks to prolong their power: to be worth having independence must be seized by force. He now proposed that the Independence Movement be united with the Vietnamese rebels

batman, on foot from Paksane to Napé and to Tha Thom, without any other danger than the stray Japanese or tiger.' Charles Rochet, *Pays Lao, le Laos dans la tourmente* (Paris, 1946), gives many examples of Laotian loyalty to the French at this time.

[59] When the wartime dictator, Marshal Phibul, seized power and forced Pridi Phanamyong, one of the originators of the constitutional régime of 1932, and wartime resistance leader, to flee the country. Pridi eventually sought asylum in Communist China.

[60] O. Meeker, *The Little World of Laos* (New York, 1959), pp. 129–32.

[61] See Katay, *Contribution à l'Histoire du mouvement d'indépendance national Lao* (Bangkok, 1948). *Katay* in Laotian means *rabbit*.

under Ho Chi Minh. This led to a decisive break between the prince and his colleagues.

Prince Souphanouvong was born in 1912 to the eleventh wife of Prince Boun Khong. He had lived and worked in Vietnam ever since 1937 when, having shown himself an outstanding student, he took a civil engineering degree in Paris. Souphanouvong had seen much of France, and before he returned home he had also studied irrigation works in North Africa, undergone courses in practical engineering, and made the acquaintance of the anti-Fascist Popular Front.[62] Naturally of a brilliant, inquiring intellect, outclassing most of his French contemporaries in Paris, he found the conditions of his work in the Public Works service of Indo-China galling. Considering that Laos had no prospects, he chose to serve in Vietnam. Here his local origin restricted him to a lower status and salary than were enjoyed by Frenchmen of similar qualifications, and he undoubtedly encountered the occasional arrogance which used to come naturally to many Europeans in the Orient. Articulate, extrovert, physically robust, his reaction was predictable.

The prince spent most of the years from 1938 to 1945 building roads and bridges in central Vietnam and Laos. He seems to have made contact with the Viet Minh soon after the Japanese action against the French in March 1945. When Japan surrendered he was at Vinh, whence he was flown by United States agents to an interview with Ho Chi Minh in Hanoi. He told the Viet Minh leader that he wanted to form a Lao national government, was given full Viet Minh support, and was soon marching into central Laos with an escort of Viet Minh soldiers dressed as Laotians.[63] Gathering a few genuine recruits and organizing anti-French resistance groups on the way, the prince reached Vientiane after the formation of the provisional government, in which he was appointed Defence Minister and Commander-in-Chief.[64]

In this capacity Souphanouvong organized such Lao resistance as there was to the French return in March 1946. After sharing in

---

[62] A. Dommen, *Conflict in Laos* (London, 1965), p. 21. Dommen gives what is probably the fullest Western account of the career of Prince Souphanouvong; he does however reproduce some popular inaccuracies.

[63] Michael Field, *The Prevailing Wind* (London, 1965), p. 42.

[64] Dommen, op. cit., p. 24. He was later Foreign Minister in the 'government in exile' in Bangkok, ibid., p. 27.

the Viet Minh defeat by French forces at Thakhek he fled across the Mekong with some of his partisans. A French plane machine-gunned the boat and killed thirty of his men. He himself was wounded and perhaps owes his life to friendly Siamese who rescued him and three other survivors from the sinking craft.[65] A few months later he was seen by a United States representative in the house of the Governor of Nakawn Panom,[66] his arm in a sling, evidently directing partisan raids across the river. In July 1946 he went to Hanoi which the Viet Minh still shared uneasily with the French. Ho Chi Minh, who might at this stage have counselled prudence, was in France and the prince was exposed to the full militancy of the Viet Minh under their military leader Vo Nguyen Giap. He returned to join the Lao Independence leaders in Bangkok, much strengthened in his view that for Laos armed rebellion in alliance with the Viet Minh was the only way to independence.

At the beginning of 1947, after the outbreak of hostilities be-tween France and the Viet Minh, Souphanouvong went back to Laos to try and raise the country against the colonial power. There was some response from sections of the Khas and Meos, for the hill minorities were already beginning to be uneasy under the authority of the Lao which was rapidly replacing that of the French.[67] The prince made contact with Sithone Khamadam, the only significant Kha leader, and the Meo chieftain Faydang, tribal enemy of Touby Lyfoung who had assisted the French return to Xieng Khouang and was now a member of the Laotian civil service.[68] But there was no general rising and some of the partisans Souphanou-vong himself had brought back to Laos strayed home to their villages.

After a few months, therefore, the prince returned to Bangkok. His Chief of Staff, Phoumi Nosavan, visited Vietnam to plan a common offensive against the French with Ho Chi Minh and Giap. Fifteen mixed Lao-Viet Minh companies began to be raised in

[65] Denis Warner, *The Last Confucian* (Penguin, 1964), p. 244.

[66] Dommen, op. cit., pp. 26–27, who, however, incorrectly places the meeting at Nongkhay.

[67] See additional note 4.

[68] See Lucien Bodard, *La guerre d'Indochine, l'enlisement* (Paris, 1963), pp. 346–9, for an account of Prince Canh, chief of the Black Thai at Son La, who, like Khamadam, had been released from a French prison by the Japanese. Prince Canh became a Viet Minh colonel.

Siam. Throughout 1947 partisan groups based in security on the Siamese bank of the Mekong, harassed the French with raids and propaganda. One such raid captured and killed the French adviser to the chaokhoueng of Savannakhet who was on his way to the Constituent Assembly in Vientiane. Two Laotians in the party were 'executed'. The third, M. Kou Voravong, chaokhoueng of Thakhek, was severely wounded and left for dead, but when the raiders had gone he found a pirogue which he was able to paddle with his hands to safety down a small river to the Mekong.

Grievous as such incidents could be, they did but dent the armour of the French, who were still confident that they would eventually re-establish themselves not only in Laos but throughout Indo-China, even if they had not done so already.

Most of the Lao leaders in Bangkok were in favour of some link with the Viet Minh, in spite of the traditional Lao fear and hatred of the Vietnamese,[69] for it must have seemed that the prosperity of Laos would continue to depend to some extent on a large Vietnamese domestic community. Prince Souphanouvong's proposal that the Independence Movement should combine with the Viet Minh was nevertheless regarded as outrageous, for it would serve the Vietnamese ambition to inherit French control of Laos and Cambodia. Although his colleagues did not formally remove him from the government-in-exile until May 1949, the prince broke off relations with it in 1948 and went his own way.

The moderate rebels were meanwhile beginning to view the progress of Laos towards independence as the outcome of their own efforts and increasingly as the satisfaction of their aspirations. Phetsarath had said in 1947 that he was not against negotiations with France and secret exchanges had taken place throughout 1948. 'We can say', wrote Katay, 'that broadly the structure of the new

[69] There is a Lao proverb: 'Dog and cat, Annamite and Lao.' Fear of Vietnamese encroachment was still very apparent in Laos. Early in the war Phetsarath himself had objected to the adoption of a Roman script for Lao, remarking that it would deliver the country into the hands of the Vietnamese. For anti-Vietnamese attitudes of leaders and people in Laos see Gentil, op. cit., p. 43, Halpern, op. cit., p. 148, Dommen, op. cit., p. 29, Rochet, op. cit., *passim*, and Caply, op. cit., *passim*. An officer present at the battle between Franco-Lao forces and Viet Minh at Thakhek in March 1946 has said that it turned into a savage demonstration of Lao hatred for the Vietnamese, which the French were unable to stop.

Lao state . . . is in a great measure our work. At least it is inspired by the clear and firm position we have taken and takes account of the claims we have consequently presented and defended.'[70] Phetsarath's reconciliation with the king he had dared to dethrone presented its own problems,[71] but after the Franco-Laotian convention was signed in July 1949, there seemed no good reason why his colleagues should not return home. Knowing that they could not take Phetsarath with them and exasperated by the way in which they considered he had exploited his position among them, the exiles formally broke their connexion with the ex-viceroy on 19 October, proclaimed the dissolution of their Independence Movement and its activities, and in November 1949 returned to Vientiane.

In the general reconciliation of families and factions that followed, it seemed that Laos could at last resume the progress towards united nationhood under French guidance, which had been interrupted by the Japanese *coup de force* in 1945. As the ministers, officials, and governors of the kingdom swore once more their loyalty to the king, and undertook, on pain of the direst calamities, 'not to stir up plots with unbelievers or foreign enemies . . . not to seek to kill the representatives of the government by means of spells, not to give secret shelter to rebels',[72] the dissidence of Prince Souphanouvong seemed hardly worth a thought.

[70] Katay, *Le Laos*, pp. 69–70, quoting an article he wrote in 1949.

[71] In spite of his active role in 1945–6, Prince Phetsarath had been a reluctant exile. However, his deposition from the office of viceroy in 1945, and the failure of the new Laotian constitution to include a viceroy, made it additionally difficult for him to compromise. He visited Laos on family business in 1956 and returned in 1957 on his reinstatement as viceroy. He died in retirement in 1959.

[72] The oath, a picturesque and very long recitation, is substantially that taken to Prince Anou of Vientiane in the early nineteenth century and to the President of France under French rule. For texts, see de Reinach, op. cit., vol. I, pp. 167–8 and *Lao Presse* of 2 November 1960.

ADDITIONAL NOTES TO CHAPTER III

1. A family tree of the royal family of Luang Prabang is at Appendix III. On the death of King Zakharine in 1904, the French had decided after some debate to retain the monarchy. They chose the dead king's young son, Prince Sisavang Vong, who was just completing a course at the École Coloniale in Paris, in preference to the elder Prince Sisaleumsak, as

Zakharine's successor. Prince Boun Khong, the viceroy or 'second king', was son of the viceroy Prince Souvannaphouma who had been killed in the attack on Luang Prabang by Deo-van-Tri in 1887. Boun Khong had done well as viceroy, an office in which, by tradition, he had much more to do with government than the king whose concern was more ceremonial and religious, and was credited with hopes of the crown after the death of Zakharine who was his second cousin.

2. C. D. Chennault, *The Way of a Fighter* (New York, 1949), p. 342; G. Sabattier, *Le destin de l'Indochine, souvenirs et documents 1941–51* (Paris, 1952), pp. 205–7, General de Gaulle, *Mémoires de guerre, le salut 1944–46* (Paris, 1959), p. 166, and General Wedermeyer, *Wedermeyer Reports!* (New York, 1958), p. 340, make it clear that this was a deliberate act.

3. In W. S. Churchill, *The Second World War*, vol. VI (London, 1954), p. 632, appears a memo by Mr. Churchill dated 19 March 1945, initiating a suggestion to General Marshall that the French in Indo-China should be assisted with ammunition; a footnote says that General Marshall 'acted next day'. However General Chennault, who was commanding the U.S. 14th Air Force in Yunnan, says (op. cit., p. 342) that the order not to supply the French came direct from the U.S. War Department, and his immediate superior General Wedermeyer (loc. cit.) reports a personal instruction to this effect from Roosevelt.

4. See Gentil, op. cit., pp. 161–6 for Kha unrest in the Muong Sai area in 1947. During the course of a visit, M. Gentil, then a French adviser in Luang Prabang, had reason to criticize the head Lao official as follows:

If you had brought the rule of justice, or more simply if you had looked after your area, the hillmen might not have become restive. But you have never toured your territory, you have not maintained the tracks, you have requisitioned labour (and then always Kha labour) only to maintain your own houses. The only information we receive in Luang Prabang about your area, we get from the head of another province . . . .

CHAPTER IV

Laos and the Indo-China War

As the Laotian leaders rejoiced in their reconciliation, Mao Tse-Tung at the head of his Communist armies was sweeping away from China the Kuomintang and Marshal Chiang Kai-Shek. In January 1950 the Communist leader recognized the Viet Minh régime and in 1951 he intervened against the United Nations' forces in Korea. These events brought him into conflict with the United States, who had supported Chiang Kai-Shek to the last and were the mainstay of the United Nations' effort. The Americans had hitherto viewed the war in Indo-China as a colonialist affair in which they must not dirty their hands. From 1950 onwards they regarded it more and more as part of their confrontation with the Communist Chinese and therefore gave increasing support to the French.

France was nevertheless doomed to defeat. To her American allies, the Viet Minh victory at Dien Bien Phu, won with Chinese help, and the surrender of North Vietnam to a Communist régime as part of the peace settlement signed at Geneva in 1954, were bitter pills indeed. The United States and their friends reacted by forming the South-East Asia Treaty Organization, which aimed to prevent a further extension of Communist power from the north. The centre of S.E.A.T.O. and the site of its headquarters was Siam. Siam's consciousness of her old Vietnamese enemy, newly backed as he was by a resurgent China from whom there had been nothing to fear for a century, now coincided with the chief concern of the new alliance, and thus became one of the elements in the confrontation of the United States with Communist China.

At the heart of this confrontation lay the kingdom of Laos, which the Geneva Agreement sought to establish as a neutral buffer between pro-Western Siam and the Communist enemy to the north. But the Indo-China War had made Prince Souphanouvong and his Pathet Lao a force to be reckoned with. Laos had emerged from the war politically divided and deeply impressed by the new power of the Viet Minh. The French defeat at Dien Bien Phu left her exposed as never before. Whether the kingdom could ever become stable enough to act effectively as a buffer state was indeed the question.

*   *   *

The French had slipped into the Indo-China War almost by inadvertence. After the first savage outburst at Haiphong and Hanoi at the end of 1946, Ho Chi Minh had withdrawn into the hills of north Tongking, where his troops could be safely augmented and trained. He and his military commander, General Giap, had studied too well the doctrines of Mao Tse-Tung to risk their main force until the foundations of French strength had been rotted away, until the population was under their control, and until their soldiers were prepared and properly armed. By the end of 1947 Giap had created wide guerrilla zones largely impervious to French military action, but activity outside them was limited to raids by isolated groups of guerrillas, intended as often as not to capture arms.

Even now Ho Chi Minh was not entirely committed to war with France. He would still, some believe, have preferred negotiations. Given a readiness to face the facts, France could still have obtained a settlement which safeguarded her economic interests. She could also have won the war militarily if budgetary and political factors had allowed her to make the necessary effort.

The endless restricted war she waged instead drove more and more people whom Communism would not otherwise have attracted into the Communist camp. When the Viet Minh struck they struck at the French. But the rebels were intermingled with the village people, so that when the French struck back they seemed to strike at the inhabitants in general. Every innocent killed or injured, every hut burned, and every village razed confirmed to the people what the Viet Minh were telling them about the French. The control of the population which he sought as a basis of victory thus passed with the minimum of effort to Ho Chi Minh, much as it had passed to Mao Tse-Tung over a much longer period in his struggle with Chiang Kai-Shek.

The arrival of the Chinese Communists on the frontier of Tongking in December 1949 changed both the political and the

military outlook. Ho Chi Minh won recognition by Peking and
Moscow in January 1950.

From then on, the Viet-Minh possessed, like the Reds in Korea, a
'sanctuary' where they could retrain and refit their troops with full
impunity in Chinese Communist training camps at Nanning and the
artillery firing ranges of Ching-Hsi. Soon, Viet-Minh battalions began
to appear in full field formations, equipped with heavy mortars and
pack howitzers, followed shortly thereafter by complete artillery battalions using American-made recoilless rifles and 105 mm howitzers.[1]

By the beginning of 1951 the French had lost control of all Tongking north of the Red River delta, the bridgehead without which
they could not continue the war. The Viet Minh had already
formed six divisions and 'felt ready to throw the French into the
sea'.[2]

Chinese Communist involvement, first on the side of the Viet
Minh and then in Korea, progressively changed the attitude of the
United States. Substantial American aid began to arrive for the
French in Indo-China. France's greatest serving soldier, General
de Lattre de Tassigny, took command. There followed hard fought
battles on the fortified line defending Hanoi and the delta, pitched
battles which de Lattre won. Giap realized his mistake and returned
to guerrilla operations, steadily building up within the delta itself
well-armed battalions and even regiments which methodically
harassed French communications and melted into the countryside
when the French attacked.

At the end of 1951 General de Lattre went home to die. During
1952 the French under General Salan were ever more immobilized
by rebel infiltration and by the turmoil of their home politics. The
population of North Vietnam passed under Viet Minh control.
Giap's striking force systematically, brilliantly, avoided battle as it
grew.

After the rains of 1952 three Viet Minh divisions overran most
of the hill country of north-west Tongking, the old Sipsong Chau
Thai, now the Thai Federation ruled by a son of Deo-van-Tri.[3]

---

[1] Fall, op. cit., p. 27.   [2] Ibid., p. 29.

[3] The administration of the semi-autonomous Thai Federation, formed
in 1948 under Deo-van-Long as a condition of his support of the French
against the Viet Minh, had been handed over to the Vietnamese government of Bao Dai on 27 May 1952.

'The frugal and indefatigable Viet Minh troops', says Lancaster,[4] 'accompanied by hordes of porters, were able to range at will throughout the mountainous region where the forests and a canopy of morning cloud provided protection from air attack.' In March and April 1953 they entered Laos, occupying Sam Neua and penetrating from Dien Bien Phu, down the valley of the River Ou, to within striking distance of Luang Prabang. With them into Sam Neua came Prince Souphanouvong who had by now turned his splinter group of the dissolved Lao Independence Movement into a politico-military organization known as the Pathet Lao.

Although the prince himself was not a Communist, the heart of the Pathet Lao was a small group of Laotian members of the Indo-Chinese Communist Party, die-hard Communists like Nouhak Phoumsavan and Kaysone Fasan,[5] who formed the Laotian Communist Party, the Phak Khon Ngan, in 1953 and are believed to be the real directors of the Pathet Lao today. In any case the prince's total dependence on Viet Minh support at this time made actual membership of the Communist Party irrelevant; effective direction of the Pathet Lao by the Viet Minh was inevitable. Prince Souphanouvong might think that he was using the Viet Minh for Laotian nationalist purposes, but to the Viet Minh he and his movement were simply the agents through whom Vietnam would inherit French power over Laos.[6] On 19 April 1953 the prince set up what he called a resistance government at Sam Neua, and began to take control of the population, his personal gift for leadership and his traditional prestige being backed by the now classical methods of peasant revolution which the Viet Minh had borrowed from Red China.

At the cost of further dispersion of their scanty forces, the French reinforced Luang Prabang and Xieng Khouang, where a fortified camp had been hastily constructed round the small airfield in the centre of the plateau, close to the jumble of huge,

[4] Op. cit., p. 257.
[5] For a short account of Nouhak, see Dommen, op. cit., p. 76. For Kaysone, see additional note 1 at end of chapter. Prince Souphanouvong went to China on a Communist indoctrination course after moving his headquarters from Bangkok to North Vietnam in 1950. Dommen, op. cit., pp. 84–85 and 92–93 gives an account of the Phak Khon Ngan.
[6] See additional note 2.

mysterious stone urns from which the Plain of Jars takes its name.[7] These measures kept the Viet Minh away from the Mekong until the onset of the rains, when their main forces returned to their base areas around the Red River delta. Much of Laos remained, however, if not wholly controlled by Prince Souphanouvong, his tribal allies, and the Viet Minh, at all events a dangerous no man's land. In the greater part of Phongsaly and Sam Neua provinces and throughout a broad belt of Kha territory along the mountainous border with Vietnam as far south as Saravane, the writ of the Laotian government ceased to run. The Viet Minh left depots of rice and ammunition in some of the areas they abandoned, thus clearly indicating their intention to return.[8]

Invasion by the Vietnamese enemy, whose exploits in modern warfare against the French had lost nothing in the telling, had caused consternation in Laos. When the danger to Luang Prabang seemed greatest, the aged king, like his grandfather in 1887, had with a kind of desperate firmness resisted pleas that the royal family should move to safety, and the blind monk of the royal city accurately prophesied that the Viet Minh would not come nearer than the Nam Suong, ten miles away.[9] Although comparatively little fighting had taken place it was clear to all that France had once more saved the kingdom, and it was therefore natural that when in October 1953 all remaining qualifications on Laotian independence were removed,[10] Laos should reaffirm its continued membership of the French Union. As neither Vietnam nor Cambodia appeared likely to offer the French this consolation for their loss of empire, France felt particularly responsible for Laotian defence.

General Salan had meanwhile been succeeded as Commander-in-Chief in Indo-China by General Navarre. At home in France

[7] See H. Deydier, *Introduction à la connaissance du Laos* (Saigon, 1952), pp. 9–10, for a brief account. It is now generally thought that they are funerary urns of the Bronze or Iron Age.

[8] Lancaster, op. cit., p. 262.

[9] For an account of Luang Prabang during this crisis see H. Deydier, *Lokapala* (Paris, 1954), pp. 158–84. As an anthropologist well known in Laos, M. Deydier was able to visit the blind monk freely and seems to have had no doubt that he had telepathic powers.

[10] By the Franco-Laotian Treaty of 22 October 1953, which contained provisions for mutual defence; see De Berval (ed.), *Kingdom of Laos* (Saigon, 1959), p. 49.

there had been some optimism that the war could be brought to an end before the general elections of 1956, although the predominant desire was now only for a situation that would allow France honourably to quit. In the field, however, the French were already at a substantial disadvantage. Navarre found most of his available forces—all but a quarter of the near half million men the French Union had committed—taken up by thousands of guard-posts trying to maintain what was left to him in North Vietnam.[11] To hold a stretch of road twenty to forty kilometres long required on the average a battalion of infantry and a battery of guns. The enemy could keep the same area in a state of insecurity with one or two infantry sections. Less than a quarter of the Red River delta was firmly in French hands, more than half of it was controlled by the Viet Minh, five French divisions were immobilized there and yet it was now itself the main enemy base. Against an enemy battle force of nine divisions, France could move no more than three.

In these circumstances Navarre proposed a two-year plan, not to win the war—that was already impossible—but to demonstrate that the Viet Minh could not win it and so prepare the way for a negotiated settlement. In the first year, by means of reinforcements from France, by raising new Laotian, Cambodian, and Vietnamese units and by reorganization on the ground, he would seek to restore freshness and mobility to his troops while avoiding major battles with the Viet Minh. In the second year, after the rains of 1954, he would go over to the offensive.[12]

The essence of the secret discussions of this plan in July 1953, during which Navarre had warned of the difficulties of defending Laos if the Viet Minh should renew their attacks on it during the next winter before he was ready, was revealed within a week in the Paris newspaper *France Observateur*.[13] By October there was evidence that the Viet Minh were in fact preparing for the campaign which Navarre feared. They calculated that a spectacular success in Laos such as the capture of a Mekong town would have a disproportionate effect on public opinion in France, and so accentuate the rising French disposition to quit.

To abandon Laos was unthinkable.[14] Navarre therefore decided to hurry forward the occupation of Dien Bien Phu, an operation

[11] H. Navarre, *Agonie de l'Indochine* (Paris, 1956), p. 46.
[12] Ibid, p. 82.
[13] Ibid., pp. 115–16.   [14] See additional note 3.

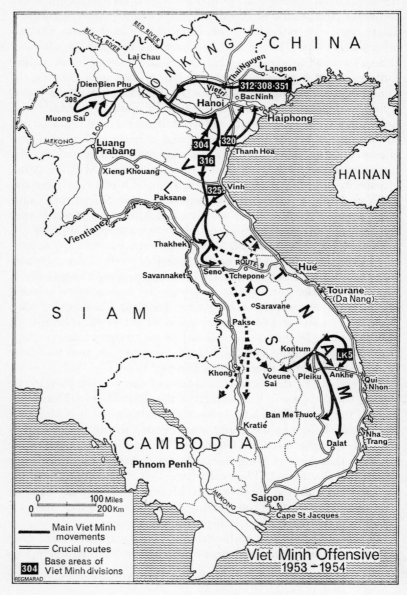

From General H. Navarre, *Agonie de l'Indochine* (Paris, 1956), p. 165.

he intended in any case, and so block the Viet Minh on their way to the River Ou and Luang Prabang. The occupation was carried out in November and December 1953 by parachute troops, and also by the move southward of the strong but isolated garrison hitherto maintained at Lai Chau on the Black River, capital of the Thai Federation. As the fortified camp was created round the old disused airstrip in the Dien Bien Phu valley, the Viet Minh build-up against it began, supported by unprecedented material assistance from China. General Navarre changed his mind; he had succumbed to the prevailing French military over-confidence in Indo-China and now waited confidently for the set-piece battle by which he would end the war.

The Viet Minh meanwhile launched diversionary attacks elsewhere in Laos. On 20 December 1953 the Viet Minh 325th Division moved from Vinh south-west over the Keo Neua Pass and across the Kam Mon Plateau to the Mekong. French and Laotian covering forces were brushed aside. On 26 December 1953 the enemy was in Thakhek and on 5 January 1954 was thought to be threatening the French air base at Seno, twenty miles east of Savannakhet. But this was all the Viet Minh intended to do and their forces moved away to the south-east.[15] Their presence even for a few days astride French communications in the Mekong valley had forced a further dispersion of French forces and had sounded the trumpets of panic in Paris.

A few days later, when an attack on Dien Bien Phu by the main Viet Minh battle force now concentrated around it seemed imminent, troops of the 308th 'Iron' Division, lightly equipped, barefoot, each with his sling of rice, suddenly turned on the Franco-Laotian forces twenty miles to the south-west and drove them back down the River Ou upon their air-heads at Muong Sai and Luang Prabang. The Viet Minh followed no further than the Bac River, content that they had diverted even more precious French reinforcements.[16] By 23 February their main force had returned to Dien Bien Phu, leaving irregulars in the Ou River valley and a screening force on the border, to prevent the movement of relief columns from Laos.

The epic, decisive battle of Dien Bien Phu followed. The

[15] See Vo Nguyen Giap, *Dien Bien Phu* (Hanoi, 1962), pp. 53–54, and 67–68.
[16] Ibid., p. 72.

French had underestimated the extent of Chinese assistance to the rebels, ignored the possibility that Viet Minh guns could be deployed so as to dominate the French positions in absolute security, discounted above all the devoted, ant-like industry of the Viet Minh themselves, and overestimated their own technical advantages. The painful story of miscalculation, suffering, and heroism will long be told.[17]

To the Laotian who watched, it was not so much a matter of suffering as of disillusion. In proportion to his resources his own war effort had been greater than that of his Cambodian and Vietnamese neighbours.[18] Now the hated enemy of his ancestors had defeated the all-powerful friend and protector in whom he had placed his confidence. Moreover, this latter-day battle of the giants and the pygmies had been fought in the high valley of Muong Theng, Dien Bien Phu, legendary cradle of the Lao people. Even the phis,[19] the primal forces of mother earth, might thus be said to be fighting on the enemy's side. If France could not stand up to the Viet Minh, how much less could the Laotian do so on his own? A deep feeling of inferiority, intensified by propaganda, was to leave the newly independent Laotian army singularly unqualified to deal with the Pathet Lao, backed as the rebels were if not with the armed strength at least with the potent myth of the Viet Minh.

From a hardly greater distance the Siamese watched with almost equal anxiety. In December 1953 the Viet Minh had reached the Siamese frontier on the Mekong at Thakhek. They had come by an ancient route; Vietnamese had been passing over it into the Mekong valley for centuries. The word *Thakhek* itself means *foreigners' landing*. Since 1945 the old Vietnamese communities on the Mekong in north-east Siam had been increased by refugees from Laos and from the Indo-China War to a total of 60,000 people,[20] and now represented a well-established Vietnamese bridgehead in the Mekong valley. Vietnamese from Nakawn

[17] See Jules Roy, *The Battle of Dien Bien Phu* (London, 1965), an account which tends perhaps to overestimate the Viet Minh, and B. B. Fall, *Hell in a Very Small Place* (London, 1967).

[18] Navarre, op. cit., p. 123.

[19] Spirits, mischievous or benign, of the animism which underlies the tolerant Buddhism of Laos. A near equivalent would perhaps be *fairies*.

[20] Thailand's letter to the U.N. Security Council, 29 May 1954. U.N. document S/3220.

Panom were said to have helped the Viet Minh in their occupation of Thakhek.[21]

Traditional Siamese apprehensions about the Vietnamese now came sharply into focus. It was not simply that seven thousand of the Vietnamese lived in Siam close to Thakhek itself, where they could be subverted against Siamese interests as the later submission to the Security Council implied, though that was bad enough. Siam also felt herself at a disadvantage because of her large Lao population in the north-east. The Lao people of Siam had at one time been almost as numerous as the Siamese. In spite of all efforts at assimilation, the great majority of the people of the north-east were still distinctively Lao, and still had more in common with their kinsmen across the Mekong in Laos than with the Siamese whose domination they still faintly resented.[22] Sixty years of French rule had not in fact changed the ethnic unity of the Mekong valley. What, Siam asked herself, would be the influence of the Viet Minh in Laos upon her own Lao population?

The most immediate effects of the battle of Dien Bien Phu were, however, felt in Europe. While French military confidence in beating the Viet Minh had mounted in Indo-China, opinion at home had moved towards the idea of a negotiated settlement. The war France had never intended had lasted too long. It had cost vast sums of money that would have been better used at home and the casualties were mounting steadily towards the figure of 172,000 which they would finally attain. Immediately after the Korean Armistice in July 1953 the French government had decided on eventual negotiations,[23] and when in September a Vietnamese Congress in Saigon declared independence outside the French union as the national aim, France realized that even victory could not now prolong her presence in Indo-China.[24] Navarre's confidence that the military situation would have improved by the spring dissuaded the French premier from opening negotiations in December,[25] but the move could not long be delayed. At the Berlin four-power meeting in February 1954, France secured international agreement

[21] B. B. Fall, *The Two Viet-Nams* (London, 1963), p. 125.

[22] See Katay D. Sasorith, *Le Laos* (Paris, 1953), pp. 17–21. For a numerical comparison of populations see additional note 1 to Chapter II, pp. 48–49 above. See also map on p. 47.

[23] J. Laniel, *Le drame Indochinois* (Paris, 1957), p. 17.

[24] Lacouture et Devillers, *La fin d'une guerre* (Paris, 1960), p. 43.

[25] Laniel, op. cit., p. 41.

to the discussion of Indo-China at the conference on the Korean
War that was to meet at Geneva in April.

The Americans had agreed to this course with some reluctance,
for they were still confident that, with the help they were now
giving to the French, the Indo-China War could be won. This
view had been consistently held ever since the Washington conference of Foreign Ministers in July 1953. Franco-American discussions at that time had resulted in an increase of United States'
aid for Indo-China to a figure that covered seventy per cent. of the
running costs of the war. The French had undertaken in return
to 'make every effort to break up and destroy the regular enemy
forces',[26] a promise which reflected American criticism of their
war effort, and to respond to American military advice.

Once having stationed military advisers in the war zone, the
United States became even more optimistic about French military
prospects. When, therefore, in March 1954, General Ély arrived
in Washington with the warning that defeat at Dien Bien Phu was
possible, the shocked Americans appeared to believe that unless
immediate action were taken, Indo-China would fall into Communist hands, with dangerous consequences for the strategic position
of the United States in the Pacific. From the Communist point of
view, said Mr. Nixon, then vice-president:

the war in Korea is about Japan . . . and so is the war in Indo-China,
which is essential to Japan's economic survival. Without trade with
Indo-China and Korea, and with these countries under Communist
control, Japan would become an economic satellite of the Soviet Union,
which is the Communist aim.[27]

Lacouture and Devillers put it even more plainly:

Le Sud-Est asiatique fournissait au monde libre un certain nombre de
produits vitaux. Il constituait d'autre part pour le Japon un partenaire
commercial de premier ordre et s'il tombait, il serait difficile pour le
gouvernement de Tokyo de rester l'allié des États-Unis. Le Sud-Est
asiatique devait être tenu absolument. Or l'Indochine en etait la clé.[28]

Short of sending their own troops to Indo-China, an action to
which President Eisenhower was opposed,[29] there were two possi-

[26] Joint Franco-American communiqué, 30 September 1953.
[27] *New York Times*, 17 April 1954.
[28] Lacouture et Devillers, op. cit., p. 72. See additional note 4.
[29] Sir Anthony Eden, *Full Circle* (London, 1960), p. 90.

bilities open to the Americans: they could intervene with sea and air forces in the hope of saving Dien Bien Phu, a course that was proposed by General Ély,[30] and they could organize an international united front to prevent any further extension of Communist power in South-East Asia. While military planning for the first of these courses proceeded, Mr. Dulles embarked upon the second on 29 March:

Under the conditions of today the imposition on South-East Asia of the political system of Communist Russia and its Chinese Communist ally, by whatever means, would be a grave threat to the whole free community. The United States feels that that possibility should not be passively accepted but should be met by united action. This might involve serious risks. But these risks are far less than those that will face us a few years from now if we dare not be resolute today.[31]

By the time the French had accepted the American offer of air support at Dien Bien Phu on 5 April, however, it had transpired that the United States Congress would only consider such a venture if a number of conditions were met. The first was that it should be supported by America's allies. Accordingly the United States proposed that Britain, Australia, New Zealand, Siam, the Philippines, and the Indo-Chinese states should join with the United States and France in an *ad hoc* grouping which, before the Geneva Conference, should issue:

a solemn declaration of readiness to take concerted action under Article 51 of the United Nations Charter against continued interference by China in the Indo-China war.... The proposed warning would carry with it the threat of naval and air action against the Chinese coast and of active intervention in Indo-China itself.[32]

The most important of those concerned, apart from France and the United States, was of course Britain, who was only now beginning to master the Communist rebellion in Malaya, and whose interest was to keep an effective barrier against Communist

[30] General Ély, *L'Indochine dans la tourmente* (Paris, 1963), pp. 65–77. The story of the projected intervention is well and analytically told by Geoffrey Warner in 'Escalation in Vietnam, the Precedents of 1954', in *International Affairs*, 1965, pp. 267–77.

[31] Speech to the Overseas Press Club, text in *American Foreign Policy 1950–55* (Dept. of State publication 6446, Dec. 1957), pp. 2373–81.

[32] Eden, op. cit., pp. 92–93. See also D. D. Eisenhower, *Mandate for Change* (London, 1963), pp. 346–7.

power as far to the north of Malaya as possible.[33] The British objected to the American proposal on three grounds. They considered that the warning to China would be ignored, that the retaliatory action planned would be militarily ineffective and politically dangerous, and that the whole procedure would prejudice the chances of success at Geneva.[34] France, principally concerned with ending her costly and unpopular war, was equally opposed to the constitution of a united front before the conference.[35] She saw no inconsistency, however, between her opposition on this score and United States' air intervention to save Dien Bien Phu, and on 23 April she made a last desperate call for unilateral United States action.[36]

Dulles had already rejected the French appeal when, on 24 April, he pressed Britain once more to agree to a collective declaration. Sir Winston Churchill remained adamant, but so by this time was President Eisenhower who later wrote that 'air strikes against Dien Bien Phu would not have been effective',[37] and the Indo-Chinese sessions of the Geneva Conference began, on 8 May, in the shadow of the overwhelming Viet Minh triumph of the day before.

Differences of view between Britain and the United States both on the usefulness of the conference and on the priority to be accorded to a collective defence pact for South-East Asia, were to persist throughout May and June. Although President Eisenhower had himself stated on 29 April that the United States would take no action in Indo-China pending the outcome of the Geneva Conference,[38] Dulles persisted in his belief that no agreement acceptable to the United States could be reached there, and the negotiations were accompanied by uneasy rumblings from across the Atlantic.[39] The reality of American nuclear power was indeed a major influence.[40] Molotov, who was to alternate with Mr. Eden as chairman of the conference, early showed that he shared British

[33] Eden, op. cit., p. 87.

[34] Eden, op. cit., pp. 93–94. See also additional note 5.

[35] Ély, op. cit., p. 88, Eden, op. cit., p. 93. See also *Survey of International Affairs, 1954* (London, R.I.I.A., 1957), pp. 28–29 for a summary of French opinion.

[36] Lacouture et Devillers, op. cit., pp. 88–89, Eden, op. cit., pp. 101–6. See also additional note 6.

[37] Eisenhower, op. cit., p. 373.

[38] *The Times*, 30 Apr. 1954.

[39] Eden, op. cit., pp. 107–20.

[40] Ibid., p. 123.

apprehensions of the risks of a world war and that Russia wanted a settlement.[41]

It was not, however, until 16 June, when a partition of Vietnam, which was to prove the eventual solution, was already under discussion between France and the Viet Minh,[42] but when the conference was nevertheless close to breakdown over the future of Cambodia and Laos, that the Chinese showed a similar disposition. Chou En-Lai told Mr. Eden 'that he thought he could persuade the Vietminh to withdraw from . . . [Cambodia and Laos] . . . and that China would recognize their royal governments, provided that there were no American bases in the territory'.[43] Thus were revealed China's conditions for peace, based on her own apprehension of American power, which were to be repeated to the French prime minister a week later. The American conditions were formulated during the visit of Sir Winston Churchill and Mr. Eden to Washington on 29 June. This visit, to settle, as Sir Winston put it, a few family differences, resulted in the establishment of a study group for a South-East Asia collective defence treaty, and in a joint communication to the French government stating the willingness of the United States and Britain to respect an armistice on Indo-China which:

1. Preserves the integrity and independence of Laos and Cambodia and assures the withdrawal of Vietminh forces therefrom.
2. Preserves at least the southern half of Vietnam, and if possible an enclave in the delta; in this connection we would be unwilling to see the line of division of responsibility drawn further south than a line running generally west from Dong Hoi.
3. Does not impose on Laos, Cambodia or retained Vietnam any restrictions impairing their capacity to maintain stable non-communist régimes; and especially restrictions impairing their right to maintain adequate forces for internal security, to import arms and to employ foreign advisers.
4. Does not contain political provisions which would risk loss of the retained area to communist control.
5. Does not exclude the possibility of the ultimate reunification of Vietnam by peaceful means.
6. Provides for the peaceful and humane transfer, under international supervision, of those people desiring to be moved from one zone to another of Vietnam; and

[41] Eden, op. cit., p. 121.   [42] Lacouture et Devillers, op. cit., pp. 188–90.
[43] Eden, op. cit., pp. 132–3.

7. Provides effective machinery for international supervision of the agreement.[44]

In the meantime the lack of progress at Geneva and the continuing slow deterioration of the French military position in Indo-China had led to a change of government in France. The new prime minister, M. Mendès-France, set himself a limit of a month for the achievement of an armistice, making it clear that an all-out French military effort would be required if he failed. This new firmness, the clarification of Anglo-American policy in Washington, together with decisive Chinese and Russian pressure on the Viet Minh, led to a hard-fought but not unsatisfactory agreement on 20 July 1954.[45]

The Geneva settlement was indeed the best obtainable in the circumstances. Dien Bien Phu had admittedly only been a battle. Viet Minh control of the Tongkingese countryside, however, made it inevitable that unless the United States intervened with ground forces, France would concede the war. The immediate problem was settled by the agreed partition of Vietnam under international control, pending supervised elections for the whole country in July 1956.[46] But the wider, historic problem of international relations in the Indo-Chinese peninsula was also recognized at Geneva, at least by Mr. Eden.[47] All were agreed that Vietnam must eventually be united. In the short term, while the problem of over-population remained, a united Vietnam would certainly be aggressive, expansionist. What could be done to prevent the ancient conflict between Siam and the Vietnamese from bursting out again now that, as in 1893, great powers were engaged on both sides?

The attractive, obvious answer was to create what Mr. Eden called a *protective pad* by neutralizing Cambodia and Laos.[48] The immediate problem was in the north, for North Vietnam was now Communist and would clearly remain dependent on China. 'The essence of the settlement', said Eden, 'was that Laos should

[44] Eden, op. cit., pp. 132–3.

[45] Lacouture et Devillers, op. cit., pp. 264–74, have the fullest account of the final stages. The unusual willingness of Molotov to compromise and of Chou En-Lai to exert decisive pressure on the Viet Minh, as M. Mendès-France's deadline approached on 19 and 20 July, does not appear to have been brought out as clearly elsewhere.

[46] See additional note 7.   [47] Op. cit., pp. 77–79.

[48] Ibid., p. 123.

remain as an independent and neutral buffer between China and Siam. It was therefore essential that the United States should not attempt to establish any military influence [there]. Any attempt to do so was bound to provoke some counter-move by China.'[49]

While Vietnam was partitioned by the Geneva Agreement, therefore, Cambodia and Laos were cast for a neutral role. They were to join no military alliances except as envisaged by the United Nations' Charter, ask for no foreign military aid, and tolerate no foreign bases on their soil unless their security was threatened. The Pathet Lao, regrouped into the provinces of Sam Neua and Phongsaly, were to be integrated into the Laotian national life. Except for a total of 5,000 French defence and training forces in Laos, all foreign troops were to be withdrawn from the two countries under the supervision of international control commissions furnished, as in Vietnam, by India, Canada, and Poland.[50] These commissions, under Indian chairmen, would report to the co-chairmen of the Geneva Conference, the foreign ministers of Britain and Russia, who thereby retained a continuing responsibility for the settlement. All this was enshrined in cease-fire agreements, declarations by the parties, and the final declaration of the conference, eleven documents in all.

The settlement gave the Viet Minh less than at one time they had hoped. Their first reverse had been the Western refusal to seat at the conference the Pathet Lao and Free Cambodian elements they had been fostering as part of an Indo-Chinese national front since 1945. Their second was when Chou En-Lai 'persuaded' them to withdraw from Laos and Cambodia on the understanding that no American bases would be established there. Success at either of these two points would have gone far to win them a legitimate and permanent influence in the two states, which could be turned to their advantage. The Chinese and Russians had then

[49] The problem was immediate only in Laos. That it is merely latent further south has often been pointed out by Prince Sihanouk.

[50] Their formal titles are 'The International Commission for Supervision and Control in Laos (or Cambodia, or Vietnam)'. The official account of the Geneva Conference and the eleven documents that constitute the agreement are in: *Documents relating to the Discussion of Korea and Indo-China at the Geneva Conference, April 27–June 15, 1954* (Cmd. 9186), and *Further Documents relating to the Discussion of Indo-China at the Geneva Conference, June 16–July 21, 1954* (Cmd. 9239).

forced them to accept a partition line in Vietnam four parallels
to the north of the one on which they had been insisting, and the
postponement of general elections until 1956, eighteen months
later than they had demanded.

Nevertheless, the Viet Minh cannot have considered the settlement unsatisfactory. They had obtained control of Hanoi and the
north. It was commonly accepted that they would win the general
elections even in 1956, and so extend their grip to the south. The
neutrality of Laos and Cambodia would then assume even greater
importance than it possessed already, for it would hold American
power and Siamese influence at arm's length while the new Vietnam was consolidated. There was thus good cause for the jubila-
tion which the Viet Minh delegates displayed when the cease-fire
agreements were signed.[51]

The position adopted by the United States with regard to
the Geneva Agreement was curious, but clear. Even as late as
13 July Mr. Dulles appears to have believed that no satisfactory
settlement was possible.[52] Then during a visit to Paris he realized
that M. Mendès-France was in some ways holding out for more
favourable terms than the seven Anglo-American points had
demanded. The Secretary of State had relented so far as to allow
his under-secretary, Mr. Bedell Smith, to return to Geneva for the
final stage of the conference.[53] But opinion in America, where the
pernicious Senator McCarthy was still at work,[54] did not allow
Dulles to associate his country fully with a settlement that handed
over territory to Communism. Furthermore, the fourth of the
seven Anglo-American conditions had not been met; Communist
North Vietnam was more populous than non-Communist South
Vietnam, and the elections in 1956 would thus clearly risk the loss
of the south to Communist control. American approval therefore
went no further than a unilateral statement implying that the
United States would not upset the agreement by force or threat
of force so long as nobody else did so.[55]

[51] Lacouture et Devillers, op. cit., p. 273.

[52] Ibid., p. 246; see additional note 8.

[53] Ibid., pp. 248–50; Eden, op. cit., pp. 138–9.

[54] The condition of American opinion is well analysed by R. P. Stebbins, *The United States in World Affairs 1954* (New York, 1956), pp.
17–24. The action by the U.S. Army which resulted in the discrediting of
Senator McCarthy had only been begun in April.

[55] See additional note 9.

There ensued, however, a change in the United States' attitude to the proposed collective defence treaty, which argues that Dulles nevertheless regarded the Geneva settlement as moderately satisfactory. The treaty had hitherto been seen to demand, like N.A.T.O., a joint military command and an organized force. The main purposes of the pact as now envisaged were:

1. To warn China that the full weight of American military power would be used to counter any overt aggression in South-East Asia.
2. To provide treaty obligations by other nations to join the U.S.A. in fighting a war of this kind, although it was realised that the main strength in meeting open aggression by China would have to come from the United States.
3. To strengthen the military and national police establishments of Siam and other countries, such as the Philippines, so that their governments could deal effectively with any internal uprising.
4. To build up the economies of Siam and the Philippines (as well as such non-member nations as Japan and Burma) in order to minimise the likelihood of local unrest and generally to demonstrate to the local peoples the value of ties with the Western powers rather than with Communism.[56]

Washington had little fear of an attack by China in the area, but if an attack came, wished to be free to react to it as circumstances permitted at the time, rather than to be bound, as in Korea, to an alliance in which American influence would inevitably be less than American responsibilities.[57]

Accordingly the South-East Asia Treaty signed at Manila[58] on 8 September 1954 by the United States, France, Britain, Pakistan, Siam, the Philippines, Australia, and New Zealand, set up no joint command and no military force. The main military provisions were that:

1. The parties would recognize aggression by means of armed attack against any one of them, or against Laos, Cambodia, or South Vietnam

[56] *New York Herald Tribune*, 8 August 1954, quoting officials at the State Department and the Pentagon. The new mood had been indicated at a press conference by Mr. Dulles on 23 July 1954; *The Times*, 24 July 1954.

[57] *Survey of International Affairs 1954* (London, R.I.I.A., 1957), p. 74.

[58] *South-East Asia Collective Defence Treaty, Manila, September 8, 1954* (Cmd. 9282), London, H.M.S.O., 1954.

which were designated for protection in a protocol to the treaty, as endangering their own peace and security, and would act to meet it according to their several constitutional processes.

2. In the case of threats other than by armed attack in the treaty area, the parties would consult immediately on measures for the common defence. But no action would be taken in the protocol states except at the invitation or with the consent of the government concerned.

The nature of the guarantee they were to receive under these provisions disappointed both the Philippines and Siam. In order to satisfy Filipino sentiment, the United States had assured the Philippines, before formal discussions began, that American forces would 'automatically react' if the Philippines were in danger of Communist aggression. But no such undertaking was contemplated for Siam, whose suggestion at Manila that Western troops should be stationed in Siam was turned aside.[59]

Nevertheless, Siam was the only one of the S.E.A.T.O. powers against whom, because of its proximity to the zone of recent operations, an immediate threat could be held to exist. Siamese anxiety had been expressed at the end of May in a request to the Security Council that the Peace Observation Commission of the United Nations keep the situation on the frontiers of Siam under observation. This had been considered by the Security Council on 16 to 18 June. Contemptuously, the Russians had vetoed it; nobody, they said, was threatening Siam.[60] The United States had hastened to reassure Siam by granting her an increase in military aid sufficient to raise the strength of her armed forces from 45,000 to 90,000,[61] and other substantial assistance.

An article by Pridi Phanamyong, the Siamese statesman and wartime resistance leader, now acknowledged to be a political refugee in Communist China, was broadcast by Radio Peking as part of its campaign against the collective defence treaty on 30 July.[62] This had contributed further to fears on Siam's behalf. A Siamese government spokesman said in Bangkok on 9 September that the government believed that aggression was imminent from a free Thai army, organized by Pridi in the Thai autonomous repub-

[59] See *Survey of International Affairs 1954* (London, R.I.I.A., 1957), p. 77.

[60] *U.N. Security Council 674th Meeting Official Record*, pp. 4–10.

[61] *Survey of International Affairs 1954* (London, 1957), p. 291.

[62] *The Times*, 31 July 1954.

lic set up eighteen months earlier by the Communist Chinese in Yunnan.[63] There were other reports of a resistance movement being recruited in Siam's nervous north-eastern provinces, and that its leader, Tiang Sirikhand, had been seen with the Communists in northern Laos.[64] The Siamese statesman Prince Wan said on 23 October that Siam was 'next on the Communist time-table'.[65] In the United States during November he asserted that thousands of Chinese who had lived in Siam were being trained in Yunnan.[66]

Despite the American failure to react with a more specific guarantee for Siam, therefore, and although there was little evidence for the alleged subversive activity,[67] the anxiety of Siam and the security of the Siamese Mekong frontier were from the first serious preoccupations for S.E.A.T.O.; and from the first Laos was the protocol state which seemed most likely to need its protection.

The formation of S.E.A.T.O. was by no means the last of the consequences of the Indo-China War, but it marked an epoch. Communist China's support for the Viet Minh in the war itself had drawn in the United States to support France. Now they were also brought, together with their allies, to the defence of Siam against the Chinese and Vietnamese Communists who might seem to threaten her, across neutral Laos, to the north. Upon the old conflict of Siam and the Vietnamese was thus superimposed the modern confrontation of Communist China and the United States. Between the two lay the kingdom of Laos which the Indo-Chinese struggle had left divided as never before. The Viet Minh had used Prince Souphanouvong and the latent ethnic divisions in the country which French rule had failed to heal, to form a weak but credible nationalist movement, a Vietnamese mortgage on the neutrality of Laos. Unless the Pathet Lao could be integrated into the fabric of the nation, unless neutrality could be established and maintained, there was a danger that the Viet Minh would foreclose.

[63] *The Times*, 10 September 1954.

[64] *Daily Telegraph*, 20 September 1954. Tiang Sirikhand, one of the war-time Seri Thai leaders, is said to have been murdered while under interrogation by the police under General Phao in Siam, *Bangkok Post*, 27 December 1957.

[65] *Survey of International Affairs 1954* (London, 1957), p. 290.

[66] Ibid., p. 294.

[67] Ibid., p. 293.

ADDITIONAL NOTES TO CHAPTER IV

1. Kaysone was born at Savannakhet in 1925 of mixed Lao and Viet-namese parentage. He studied medicine at Hanoi University which he left in 1945 to join the Lao Independence Movement at Savannakhet. Having received military training in Vietnam, he served on the Viet Minh/Pathet Lao side in North Laos and became defence minister in Prince Souphanouvong's 'governments' of 1950 and 1953. A convinced Communist and long a member of the Indo-Chinese Communist Party, he is considered the most powerful of the Pathet Lao leaders.

2. See Dommen, op. cit., p. 71. From 1945 the Vietnamese-dominated Indo-Chinese Communist Party had sought to form a united front against the French in Laos, Cambodia, and Vietnam. After its transformation into the Lao Dong Party in 1951, its policy included the formation of a federa-tion of the three states, which the Vietnamese were determined to domi-nate. Brian Crozier, in 'Peking and the Laotian Crisis' in *China Quarterly*, 1961, p. 136, refers Communist ambitions in Laos and Cambodia back to the foundation of the Indo-Chinese Communist Party by Ho Chi Minh in 1930; these ambitions are of course as much Vietnamese as Communist

3. B. B. Fall, op. cit., pp. 281–4, deals with disagreements as to General Navarre's orders on this point. When all is said, it is clear that no show-down battle had been contemplated for 1953/1954. On this all authorities agree. It would appear that the general disregarded the spirit of his orders; however, it can at least be said that the French government was aware of this in ample time for action if it had had the will to disagree with him.

4. See R. P. Stebbins, *The United States in World Affairs 1954* (New York, 1956), p. 290, quoting a speech by President Eisenhower on 22 June 1954: '. . . it becomes absolutely mandatory to us, and to our safety, that the Japanese nation do not fall under the domination of . . . the Kremlin. If the Kremlin controls them, all of that great capacity would be turned against the free world. . . . And the Pacific would become a Communist lake.'

5. A hidden element in British and French reluctance to follow the American initiative in Indo-China may have been suspicion of American motives. The point was made by Walter Lippmann in the *New York Herald Tribune* on 8 June 1954: '. . . the interventionists . . . have an unlimited objective—namely the overthrow of Red China. For this . . . Dulles can never hope to organise a united front in Europe and Asia', or even, he continued, in the U.S.A.

6. The exact sequence of events is still not entirely clear. It appears likely, however, as Stebbins concluded in 1956 (op. cit., p. 225), that the plan was dropped even before a definite 'No' was received from London. General Ridgway, the Army Chief of Staff, who was known to be opposed to it at the time, states in *Soldier—the Memoirs of Matthew B. Ridgway* (New York, 1956), pp. 275–7, that a full report he had sent to President

Eisenhower 'played a considerable, perhaps a decisive, part in persuading our government not to embark on that tragic adventure'. This is to some extent supported by the president's remark quoted on p. 94, that air intervention would not have worked.

7. Until the late afternoon of 20 July the French negotiators had hoped to avoid the mention of a date for the elections, and to leave this to be fixed by the International Control Commission when conditions were right. The final compromise between the Viet Minh demand for elections in six months and the French position, was suggested by Molotov (Lacouture et Devillers, op. cit., p. 268). The last-minute change from what the French had hoped to what they accepted seems to be reflected in the curious drafting of para. 7 in the final declaration of the conference:

... In order to ensure that sufficient progress in the restoration of peace has been made, and that all the necessary conditions obtain for free expression of the national will, *general elections shall be held in July 1956.*

As it stands, this is a *non sequitur*. The sentence would have read more naturally and have made more sense if, instead of the words italicized, it had contained some formula such as:

the date of the elections will be left to be fixed by the International Control Commission.

8. Mr. Dulles informed the French ambassador in Washington on 9 July that he feared the French would accept even the 12th Parallel as the line of partition in Vietnam. This would have brought the Viet Minh to within 100 miles of Saigon. M. Mendès-France was, however, negotiating for the 18th Parallel and finally accepted a line just below the 17th.

9. 'Since Dulles had been at least as responsible as ourselves', says Eden, 'for calling the Geneva Conference, this did not seem to me reasonable. I also feared that it might lead to difficulties at our final meeting, for the Chinese had indicated that they would insist upon signature of the final declaration by all the delegations.' Eden, op. cit., p. 142. Mr. Eden accordingly arranged with Molotov that the final declaration would have a heading in which all the participating countries would be listed, thus obviating the need for signatures. If this now seems a somewhat haphazard way of sealing an important international arrangement, it should be remembered that the overriding concern for most of the negotiators was to bring nine years of costly fighting to an end; this was achieved in the cease-fire agreements which had been signed in due form by the belligerents.

CHAPTER V

The Problem of Neutrality

THE role of neutral buffer between the peoples to the north-east and south-west of the Annamitic Chain, which Laos was now asked to assume, demanded an internal stability and strength that the kingdom did not possess. A buffer must absorb shocks from both sides. If it is to do this safely there must be no internal stresses.

Laos as formed by the French was unstable because it included mutually hostile ethnic elements closely connected with the populations it was required to separate. The dominant Lao valley people feared and disliked the Vietnamese, as did their Lao neighbours in north-east Siam. The hill folk in upper Laos, on the other hand, disliked the Lao and tended to look for support towards their close kinsmen across the border in North Vietnam, who themselves were not unfavourably disposed towards the Vietnamese, because the Viet Minh had taken pains to conciliate them. On the one side was the Lao-dominated government, on the other the highland Pathet Lao.

Laos could only achieve the stability essential for its new international role if the two factions could be reconciled. The task was not impossible; time, patience, and good faith were needed. But the external strains proved too great, the partisans too pressing. The Viet Minh were already using one side; Siam and the United States were soon involved on the other. It took from 1954 to 1957, with several false starts and nervous hesitations, for Laos to agree on the integration of the Pathet Lao into the life of the country. The degree of integration achieved, and the limited success of the Pathet Lao at partial elections which followed in 1958, then so alarmed the non-Communist side that the government which had brought the agreements about was replaced by openly anti-Communist rule. Inevitably, perhaps, the Pathet Lao returned to insurgency. By the middle of 1960 the rigging of general elections by a right wing group which had meanwhile supplanted the new régime, had alienated even the moderates, and the country was sliding towards civil war. The confrontation between China and the United States was thus transferred from the conflict between Siam and the Vietnamese to the inner divisions of Laos.

*　　*　　*

At the Geneva Conference the Viet Minh had tried to assert that the Pathet Lao and Free Cambodian movements should be given the same status as themselves. The West was able to resist this claim, which rested on the Vietnamese and Viet Minh ambition to inherit French power in the whole of Indo-China. Neither the Pathet Lao nor the Free Cambodians were therefore seated at the conference. Rebel control of Cambodian territory was insignificant but Prince Souphanouvong was able to claim that the Pathet Lao needed Phongsaly and Sam Neua provinces as regroupment areas pending an internal Laotian political settlement. As the Viet Minh were in possession of the two provinces this claim had been con-ceded. The Laotian government stated in a declaration of its own that it was resolved 'to integrate all citizens, without discrimination, into the national community and to guarantee them the enjoy-ment of the rights and freedoms'[1] for which the constitution pro-vided. It also undertook to arrange for special representation of Pathet Lao interests in the administration of Phongsaly and Sam Neua until the general elections scheduled for 1955 should complete the process of national reconciliation. These promises were brought into the general framework of the Geneva settlement.

In Laos itself, politics had changed but little since the return of Prince Souvannaphouma and his fellow-exiles from Bangkok in 1949. Political life was still dominated by a few families and its issues were narrow. Phoui Sananikone, head of an important Vientiane business family, capable, eloquent, moderate, with a long record of public service, had succeeded Prince Boun Oum as prime minister in February 1950. Prince Souvannaphouma was a member of Phoui's[2] government and in November 1951 himself

---

[1] *Further Documents relating to the Discussion of Indo-China at the Geneva Conference, June 16–July 21, 1954* (Cmd. 9239), London, H.M.S.O., 1954, p. 41.

[2] The use of given names to refer to individuals is normal in Laos, where family names have been general only since 1944.

formed an administration which included his old colleague in exile, Katay.

The prince had still been prime minister when the Viet Minh invaded Laos in 1953, he had negotiated the final independence conventions with France, and been in office during the Geneva Conference. It was to be expected that he would now preside over the integration of the Pathet Lao and of their leader, his half-brother Prince Souphanouvong, into the national life of Laos. Prince Souvannaphouma's policy was one of strict neutrality abroad and of reconciliation at home. He was little inclined to compromise with either Vietnamese or Siamese interests and regarded both nations with suspicion.[3] He was not afraid of Communist domination through Pathet Lao power because he felt that, once reconciliation had been achieved, the civilizing influence of normal Laotian life would sift out and isolate the committed, hard-core Communists, of whom there were fewer than twenty.

This was not an unreasonable view. Souphanouvong was, after all, a Laotian royal prince, grandson of that Prince Souvannaphouma who had died defending the royal city in 1887. In spite of his obligations to the Viet Minh, his Communist indoctrination course in China, his Vietnamese wife,[4] and his great days in the jungle, the fundamental interests of Prince Souphanouvong were no different from those of any other son of his father. Once he was back in a Laotian atmosphere and his day to day reliance on the Viet Minh was ended, there was a chance that the deeper interests would prevail.

Mr. Dulles had no sympathy with this point of view, and as the United States was now replacing France as chief contributor to the Laotian budget, his opinions quickly became an important political factor in Vientiane. He was deeply mistrustful of Prince Souvannaphouma and sought 'to improve upon the then Laotian government, i.e. to see the succession pass to one more sympathetic to his opinions'.[5] In this he was helped by events, for in September 1954, just as Prince Souvannaphouma had successfully begun his difficult task, the stout-hearted Laotian defence minis-

[3] E. H. S. Simmonds, 'Independence and Political Rivalry in Laos 1945–61' in *Politics in Southern Asia*, S. Rose (ed.), (London, 1963), p. 178.

[4] Le Thi Ky Nam, daughter of a postal employee who was a Communist sympathizer; Lancaster, op. cit., p. 432.

[5] Lord Avon, letter to *Sunday Times*, 19 April 1964.

ter, Kou Voravong, who was believed to be the strongest supporter of the policy of reconciliation towards the Pathet Lao,[6] was assassinated in Vientiane. The murder has never been explained, but in the tumult of charge and counter-charge that followed, Prince Souvannaphouma resigned and national reconciliation became infinitely more difficult.[7]

A new government was formed in November under the forceful and active Katay, a man of middle class, partly Vietnamese origin, firmly attached to the traditions of southern Laos. Like many southerners Katay had a strong sense of the unity of the Lao people on both sides of the Mekong. He felt that the imposition of different régimes on the two river banks was unjust, and looked forward to the day when political differences could be reduced to a minimum. The links with Vietnam imposed upon Laos by France were contrary to tradition and geography, and must be replaced by the close relations with Siam and to a lesser extent Cambodia, which language and history dictated.[8] Laos accordingly withdrew, as did Cambodia, from the joint Indo-Chinese economic arrangements negotiated with France in 1950, and the resulting budgetary deficit was covered by United States aid.

The new prime minister did not go so far as to advocate the union of Laos with Siam. He had returned from exile in Bangkok convinced that the Lao people of Siam were still treated as second-class citizens by the dominant Siamese.[9] But he did share the Siamese view that the Pathet Lao represented a veiled threat from Vietnam to the Mekong valley. He had been among those who had expelled Prince Souphanouvong from the Lao Independence Movement in 1949 'because of his complete dependence on

[6] Simmonds, op. cit., p. 177.

[7] However, the murder was 'obviously directed at the government as a whole' (*Survey of International Affairs 1954* (London, 1957), p. 95). Prince Souvannaphouma has said that his fall at this time was due to foreign interference (speech at Geneva Conference, 14 June 1961).

[8] Katay, *Le Laos*, p. 92. See also *Contribution à l'histoire du mouvement d'indépendance national Lao* (Bangkok, 1948).

[9] *Le Laos*, pp. 17–21. Mr. E. H. S. Simmonds has said: 'Hesitations about too close *political* involvement with Thailand had caused Laos to look askance . . . in 1955, at Thailand's "helpful" move to internationalize the Pathet Lao question by bringing up the matter at a S.E.A.T.O. meeting.' 'The Evolution of Foreign Policy in Laos since Independence', *Modern Asian Studies*, II, 1 (1968), p. 8.

foreign elements and powers',[10] and the prince's subsequent activities had confirmed that verdict. Katay's natural reaction now was to draw closer to the Siamese, who were rapidly doubling their military forces with the help of the United States. He discussed defence and the promotion of trade and communications during a state visit to Bangkok in February 1955; he later set up a Thai-Lao trading association, and a Laotian defence mission visited Siam in October. The extension of the Siamese railway system to Nongkhay, eleven miles by road and ferry from Vientiane, which was completed at the end of the year, did more than anything else to consolidate the link.

Transfer of government responsibility from Prince Souvannaphouma to Katay in November 1954 had meanwhile been followed by difficult negotiations with the Pathet Lao. Discussions between the two princes in August and September had been promising. The withdrawal of French and Viet Minh forces from Laos and the regrouping of the Pathet Lao in the two northern provinces had been completed in November. The French officers sadly left their Laotian units; some remained in the French military organizations allowed by the Geneva Agreement for training and defence purposes. The Pathet Lao had admitted on 4 November, in the last days of Prince Souvannaphouma's authority, that their administrations in Phongsaly and Sam Neua came under the authority of the government in Vientiane.[11]

Prince Souvannaphouma was minister of defence in the new government; but the atmosphere was now quite different. The political talks which began at the Plain of Jars airfield on 3 January 1955 proved long and laborious. In March they were transferred to Vientiane and here they stumbled to a close. The chief issue was the right of the government to take over the administration of Phongsaly and Sam Neua provinces before the general elections due in August. Katay maintained that this was essential if the elections were to be properly run. The Pathet Lao argued, against the obvious intention of the Geneva Agreement, that the provinces were theirs until a full political settlement was reached. The talks were broken off by Katay at the end of April.

Scarcely a week earlier, in the Afro-Asian Conference at Ban-

[10] Speech by Phoui Sananikone at the Geneva Conference: Cmd. 9186, p. 116.

[11] *First Interim Report of the International Commission for Supervision and Control in Laos* (Cmd. 9445), London, H.M.S.O., 1955, p. 45.

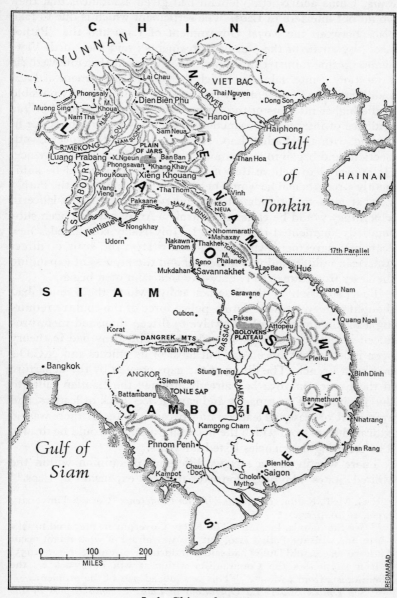

Indo-China after 1954

dung, China and North Vietnam had given assurances that they would not interfere in Laos. 'The settlement which is due to take place between the Royal Government of Laos and the "Pathet Lao", by virtue of the Geneva agreements', said the North Vietnamese prime minister in the written agreement that followed, 'is a question of internal order which the Royal Government of Laos and "Pathet Lao" are entirely free to solve in the best way possible in the higher interests of the country and people of Laos.'[12] This evidence of international sanction gave Katay some confidence in dealing with the Pathet Lao. He now decided to proceed with elections and began to move more troops into Sam Neua province. He appeared to believe that if the Laotian army could be sufficiently strengthened he would be able, if not to suppress the Pathet Lao, at least to intimidate them and reach a political balance in which they would be easier to control.[13] Army pay had been substantially augmented in January. In July Katay concluded a new economic agreement with the United States; the scale of direct American military aid was increased and the process of expanding the army from fifteen to twenty-five thousand men began.

The expansion of the Laotian army, which the French had thought of merely as the future police force of the country requiring a maximum strength of twelve to fifteen thousand men, produced insoluble problems of leadership. The army had in theory been independent since 1950 but most of its officers and N.C.O.s had been French. The filling of the gaps created by the departure of the French in 1954 had already strained the Laotian cadre to the maximum of its capacity and experience. Lack of leaders, and even more of seasoned leaders, now became acute, for there was no educated class from which the necessary numbers could be drawn. The resulting deficiencies lasted for years.

There was in fact a serious difference of opinion within the United States administration over military expansion in Laos.[14]

[12] G. McT. Kahin, *The Asian-African Conference* (Cornell University Press, 1956), p. 27.

[13] See Simmonds, loc. cit.; 'The Katay Government prepared to take a firm line with the Pathet Lao, but . . . was afraid of what might occur if it were successful.' Dulles had said of it during a visit in Februrary 1955: ' "If it suppresses the Communists within it will be struck by the Communists from without." ' This was indeed part of the problem.

[14] See *United States Aid Operations in Laos: Seventh Report by the Committee on Government Operations, June 15, 1959*, Washington, 1959, p. 8.

The State Department supported the build-up for political and economic reasons; it was a means of consolidating the verges of the S.E.A.T.O. system; furthermore, aid administered in the form of army pay reached more people more quickly than aid in any other form. But the American military authorities saw no reason for increasing the number of soldiers. They did not consider that the Laotian army had any role to play in mutual defence and agreed with the French as to its size and function. Their judgement was to be amply vindicated; it was not military but political action that was needed.

Faced with what looked like determination on the part of Katay, the Pathet Lao had on 6 June called on the government to stop the despatch of troops against them in Sam Neua, to postpone the elections and resume political talks.[15] The elections were duly put off until December and further negotiations commenced in July; however, Pathet Lao insistence on major changes in the electoral law and on retaining control of the provinces they considered theirs led to the suspension of these talks on 5 September.[16] A meeting between Katay and Prince Souphanouvong at Rangoon in October brought about a new cease-fire in Sam Neua, but subsequent discussions in Vientiane were terminated on 4 November.[17] There was clearly no basis of confidence between the two sides. Only the patient mediation of the International Control Commission had kept the dialogue going at all.

The general elections therefore took place in December 1955 in the ten provinces held by the government, without Pathet Lao participation. None of the four parties involved gained an outright victory and, when the new Assembly met, Katay found himself without the two-thirds majority then required for the formation of a new government.[18] His strong measures had brought the kingdom no nearer to peace and it was Prince Souvannaphouma who was eventually able to muster the necessary parliamentary support. On 20 March the prince pledged himself once more to bring about

[15] Cmd. 9630, p. 11.
[16] *Third Interim Report of the International Commission for Supervision and Control in Laos* (Cmnd. 314), London, H.M.S.O., 1957, pp. 5–7.
[17] Ibid.
[18] This rule was modified after the crises of 1956 and 1957. A simple majority is now required: *Laos*, C.O.I. pamphlet R3706, February 1958, p. 7.

national reconciliation.[19] He had most of his work to do again, but
in spite of many obstacles and open Siamese and American disapproval, it was done, perhaps with the help of Soviet influence.[20] In
August 1956 Prince Souphanouvong came to Vientiane; mixed
military and political committees were set up and on 28 December
there was an agreement in principle on the basis of neutrality,
guaranteed democratic freedom, and peace. Supplementary elections would be held to give the Pathet Lao a chance of representation in the Assembly, and in the meantime there would be a
coalition government.[21]

Fears in the United States of a 'conquest by negotiation'[22] on
the part of the Communists, now began to affect opinion in Laos,
where the American ambassador, as he was later to admit, was
already struggling to prevent a coalition.[23] The first three months
of 1957 saw an intensive agitation led by Katay who had just
returned from the United States, against the excessive demands of
the Pathet Lao and the dangers of Communism. Mutual suspicion
returned. In March talks on the implementation of the agreement
were adjourned because, said Prince Souvannaphouma, of Pathet
Lao intransigence,[24] and at the end of May the prince resigned
when the Assembly gave him a qualified vote of confidence, that is,
'it approved of the results so far achieved, but it expressed its dissatisfaction with the protracted negotiations and the closeness with
which Souvannaphouma and Souphanouvong were associating
themselves'.[25]

After a prolonged crisis, when neither Katay nor the left-wing
leader Bong Souvannavong had been able to form a government,
Prince Souvannaphouma returned to power in August, making the

[19] Cmnd. 314, pp. 52–53.

[20] *Survey of International Affairs 1955–56* (London, R.I.I.A., 1960), p.
274.

[21] Cmnd. 314, pp. 66–67.

[22] E. H. S. Simmonds, 'A Cycle of Political Events in Laos' in *The
World Today*, 1961, p. 59. Americans had been talking of this danger as
early as January 1957.

[23] *United States Aid Operations in Laos: Hearings before a Subcommittee
of the Committee on Government Operations, House of Representatives,
Eighty-Sixth Congress, First Session,* Washington, 1959, p. 195: 'I struggled
for sixteen months to prevent a coalition'.

[24] Broadcast, 8 April 1957; *Laos*, C.O.I. pamphlet R. 3706, p. 12.

[25] Roger M. Smith, 'Laos' in *Governments and Politics of Southeast
Asia*, G. McT. Kahin (ed.), (Cornell, 2nd edn. 1964), p. 543.

strength of his own stand against Pathet Lao pretensions clear.[26] The negotiations were resumed and there was signed on 12 November a detailed political and military settlement, the Vientiane Agreements.[27] On 18 November Prince Souphanouvong handed over the two northern provinces and swore allegiance for himself and his party to the king of Laos. Next day, together with his associate Phoumi Vongvichit, he entered a government of national union headed by Prince Souvannaphouma.

For a time all seemed to go well. In spite of undisguised American and Siamese disapproval of the Vientiane Agreements,[28] the United States did not stop their economic and military aid. Prince Souphanouvong proved an efficient and honest Minister of the Plan. He would, he said, follow a policy of co-operation with the United States, since Laos needed aid 'not for several years but for several decades'.[29] He instituted monthly accounting and monthly progress reports in his department, a thing previously unheard of, and took a particularly keen interest in the United Nations' project to harness the Mekong for the benefit of the Mekong states. Demobilization of the Pathet Lao, some three thousand regulars and three thousand auxiliaries, proceeded.[30] Three-quarters of them went back to their villages, while the fifteen hundred chosen for integration into the national army were grouped into two battalions which were stationed at Xieng Ngeun and on the Plain of Jars. The Pathet Lao leaders settled down in Vientiane. They became leaders of a political party, the Neo Lao Hak Sat (N.L.H.S.). Normality began to work on them as Prince Souvannaphouma had foreseen.

It remained to hold the supplementary elections which would provide for representation of the new party in the Assembly and so complete the process of national integration begun at Geneva. Twenty additional parliamentary seats were created for this purpose and the elections were fixed for May 1958. At the end of 1957, as he considered the dangers of these elections, the American

[26] *Fourth Interim Report of the International Commission for Supervision and Control in Laos* (Cmnd. 541), London, H.M.S.O., 1958, pp. 44–51, the prince's investiture speech, 8 August 1957.

[27] Texts in Cmnd. 541, pp. 59–61.

[28] Sisouk Na Champassak, op. cit., p. 60. See also D. E. Nuechterlein, *Thailand and the Struggle for Southeast Asia* (Cornell, 1965), p. 145.

[29] Oden Meeker, op. cit., p. 209.   [30] Cmnd. 541, p. 153.

ambassador to Laos, Mr. J. Graham Parsons, had feared that the
manifest failure of past United States' aid to cater for the needs of
the rural population might play into the hands of the Pathet Lao.[31]
He therefore inaugurated a crash programme of rural aid, Operation Booster Shot, over ninety simple rustic projects which he
hoped might counteract anti-American election propaganda in the
villages. The programme, which cost less than a tenth of total
American aid to Laos in 1958, was extremely successful. Never
before had United States' aid in any quantity reached the countryside. The ambassador was confident of a heavy election defeat for
Prince Souphanouvong.[32]

Electoral battles in Laos had, however, hitherto been fought in
terms of family or personal rather than political rivalries. The four
traditional parties saw no need to sink their differences, and duly
nominated eighty-four candidates for the twenty new seats and
one vacant seat that were to be contested. In consequence the
N.L.H.S., with its electoral ally, the left-wing Peace Party,
won thirteen of the seats with only thirty-two per cent. of the
votes.[33]

The significance of these figures was lost in the ensuing uproar.
The left wing had gained a spectacular victory. Those who had
watched their single-minded efforts were not surprised; for political
penetration of the rural districts of Laos was not difficult, it was
only new. When the Pathet Lao, backed by the Viet Minh, first
arrived in Sam Neua they behaved with propriety, with respect
for tradition, and with the utmost friendliness as far as the people
were concerned. Their soldiers were well-disciplined and orderly
like the Viet Minh themselves. They removed the provincial and
district administrators who were appointed by the government,
making the most of local feeling against domination by the Lao.
Some of these men they 'executed' after summary trials before

[31] Over the period 1955–63, less than 1 per cent. of aid funds was spent
on improving agriculture, an activity that provided the living of 96 per
cent. of the population: Dommen, op. cit., p. 107.

[32] *United States Aid Operations in Laos: Seventh Report by the Committee on Government Operations, June 15, 1959* (Washington, 1959), pp.
45–47.

[33] E. H. S. Simmonds, 'Independence and Political Rivalry in Laos
1945–61' in *Politics in Southern Asia*, S. Rose (ed.), (London, 1963), p. 181.
Mr. Dommen, whose work is otherwise so detailed, fails to mention this
figure.

'people's tribunals'.[34] Where they removed unpopular village headmen, they were careful to replace them by election in accordance with custom.

The new leaders—all, of course, Pathet Lao sympathizers—would first seek to revive and deepen the traditional socialism of the villages. The pooling of labour to clear forest, the co-operation of neighbours in house-building, and the allocation of agricultural produce from the common fields according to size of family were already normal. It was also normal for the village and district headmen to have their perquisites, their percentage of the taxes collected and labour requisitioned. Some had taken more than others; some had 'made their harvests on the backs of the people',[35] some had insisted on the *droit de cuissage* when they were on tour.[36] It was often easy for the Pathet Lao to improve on the traditional system from the villagers' point of view.

Inevitably labour still had to be requisitioned; but now, in addition to the wearisome road-making and porterage, some of the common effort was directed to the building of schools and medical centres, benefits which had an impact out of all proportion to their cost because they had rarely been available to the hill people in the past. Promising children were taken to North Vietnam or China where they would be given schooling in their own languages and whence they would return, some to teach in the new schools, others to act as political cadres, all ready to explain that the new benefits were due to the Pathet Lao and their disinterested friends the Viet Minh.

This was an adaptation of the classic method of population

[34] For example, the acting governor of Sam Neua and the district officer of Xieng Kho were murdered in this manner: Dommen, op. cit., p. 40.

[35] A traditional phrase for the misuse of perquisites. In 1861, when the explorer Henri Mouhot was crossing Siamese Laos on his way to Luang Prabang, he met a Siamese official who was about to make his fortune (or so he thought) out of requisitioning labour for the transit of a sacred white elephant through his village. He explained the system, which was to requisition more labour than was needed and then to release some of the labourers on payment of a fee which he kept. 'It is called', he said, 'making one's harvest on the backs of the people. Have you not, respected stranger, a similar saying in your language?' H. Mouhot, *Voyages dans les royaumes de Siam, de Cambodge, de Laos*, F. de Lanoye (ed.), (Paris, 4th edn., 1883), p. 276.

[36] Gentil, op. cit., p. 95.

control used by Mao Tse-Tung and Ho Chi Minh to obtain a solid basis of support for a people's army. It needed no sinister pressures on the easy-going Laotian, no threats of cruelty.[37] The people were simply being governed intelligently for the first time. The tragedy was that the government could offer no competition. Sam Neua, with its traditional dislike of Lao domination, with its leaning towards and easy access to North Vietnam, and with a hill-Thai population that had suffered more than most from political instability both before and after the arrival of the French, was particularly fertile ground for the Pathet Lao. Furthermore Souphanouvong generally, Sithone Khamadam and Faydang within the Kha and Meo communities, were leaders in the old tradition; the influence all three exerted was to some extent founded on genuine popularity.

Of importance too was the success of the Viet Minh in conciliating the hill-Thai and other tribesmen across the border in Tongking, by methods similar to those which the Chinese were using in Yunnan. The Viet Minh have defined their country as 'one nation composed of several peoples', and have guaranteed the mountain folk the right to preserve their customs, languages, and systems of writing. 'As in other poly-ethnic states of the Soviet bloc, the approach to the minorities has gone beyond the realm of theory and has given the D.R.V.N. a competitive advantage over all its neighbours who still persist in a forced-assimilation policy.'[38] The Pathet Lao enjoyed the same advantage in competing with the Laotian government for the allegiance of the hill peoples. 'To the many ethnic minorities' in Laos, says Mr. Field, 'the government symbolised only the oppressive, exclusive ambitions of the Lao majority. Despite the exaggerated claims of the nationalist politi-

[37] For what is nevertheless alleged to have happened see Dommen, op. cit., pp. 80–81. Dommen's account is however based partly on refugee statements included in the case presented by the Laotian government to support its allegations of Viet Minh intervention in Laos in 1959. The other side of the story is in Burchett, *Mekong Upstream* (Berlin, 1959), pp. 259–64. On balance it is probable that comparatively little violence was used; but if this is so the reason was that violence was not needed to achieve the Viet Minh and Pathet Lao aim.

[38] B. B. Fall, *The Two Viet-Nams* (London, 1963), p. 141. See also Professor Fall's 'Problèmes des états poly-ethniques en Indochine' in *France-Asie*, Mar.–Apr. 1962; a particularly clear statement of the problem in so far as it affects Vietnam is to be found in the same author's *Viet-Nam Witness, 1953–1966* (London, 1966), pp. 190–6.

cians . . . they had few contacts in the villages and commanded practically no respect among the minorities.'[39]

The Vientiane Agreements had begun a new, open phase of Pathet Lao activity. For this there were now many agents, recruited in the north and trained with Viet Minh assistance. Their task was simple, for they were peasants themselves. An agent would come and stay in a village, helping unpretentiously with village tasks and exuding goodwill. This in itself was something new. When government officials visited a village— as a senior Lao officer said of the French—'they got the best girls, the best pigs, the best chickens. . . . When a Vietnamese agent reaches a village he doesn't take the most beautiful girls or the chickens or the pigs. He stays outside the village and helps work in the fields and harvest the rice.'[40]

In the absence of any government presence to counteract his activity the agent could often win over the village headman or, if he proved obdurate, secure the election of someone else. When he had done this it was not difficult to make it dangerous for government officials to visit the village or frustrate their efforts if they did so.

If an agent needed to reinforce his arguments he would sometimes arrange for villagers to visit Vientiane, now a sprawling conglomeration of villages containing 70,000 people, or one of the other Mekong towns, so that they could see for themselves how the new riches of the country were being spent. For not only was aid not reaching the villages, it was also being shamelessly wasted in the towns:

Corruption and extortion in the customs, banking, foreign trade, police and other administrative departments were commonplace. Blackmarket deals in American aid dollars reached such proportions that the Pathet Lao needed no propaganda to turn the rural population against the townspeople. The Chinese of Hongkong and Bangkok and a few Lao officials profited from the American aid. . . .[41]

The poor Laotian stood helplessly by and the Pathet Lao reaped the harvest.

[39] Field, op. cit., p. 54. See V. Thompson and R. Adloff, *Minority Problems in Southeast Asia* (Stanford, 1955), p. 210, for the use the Viet Minh/Pathet Lao made of gaps left by departing French administrators.
[40] Oden Meeker, op. cit., p. 211.
[41] Sisouk Na Champassak, op. cit., p. 64.

In these circumstances, the thirty-two per cent. of the votes secured by the Pathet Lao and Peace Party in the partial elections of May 1958 certainly showed no runaway trend towards Communism. Had the number of seats won matched the proportion of votes obtained the result would probably have been accepted as reasonable. The imminent reality of the thirteen new left-wing deputies in an Assembly of fifty-nine was, however, a severe blow to the government and the West. The United States authorities were particularly shaken. A Congressional inquiry into the administration of American aid in Laos was uncovering mismanagement and corruption. Mr. Parsons himself had told the inquiry that the Pathet Lao defeat he predicted in the elections would be 'value for our aid money'.[42] Now it suddenly seemed that there had been no value for money at all.

Action was urgent, for the Congressional Committee on foreign aid was to sit in June. It was essential that the administration should be able to convince the Congress of its will and capacity to stop abuses and to arrest the progress of the Pathet Lao, if it was to escape a cut in its aid programme. On 30 June, however, Prince Souvannaphouma's government with its two Pathet Lao ministers was still in office. In the face of mounting Congressional criticism of the aid programme, United States economic aid, now amounting to all but a fraction of the Laotian budget, was suspended. The pretext was the need for monetary reform; the purpose was to force Prince Souvannaphouma out of office.[43]

It had seemed at first as if the prince would be able to satisfy his critics. He had already created a united parliamentary front against the left, the Rally of the Lao People, in which he had the support of thirty-six of fifty-nine deputies in the new house. He had encouraged the formation outside the Assembly of the 'Committee for the Defence of National Interests', an anti-Communist organization of the younger, better educated officials and army officers who had hitherto played little or no part in politics. He had also declared that, now elections had been held, the International Control Commission had completed its task in Laos. This led to its withdrawal in July in spite of the dissent of its Polish

---

[42] *United States Aid Operations in Laos: Seventh Report by the Committee on Government Operations, June 15 ,1959* (Washington, 1959), p. 47.

[43] Dommen, op. cit., p. 110. See also speech of Prince Souvannaphouma at the Geneva Conference, 14 June 1961.

member who saw it as providing a measure of protection for Pathet Lao interests.[44] The West was glad to see it go.

The prince had, however, underestimated the anxiety of the Americans and Siamese about the danger of a Communist takeover, and had never gained their confidence. The Committee for the Defence of National Interests, the C.D.N.I., which had possessed it from the first, was now used against him. In the manoeuvrings that followed the inauguration of the new Assembly, 'allegedly with the enticement of monetary bribes distributed by the P.E.O. and C.I.A., a sufficient number of deputies were persuaded to block Souvanna's reappointment'.[45] On 6 August the prince gave up the attempt to form a new government and on 18 August Phoui Sananikone returned to power. His cabinet included four members of the C.D.N.I. but the two Pathet Lao members of the previous administration were of course excluded. Prince Souvannaphouma went to Paris as ambassador, Prince Souphanouvong became chairman of the new Assembly.

The Swing to the Right

M. Phoui Sananikone is one of the two or three Laotian politicians capable of holding his own in the world of statesmen. He had done this as head of the Laotian delegation at Geneva in 1954, scorning Pathet Lao pretensions and firmly standing his ground, and he now took office as prime minister for the second time. His task was to prevent further gains by the Pathet Lao and to secure a resumption of American aid.

He made an energetic start. Besides proceeding immediately with the financial reforms which were to restore the flow of American cash in October, he declared war on corruption and prolonged the hours of work in government offices. There were changes in ambassadorial posts and in governorships of provinces. 'Communist sympathisers and long time fellow travelers of the

---

[44] It adjourned *sine die* on 19 July 1958. Its important contribution to the 1957 settlement has yet to be fully acknowledged.

[45] Roger M. Smith, 'Laos in Perspective' in *Asian Survey*, Jan. 1963, p. 63. The Programs Evaluation Office (P.E.O.) was an organization staffed by soldiers out of uniform, set up in 1958 to administer U.S. military aid. It was commanded by a Brigadier General of the U.S. Army whose name had been removed from the current Army List in order to conceal his status. *New York Times*, 9 January 1962.

Pathet Lao were dismissed from government service',[46] although
some of them had been appointed under the Vientiane Agreements. Ngo Dinh Nhu, infamous brother of the ill-fated South
Vietnamese president, paid an official visit to Vientiane in September. There was talk of a law against Communism. 'As far as peaceful coexistence is concerned', said Phoui, 'we shall clearly inform
neighbouring countries that we shall coexist with the Free World
only.'[47]

After the implementation of the monetary reforms on 10
October, however, the new régime began to run into difficulties.
In addition to the left-wing critics in the Assembly, there were
those whose vested interests had been affected by the new measures
which included devaluation and the abolition of the widely abused
system of import licences. The proposed anti-Communist law was
put aside and Phoui became more cautious. The opposition
showed itself on 31 October, the day on which the Assembly was
due to go into recess. A motion was carried by 22 votes to 20 for
the prolongation of the session. The royal speech of adjournment
was nevertheless made and the Assembly broke up. During
November the political crisis gradually intensified, and by the
beginning of December Phoui felt that his government was in
danger. There was talk of a *coup d'état* by army officers and others
who affected to regard the strength of the opposition as proof of
the ineffectiveness of the government, and even of the C.D.N.I.
itself, against the left wing. Alarmed by the rumours, about
two hundred members of the Pathet Lao took refuge in North
Vietnam.

It is tempting to connect the events which followed with the
parallel political developments in Siam. A year earlier Marshal
Sarit had ousted his two main rivals for power in that country,
had installed a government of his own choosing, and had departed
almost immediately for medical treatment in the United States.
In October 1958 he was completing his convalescence in Great
Britain when a new political crisis arose in Bangkok. On 19 October
the marshal suddenly returned to Siam, dismissed the government, and assumed full powers himself. The reason he gave for his
action was the existence of a Communist threat, internal and ex-

[46] Sisouk Na Champassak, op. cit., p. 67.
[47] Quoted by B. B. Fall: 'The Laos Tangle' in *International Journal*,
16 February 1961, p. 142.

ternal.[48] An immediate sequel was the arrest of seventy Vietnamese in north-east Siam on grounds of Communist subversion.

According to reliable reports, nobody really believed that there was 'even a trace of Communist danger' in Siam.[49] The crisis was essentially economic and it was partly due to the cut of about one-third in American aid to Siam in 1958. One of the means being adopted to put the economy back on its feet was, however, 'a veiled ultimatum to the United States to increase its aid'. Hence the allegations, which were far from convincing, of Communist activity in the north-east.

Colonel Phoumi Nosavan, a relation of Marshal Sarit, had also spent the year 1957–8 in the West. He had returned to Laos in August 1958 from a course at the *École Supérieure de Guerre* in Paris. Phoumi was not popular with his contemporaries in the army, who suspected his past association with the left, and he was not given the influential military post to which he is believed to have aspired. By December he was among the officers whose political ambitions were thought to have been aroused by the turn of events.

The fears of a *coup d'état* in Vientiane proved groundless. Colonel Phoumi did not seize control. There occurred instead a series of incidents, mysterious at the time, which led through reaction and counter-reaction to much the same result a year later. On 15 December 1958 a Laotian military patrol was fired on when visiting the district of Huong Lap, a remote region on the frontier with North Vietnam some fifteen miles north of the Lao Bao Pass through the Annamitic Chain east of Savannakhet. It was a most sensitive area because so close to the demilitarized partition zone between North and South Vietnam. The frontier had been disputed even in French colonial days, when Huong Lap had been governed as part of Vietnam. The North Vietnamese had appropriated it after the departure of the French; no Lao official had ever visited it and no Laotian military post had ever been established there, although it appeared to be part of Laos on the map. To the few who knew these facts, the hostile reception of the Laotian patrol can have come as no surprise.

On 27 and 31 December, the North Vietnamese alleged that Laos had violated their border at Huong Lap. The Laotian

[48] *The Times*, 21 October 1958.
[49] *Manchester Guardian*, 3 November 1958.

government denied this and countered with charges that the North Vietnamese themselves had occupied three Laotian villages in the area. There was renewed talk in Vientiane of a *coup* by anti-Communist officers and officials. Prince Souphanouvong called for the reactivation of the International Control Commission. On 11 January the prime minister, Phoui Sananikone, stated that the frontier incursions were connected with the internal political situation and that the Pathet Lao were actively planning insurrection. On these grounds he obtained from the Assembly, on 14 January 1959, emergency powers for twelve months, a measure by which the Assembly 'virtually divested itself of legislative powers for the period'.[50] He also protested to the Secretary General of the United Nations against North Vietnamese interference in Laos.

In presenting the Huong Lap incident as a clear case of aggression by the Viet Minh, Dommen comments that 'accusations of ground violations are a characteristic tactic employed by Asian Communists when they are preparing their own military initiatives'.[51] However, it was not the Viet Minh who followed up the incident at Huong Lap, where the trouble died down as quickly as it had arisen. The sequels came in Laos and Siam. In Laos the government was remodelled on 24 January 1959 to include Colonel Phoumi and two other army officers, a definite move further to the right. In Siam on 29 January Marshal Sarit promulgated an emergency constitution, justifying his action in part by renewed references to the danger in the north[52] which, thanks to the furore in Laos, must certainly have seemed more credible than it had done in October.

Phoumi, who had in other days been chief of staff to Prince Souphanouvong, now became the dominant right-wing influence in the Laotian army and government. To the Siamese backing he already enjoyed, he soon added the powerful support of American agencies who came to regard him as the future strong man of Laos, although the American ambassador was to say a few months later that Phoumi 'was using anti-Communism, through the device of

[50] E. H. S. Simmonds, 'Independence and Political Rivalry in Laos 1945–61' in *Politics in Southern Asia*, S. Rose (ed.), (London, 1963), pp. 183–4.

[51] Op. cit., pp. 115–16.

[52] D. A. Wilson, *Politics in Thailand* (Cornell, 1962), p. 34.

the C.D.N.I., to further his personal ambitions'.[53] By June 1962 there was little doubt, as will be seen later, that Phoumi had sometimes manufactured and frequently exploited military incidents for political purposes. Whether or not the encounter at Huong Lap on 15 December 1958 was accidental, it appears to have been exploited to the advantage both of Phoumi and of Sarit.

At the beginning of 1959 a Nationalist Chinese consul had been installed in Vientiane and the South Vietnamese legation there raised to the status of embassy. These developments had inevitably given offence to North Vietnam and China, who had been persuaded by Prince Souvannaphouma in 1956 to drop their requests for diplomatic representation in Laos. The prince had pointed out during visits to Peking and Hanoi that the Nationalist Chinese were not represented in his country and that the exchange of legations between Laos and South Vietnam was a relic of pre-independence days which did not justify a similar exchange with Hanoi.[54] The reaction of the north, Peking, and eventually Moscow, to the Laotian crisis of January 1959 could therefore only be to back Prince Souphanouvong's demand for the return of the International Control Commission.

Phoui Sananikone not only rejected this demand, but stated on 11 February that Laos had fulfilled her obligations under the Geneva Agreement, and that she could no longer be bound by the limitations on foreign military aid which she had accepted at Geneva pending a political settlement in Vietnam, and had confirmed less than a year earlier.[55] The prime minister's reference was to a Laotian declaration on the military status of the country, which contained the following undertaking: 'During the period between the cessation of hostilities in Viet Nam and the final settlement of that country's political problems, the Royal Government of Laos will not request foreign aid, whether in war material, in personnel or in instructors, except for the purpose of its effective territorial defence and to the extent defined by the agreement on the cessation of hostilities.'[56] The agreement on the cessation of

[53] Dommen, op. cit., pp. 127–8.
[54] Prince Souvannaphouma, 'Le fond du problème', in *France-Asie*, Mar.-Apr., 1961.
[55] Letter of Prince Souvannaphouma to the International Control Commission, 31 May 1958: Cmnd. 541, p. 122.
[56] Cmd. 9239, p. 42.

hostilities had provided that apart from the French training and defence establishments with a permitted total of five thousand men, no reinforcements of troops or military personnel from outside Laotian territory were to be allowed at all.[57] It could therefore be argued that even if the Laotian government now felt itself free to ask for military aid, it was a breach of the cease-fire agreement if, for example, American military personnel were sent.

While the United States State Department at once supported Phoui's statement, the Communist bloc interpreted it as a denunciation of the Geneva Agreement. Their protests were redoubled when the Americans responded to a Laotian request for technical assistance by bringing into Laos eighty Filipino military technicians and establishing a training section in the Programs Evaluation Office. The Soviet Union, in a note to Britain, charged the Americans with openly inciting the Laotian government to violate the Geneva Agreement. Russia suggested that the two co-chairmen should request the International Control Commission on Laos to resume its work as soon as possible. After a number of exchanges the Soviet suggestion was rejected.[58]

Meanwhile the Laotian government had decided to bring to a head the question of integrating the two Pathet Lao battalions into the national army, a matter which had long been held up by disagreements on the number of Pathet Lao officers to be accepted and on their ranks. In April the government agreed to accept the 105 officers nominated by the Pathet Lao and named 11 May as the day on which formal integration would take place.

It is not hard to imagine how, from the Pathet Lao point of view, it seemed that a dangerous situation was beginning to arise. Their first set-back had been the departure of the International Control Commission, one of whose main duties had been to prevent discrimination or reprisals against them. Freed thereafter from international checks, and under increasing pressure from the right, the government had then abandoned the neutral policy of the Vientiane Agreements on the basis of which Sam Neua and Phongsaly provinces had been handed over by the Pathet Lao. The Pathet Lao

---

[57] Article 6, Chapter II of the agreement on the cessation of hostilities in Laos: Cmd. 9239, p. 20.

[58] *Documents relating to British Involvement in the Indo-China Conflict 1945–1965* (Cmnd. 2834), pp. 135 ff. See also *Survey of International Affairs 1959–60* (London, R.I.I.A., 1964), pp. 286–7.

then lost their representation in the administration. Finally, all possibility of their working through the Assembly had been deferred by the prime minister's assumption of emergency powers. The Pathet Lao were being forced back into insurgency.

Now Prince Souphanouvong probably knew, for there are few secrets in Laos, that the government's agreement to accept 105 of his officers contained a trick. Sisouk Na Champassak, the Secretary of State for Information at the time, makes this clear: 'Once the agreement was reached, the weapons surrendered, and the two battalions scattered throughout the country, the commissions could be nullified by demanding, for example, that the new officers pass examinations appropriate to their rank'.[59] As the educational standards of these men of the jungle were low—for few of the hillmen had been to school—they could be expected to fail.

At a time when he was no longer a member of the government, when he had lost his voice in the Assembly and when his followers were being subjected to increasing pressures, Prince Souphanouvong was thus to be deprived of the last elements of his military independence. It would appear that the two battalions had instructions not to accept integration on 11 May unless the prince or his military commander Colonel Singkapo were present. Singkapo was not invited, and in spite of a last-minute invitation the prince did not attend. On this and several other pretexts the two units refused integration.

The government decided to use force. Prince Souphanouvong and the three other chief Pathet Lao leaders were placed under house arrest, and, after an ultimatum, the two battalions were surrounded in their camps by government forces. On 17 May Prince Souphanouvong agreed to order his men to accept the government terms and one battalion did so. The other did not wait. On the night of 18 May the whole seven hundred men, complete with their families, their chickens, pigs, household possessions, and arms, slipped out of their camp on the Plain of Jars and followed a long-planned route to an isolated valley near the North Vietnamese border some forty-five miles away.[60] The

[59] Sisouk Na Champassak, op. cit., p. 78.
[60] B. B. Fall, *Street Without Joy* (Harrisburg, 1961), pp. 301–2 gives a graphic account of the escape of this battalion. A substantial part of the other battalion decamped in August. The arrangements for guarding it had been poor.

monsoon had already broken; there was contact but no serious pursuit. Nevertheless incidents were reported between the two sides in Xieng Khouang province, and Hanoi Radio asserted that the local population was rallying to the Pathet Lao. This was false but it intensified the new crisis and worried the West. On 25 May the Laotian government stated that the Pathet Lao had committed an act of open rebellion and that only a military solution now seemed possible. The furious protests of the Communist bloc were rejected.

At this point the United States Congress Committee whose inquiries had had their effect upon Laotian politics in 1958, published its report on United States aid operations in Laos. It was a sober document, examining the corruption and mismanagement which had dissipated much of the aid given to the country since 1955 and probing its causes. 'Giving Laos more aid than it could absorb hindered rather than helped. . . . Excessive cash grants forced money into the Lao economy at a faster rate than it could possibly be absorbed, causing . . . inflation . . . profiteering'.[61] On the basis of this report the Congress would now obviously press for a reduction in aid to Laos. What followed has been attributed to the efforts of those who wished at all costs to prevent such a catastrophe.

'The question for the Laotian Government at this time', says Lederer in *A Nation of Sheep*,

would be how to persuade the U.S. Congress and U.S. public that aid for Laos should not be reduced. What reasons could be offered for having an army which costs three times as much as the total cash income of Laos? Millions of U.S. dollars already had gone into the hodge-podge Laotian military, yet there was little to show for it. There was no checking-up on padded army pay-rolls; and much of the money went into officers' pockets. Only about one-fifth of the troops could be put into the field. They had no communications system, no transport system, no system of material maintenance, and precious few functional weapons, in spite of the enormous sums spent. The Royal Laotian troops were incapable of handling the pro-Reds—who were far fewer in number than themselves. . . . What went through the heads of the Lao officials we can

[61] *United States Aid Operations in Laos; Seventh Report by the Committee on Government Operations, June 15, 1959* (Washington, 1959), pp. 1–2.

only guess. But of this we are certain: within a week after the damning Congressional report was received in Laos, things began to happen.[62]

What happened was another military crisis, more extensive and more suspect than that which had occurred in January, and a further increase in American involvement. On 29 July the government announced that frontier posts in Sam Neua province had been attacked by Pathet Lao forces stiffened by Viet Minh. Prince Souphanouvong and fifteen other Pathet Lao leaders were promptly gaoled and on 4 August Laos complained to the United Nations.

The pattern of reports during the next six weeks followed closely the pattern of Viet Minh attacks against the French in the dry season of 1952–3;[63] but it was now the wet season. From 18 to 31 July the government had reported a deep thrust into Sam Neua province which threatened to cut it off from the rest of Laos. A period of general insecurity ensued, with reports of pinprick attacks throughout the country in August. Then, from 30 August to 15 September heavy attacks were reported on Lao outposts in Sam Neua, with thrusts along the traditional invasion route from the north to Luang Prabang.

As the countryside was soaking under the torrential rains which are normal at this time of year, major operations were barely possible. The press nevertheless accepted the Laotian military reports at their face value and the resulting headlines were dramatic. 'There was wild talk in Congress of sending U.S. troops to Laos, and of bombing the "invaders" with U.S. Navy and Air Force planes. Units of the Seventh Fleet were sent to the danger zone in the South China Sea. . . . State Department announced that the situation was grave.'[64] On 4 September the Laotian government asked the United Nations for an emergency force to resist Viet Minh aggression.

The truth became known gradually in September. Observers discovered that there had indeed been Pathet Lao military activity in Sam Neua province and elsewhere, but it had been on a minor scale. The technique was not new. Small armed Pathet Lao groups would approach defended villages, sending emissaries ahead to frighten the defenders with stories of approaching hordes. The

---

[62] W. J. Lederer, *A Nation of Sheep* (London, 1961), pp. 21–22.

[63] B. B. Fall, *Street Without Joy* (Harrisburg, 1961), pp. 302–3.

[64] Lederer, op. cit., p. 24.

isolated military posts, not always linked by radio and never
particularly confident in this basically hostile non-Lao country,[65]
would despatch runners with reports of massive enemy attacks or
movement, in order to excuse their own withdrawal.[66] The reports
were accepted at the army headquarters in Sam Neua, translated
into great red arrows on the situation maps, and forwarded to
Vientiane where they became even bigger arrows on ever larger
maps.[67] The press, without too much American discouragement,[68]
reproduced the stories, sometimes in an even more sensational
form; broadcasts of the resulting news items increased further the
nervousness of the men holding out against the tide of panic. As
the little garrisons and petty officials fled, the Pathet Lao substituted
their own, until by mid-September they controlled considerable
areas in half the provinces of Laos.

Whether the Sam Neua crisis was created by the Laotians
themselves, as Lederer suggests, may never be known. However
it started, few doubted that the North Vietnamese supported the
Pathet Lao in exploiting it, indeed that they had used it to reacti-
vate the Pathet Lao as a guerrilla force. This needed no greater aid
than had been given as a matter of course in the past.[69] A regular
Viet Minh invasion, on the other hand, was fundamentally

[65] See the *Carte ethnolinguistique de l'Indochine*, École française
d'extrême orient, 1949. Sam Neua province contains virtually no Lao.
The ethnic proportions for 1921, quoted by LeBar and Suddard, *Laos, its
People, its Society, its Culture* (New Haven, 1960), probably represent the
situation today: 75 per cent. Thai—that is hill-Thai—18 per cent. Kha
and 6 per cent. Man (p. 239). The north of the province where the trouble
started in 1959 is peopled by Black Thai whose traditional centre is Son
La, some twenty miles across the hills to the north. The former Son La
chief, Prince Canh, imprisoned by the French for murder, had joined the
Viet Minh after release by the Japanese in 1945 (Bodard, op. cit., pp.
348–9). It was thus nervous country for the predominantly Lao army.
B. B. Fall, 'Problèmes des états poly-ethniques en Indochine' in *France-
Asie*, Mar.–Apr. 1962, goes so far as to call the Laotian crises of both
1959 and 1960 'predominantly tribal rebellions'.

[66] See B. B. Fall, *Street Without Joy* (Harrisburg, 1961), pp. 302–4;
Lederer, op. cit., pp. 26–28; Dommen, op. cit., p. 120.

[67] Denis Warner, *The Last Confucian* (London, Penguin, 1964), pp.
255–8: the army commander in Sam Neua 'accepted as fact what the most
junior Western staff officer would have rejected as fiction'.

[68] Lederer, op. cit., pp. 24–25; see also Sisouk Na Champassak, op. cit.,
p. 115.

[69] Simmonds, in S. Rose (ed.), op. cit., p. 187.

improbable both because of the weather and because it would have attracted S.E.A.T.O. intervention, the last thing that North Vietnam could have wanted.

The United States, however, who had accepted the worst interpretation, and had substantially increased her military aid at the end of August, remained only half convinced that she had been deceived. The Programs Evaluation Office had received an additional hundred military advisers in civilian clothes, and had set up training teams at the main military centres to begin, in agreement with the French, a programme of technical and weapons training for the whole army. The strength of the army was increased to twenty-nine thousand men; so far from any reduction, United States military aid for 1959 showed an effective increase of nearly thirty per cent. on the figure for 1958.[70]

By relying on military means to combat the Pathet Lao the Laotian government and its American advisers were playing into the hands of their enemies. Pathet Lao action was more political than military; it relied on the exploitation of social and political grievances and needed to be fought by the removal of these grievances rather than by military action. The Lao soldier, with his ineradicable terror of the Viet Minh, was quite incapable of combating the fear psychosis on which the Pathet Lao relied. If well reinforced he could overrun a particular area and force the Pathet Lao to go to ground. But his behaviour then often frightened the rural people into the jungle as well, and when he left his enemies were stronger than ever. Mounting insecurity ended whatever remained of the impetus of medical and social development into the countryside: the Pathet Lao could profit cheaply by replacing it.

A factor that should perhaps be examined is the possible influence on these events of the traffic in opium. The French had never been able to prevent the cultivation of opium by the Meos and Yaos, predominantly in Xieng Khouang province, and had ended by encouraging it during the war for revenue reasons. The annual consumption of the drug in French Indo-China was esti-

---

[70] LeBar and Suddard, op. cit., p. 251, gives the figures as $19.8 million in 1958 and $11.2 million in 1959. The unit of Laotian currency had, however, been devalued in October 1958 from 35 to 80 to the U.S. dollar, a fact which reverses the proportion between these two figures.

mated at 110 to 120 tons in 1939, to which Laos had contributed amounts of up to 23 tons according to the policy and activity of the government purchasing agents. Whatever remained of the crop, over and above local needs, was bought up each year by the traditional Chinese pony caravans, for the illicit trade in North Vietnam and South China.

In 1941 the interruption of normal supplies from outside the colony and the consequent rise in prices stimulated Laotian production and attracted new growers, particularly in Sam Neua and Phongsaly provinces, where illegal cultivation by Khas and hill Thai probably contributed to a considerably increased output. The government purchased 25 tons in 1942, of which more came from Sam Neua than from the traditional opium province, Xieng Khouang. In 1945 the Japanese, and in 1946 the Chinese Nationalists, can be assumed to have accounted for most of the crop. From 1947 onwards any return to the pre-war pattern in Laos would have been distorted by the spread of Viet Minh control, but at first outside sources of supply would again have been available to the main consumers, the populous cities of Saigon and Hanoi. The Viet Minh were in control of much of the opium-growing areas of Laos in 1953 and 1954. At the end of 1954 they occupied Hanoi under the Geneva Agreement, but almost at once they were in sore straits because of the cessation of all kinds of trade with South Vietnam, including, presumably, the import of opium.

Even if the desire of an *habitué* for his opium is no stronger than that of a smoker for tobacco, the maintenance of normal supplies must, in itself, have been of some importance to the Viet Minh. But they had also been using opium to pay for Chinese military aid and to finance their intelligence services and propaganda.[71] It is therefore not surprising that they should have been reluctant to leave productive areas like Sam Neua and Phongsaly. In the event, they controlled the two provinces through the Pathet Lao in 1955, 1956, and 1957. Government troops arrived before the 1958 harvest but are unlikely to have affected the direction of the opium traffic in that year. In 1959, when perhaps they were more firmly established, trouble began again in July, a month when much of the opium is still in the villages.

The rest of Laos is of course far from uninterested in the opium trade. Consumption cannot be high, but the demand for illicit

[71] *Le Monde*, 22–23 November 1953.

opium in Siam, Cambodia, and South Vietnam ensures satis-factory profits for anyone who can securely move it from the relatively inaccessible highlands where it grows. Opium smuggling receives occasional publicity. The involvement of General Phao and of the Siamese police at one time was notorious. The traffic is certainly important and conflicts along the routes of supply between the various parties concerned must therefore be regarded as normal. Its precise influence on the events of 1959 cannot be assessed; sixty-five tons, the estimated annual production in Laos by 1960, is however an influential amount of opium.[72]

The Sam Neua crisis faded as the world realized what had occurred. Laotian statements lost their colour. As early as 23 September, when a United Nations mission was beginning to investigate the Laotian complaint, North Vietnam was no longer being accused of aggression. The autumn passed. On 29 October the old king, Sisavang Vong, died after a reign of fifty-four years. The Crown Prince Savang succeeded him. The United Nations mission produced an inconclusive report.[73] There was no evidence, it said, to support the view that North Vietnamese forces had invaded Laos or otherwise committed direct aggression, although 'varying degrees and kinds of support' appeared to have been given to dissident Laotian elements by North Vietnam. The only direct evidence which the government had been able to produce for the mission was a weapon of Communist bloc manufacture. This had in fact been taken from a Viet Minh soldier of tribal origin who had deserted across the border into Laos some time previously, and had no connexion with the Sam Neua operations.

Mr. Hammarskjold visited Laos to see for himself. The co-ordination of economic aid for the country by the United Nations seemed a promising possibility. But the Laotian government and its prime minister were ill at ease. They had been lectured by Mr. Hammarskjold and the West. Mr. Hammarskjold's wise advice was that they should return to a policy of neutrality[74] and to economic rather than military development.

[72] LeBar and Suddard, op. cit., p. 205. See also Denis Warner, op. cit., p. 283, and B. B. Fall, *Hell in a Very Small Place* (London, 1967), pp. 20–21.

[73] *Report of the Security Council Sub-Committee under Resolution of 7 September 1959*, U.N. Security Council document s/4236, 5 Nov. 1959.

[74] E. H. S. Simmonds, loc. cit. *Survey of International Affairs 1959–60* (London, R.I.I.A., 1964), p. 294.

This moderate view probably coincided with Phoui Sananik-one's own judgement. The policy of all-out commitment to the West and of repression of the Pathet Lao which had been followed since January, had been that of the C.D.N.I. The prime minister had yielded to right-wing pressure, and he had really believed that Sam Neua had been invaded by the Viet Minh. He now blamed his youthful allies, and in particular Colonel Phoumi, for the summer fiasco. There was soon a serious rift between himself and the C.D.N.I. members of the government.

A disagreement as to the date of general elections precipitated the new crisis. The C.D.N.I. believed that the situation demanded an intensification of pressure against the Pathet Lao, with dictatorial powers and an indefinite postponement of the elections. Phoui realized that this might lead to civil war. He also felt strong enough for new negotiations with the Pathet Lao before general elections early in 1960.[75] His moderate supporters, how-ever, insisted on the removal of Kamphan Panya, the senior C.D.N.I. minister, from the Ministry of Foreign Affairs. The up-shot was the exclusion of the C.D.N.I. ministers from the govern-ment in a reshuffle which was confirmed by a special meeting of the Assembly, and a *coup d'état* led by Phoumi, who had just been promoted to Brigadier General. In the middle of the crisis, on 29 December, Katay died suddenly of an embolism. With him died any hope of a compromise between the politicians and Phoumi. The dismissal of Phoui Sananikone by the king followed on 30 December.

Whether or not, as some have alleged, United States influence was responsible for the fall of the Sananikone government,[76] the Western powers were not pleased with the prospect of a military

[75] E. H. S. Simmonds, 'The Evolution of Foreign Policy in Laos', p.17. Sisouk Na Champassak, op. cit., pp. 129–30, discusses the crisis from the C.D.N.I. point of view; Roger M. Smith, 'Laos in Perspective' in *Asian Survey*, January 1963, associates Phoui's policy with disappointment in the quantity of American aid.

[76] Roger M. Smith, loc. cit., states that Phoumi's *coup d'état* was staged with P.E.O. and C.I.A. advice. Dommen, op. cit., pp. 127–8 supports this as far as the C.I.A. is concerned. He comments, however, that all American agencies did not share the optimistic C.I.A. view of Phoumi. See also *Survey of International Affairs 1959–60*, (London, R.I.I.A., 1964), pp. 286–7.

régime in Laos. Their deep concern was made clear when, on 4 January 1960, the French, British, and American ambassadors and the Australian chargé d'affaires called on the king. As the Assembly was no longer in being, His Majesty decided to name a provisional government responsible to himself. He chose the elder statesman Kou Abhay as prime minister. The new government which took office on 7 January was nevertheless dominated by General Phoumi.

Now that the army was in charge of affairs it regarded the risk of general elections as less serious.[77] It was accepted that the elections would be held in April 1960 and General Phoumi prepared to rig them. Sisouk Na Champassak, who had acted as Phoumi's official spokesman during his *coup d'état*, tells us how this was done:

The electoral districts were revised to break up Pathet Lao zones of influence and prevent the movement from forming highly compact groups. The eligibility requirements for candidates were stiffened . . . a minimum educational standard was required. . . . This . . . clause . . . contained a trick; more than half the Pathet Lao leaders and propagandists had no schooling and so were automatically excluded from the race.[78]

At the same time a joint committee was formed under General Phoumi to draw up a common list of candidates for the C.D.N.I. and the Rally of the Lao People, allegedly to prevent the splitting of the anti-Pathet Lao vote, but in fact to bring the new Assembly under Phoumi's control.

The task of ensuring security for the elections was given to the army who decided that 'wherever possible, it would suppress Communist propaganda in the provinces to insure the victory of the government candidates'.[79] In the 'least secure area', which turns out to be the notoriously unsubdued Bolovens Plateau in the south, a large scale 'raiding operation' was carried out by nine battalions: 'Their objective was not so much to clear the area of rebels . . . as to make the population aware of the presence of Royal troops, to reassure it, and to prepare a favourable climate for the elections. In the most important villages, little garrisons were installed temporarily for the protection of the candidates.'[80] 'The

---

[77] Simmonds, in *Politics in Southern Asia*, S. Rose (ed.), p. 188.
[78] Sisouk Na Champassak, op. cit., p. 139 ff.
[79] Ibid., p. 141.   [80] Ibid., p. 142.

result of this countryside campaign', comments Mr. Dommen, 'was not the mopping up of the Pathet Lao but the alienation of the peasantry.'[81]

[81] Op cit., p. 132. Dommen supplies much detail on the manner in which the election was rigged, including, allegedly, open monetary bribes by C.I.A. agents.

The election results were a foregone conclusion. The fourteen Pathet Lao and Peace Party candidates all failed, sometimes in bizarre circumstances. In one area, for instance, a candidate who voted for himself together with a dozen members of his family still polled no votes. However, says Mr. Simmonds, 'the real danger feared by the C.D.N.I. in the election had not been N.L.H.S. but the more moderate Rally Party who might have been expected to sweep the board'.[82] Although the Rally Party had been able to insist on a majority of the candidates on the common list, it had much less than a majority in the line-up of successful candidates. Again Sisouk Na Champassak explains how this was achieved.[83] After the elections a new party was formed under General Phoumi, to which Rally Party deputies who had gained their seats with army assistance now adhered. The Phoumi party thus claimed thirty-five seats in the new house and the Rally Party seventeen. It was the technique Marshal Sarit had used in the Siamese elections of 1957.[84]

Prince Souvannaphouma, who had returned from Paris for the elections and was again the member for Luang Prabang, was elected chairman of the Assembly. Partly because of renewed Western warnings of the objections to military rule in Laos, his nephew Prince Somsanith[85] became prime minister. There was, however, no doubt where power lay. Phoumi, gathering into his hands the commercial interests of Katay, and possessing in full measure the confidence of the United States, clearly intended to rule.

The new government took office on 2 June. One of Phoumi's first decisions was to have been to press on with the public trial of Prince Souphanouvong, which had been deferred on the advice of Mr. Hammarskjold in the previous autumn. Perhaps with this in mind, on the night of 23 May, the prince and fifteen other Pathet Lao leaders with him in prison had escaped with the aid of their guards. The guard company had not been changed for six months; the prisoners had been able gradually to win over enough of the gendarmes to make success possible and then certain. They

---

[82] Simmonds, in Rose (ed.), op. cit., p. 189

[83] Sisouk Na Champassak, op. cit., p. 146.

[84] Denis Warner, op. cit., p. 289.

[85] A man of moderate opinions whose appointment would allay Western anxieties but who was 'greatly indebted' to Phoumi: Sisouk Na Champassak, op. cit., pp. 147-8.

had left the prison disguised as gendarmes and in a gendarmerie lorry. By the time they were missed they had abandoned the lorry some thirty kilometres from Vientiane and were safely in the jungle.[86] It was not long before they reached an area where the local Pathet Lao organization could protect them. More than four months later, having walked some three hundred miles and visited Pathet Lao groups in several provinces, Prince Souphanouvong arrived in Sam Neua, which was by then in Pathet Lao hands.

The new Assembly that unanimously approved the Somsanith government on 2 June did so with reservations. 'We would search in vain', said a deputy, 'for any element of satisfaction in the situation that faces us. Finance? Our coffers are empty. Education? We have neither teachers nor schools. Health? We have no equipment, nurses or doctors. I shall vote nonetheless for the government because it is a government of new men and constitutes our only hope of getting out of our difficulties.'[87]

The swing to the right was now complete. It had been overwhelmingly a swing to the south, to southern Laos from which came Phoumi and most of his friends, and to Siam. Siam was indeed the key to what had happened. Just as in the nineteenth century, when faced with a direct challenge from Vietnam, the Siamese had no longer been content that states on their borders should owe a dual allegiance, so now 'their aim was to maintain an area of political influence beyond [Siamese] frontiers as a defensive measure'.[88] The natural economic links between Laos and Siam had been re-established in 1955 after the break-up of French Indo-China. Katay had been glad of Siamese support for his stand against the Pathet Lao, though with a hint of caution. But when Souvannaphouma in 1956 reverted to what was equally traditional Lao policy—'contact with all and commitment to none'[89]—the Siamese grew increasingly disturbed. Significantly it was Katay who led

[86] Anna Louise Strong, *Cash and Violence in Laos* (Peking, 1962), pp. 75–84 and Burchett, *The Furtive War* (New York, 1963), pp. 175–6, both maintain that the prisoners escaped on foot. The version adopted comes from a later prisoner in the same prison who obtained his information from the staff.

[87] Prince Boun Om, brother of Prince Boun Oum: *Lao Presse*, 6 June 1960.

[88] E. H. S. Simmonds, 'The Evolution of Foreign Policy in Laos' in *Modern Asian Studies*, II, 1 (1968).

[89] Ibid.

the agitation against the agreement with the Pathet Lao in 1957, and Phoumi Nosavan, a relation of the Siamese leader himself, who took over the reins when the grip of Phoui Sananikone, who had also enjoyed a measure of Siamese confidence, appeared to falter at the end of 1959.

United States involvement in Laos had grown out of her commitment to Siam which put Washington 'under a continuing compulsion to take actions disproportionate to the intrinsic strategic value of Laos'.[90] The Americans had moved from the outside to the inside of the Laotian problem. The basis of the Geneva settlement for Laos had thereby been removed. In one way or another the other side was bound to react, as Sir Anthony Eden had foreseen. A sign of this already was the increasing Pathet Lao strength in the country.

Yet there was to be one more chance of success for moderate policies before the country slid into civil war. On 9 August 1960, Captain Kong Lae carried out a *coup d'état* in Vientiane, and less than a month later Prince Souvannaphouma began his third attempt to bring peace to his country.

[90] Dommen, op. cit., p. 68.

CHAPTER VI

The Laotian Civil War

FEW people had better reason to understand the realities of the internal conflict in Laos than Captain Kong Lae[1]. Kong Lae was born on 6 March 1934 into a peasant Pou-Thai family in Muong Phalane, half-way along the main road from Savannakhet eastwards to the frontier of Vietnam, and close to the foothills of the Annamitic Chain, in the zone where Siamese and Vietnamese influence mingled before the coming of the French. As a boy in 1945 he saw the guerrillas who harassed the Japanese and then held out against the Viet Minh or the French. He was too young to join them, but he heard the village talk and shared the small, vital conspiracies of silence as to relatives and friends sought by one side or the other.

After primary schooling in his own district Kong Lae started his secondary education at Savannakhet in October 1950. His father had long been dead; he won a scholarship. But the scholarship was not enough to keep him and he longed for money in his pocket. He left school at the end of 1951, joined the army where 'the pay was so high that even a Private could think of getting married',[2] and was posted to the 1st Parachute Battalion. Six months later, having qualified as a parachutist, he was sent to the army cadet school whence he emerged in July 1953 as an officer on probation.

Now just over nineteen years old, Kong Lae volunteered for active service in north Laos and commanded a section of infantry in operations against the Viet Minh in the River Ou valley before

---

[1] The French spelling is Konglé, the *e* being pronounced as *ai* in *lair*, and represented by *ae* in the English spelling adopted. The account of Kong Lae's early life is his own, told to the Polish journalist Wojcech Zukrowski in 1961 and, more factually, to a Western observer in 1963.

[2] Wojcech Zukrowski, 'I was Konglé's shadow', in *Literaturnaya Gazeta*, Moscow, 28 February, 2, 4, and 7 March 1961.

and during the siege of Dien Bien Phu. He showed himself a good leader and was confirmed as an officer earlier than was usual, in March 1954.

It was at this time, he tells us, that he, a plainsman, came to know the difference between lowland and hill through personal experience, and first encountered the Pathet Lao in the field. 'A Pathet Lao force made a surprise attack on us one night. We took to our heels, leaving all our equipment behind. All I remember is that I held a compass in my hand as I dived into the dark safety of the jungle. My only desire at that moment was to get as close as possible to the Mekong.'[3] The year 1955 found him still in north Laos, and he remained there, based on Luang Prabang but fully involved in operations, until September 1957. After a short training visit to the Philippines, Kong Lae was then appointed director of the Commando School in Vientiane and sent on a three-month Rangers' course in the Philippines. When he returned in January 1958 the Commando School was being converted into the 2nd Parachute Battalion; he took his place in it as assistant to the commanding officer, whose poor health caused him gradually to leave more and more of the burden of command to Kong Lae.

Thus it was that the new parachute battalion became peculiarly that of the young Captain, already at twenty-four one of the veterans of the Laotian civil war, and already beginning to realize that the problems at the root of it were not soluble by military means. Kong Lae had much influence in choosing his officers and N.C.O.s and always commanded them in operations. Several times he was sent out 'with orders to rout the guerrillas and burn villages supporting them'. He 'shammed battles with lots of shooting and nothing else'.[4] However, his reports of enemy killed and ammunition expended were excellent and his battalion was considered one of the best. He led it in pursuit of the escaping Pathet Lao battalion in May 1959, and it was involved in the Sam Neua crisis in August. But whatever Kong Lae reported about its actions, he himself was fully aware of the facts. He saw no Vietnamese; there was no Viet Minh invasion; it was simply a matter of Laotians fighting Laotians and he had the best of reasons to know, as he and his men passed month after month among the grass-roots of the country, that Laotians did not want to fight. He knew of the corruption and place-seeking in Vientiane. What he saw of the pre-election

[3] Zukrowski, op. cit.   [4] Ibid.

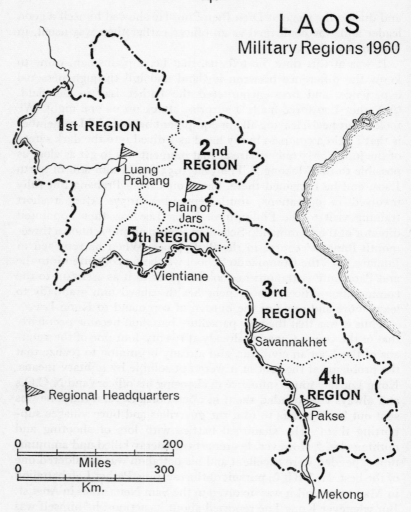

LAOS
Military Regions 1960

1st REGION

Luang Prabang

2nd REGION

Plain of Jars

5th REGION

Vientiane

3rd REGION

Savannakhet

4th REGION

Pakse

Regional Headquarters

0   200
        Miles
0   300
        Km.

Mekong

sweep across the Bolovens Plateau in 1960 ripened his realization that the Pathet Lao problem was not really military at all.

For Kong Lae it followed that eventually he and his men might have to take action. The simple facts were clear, but not perhaps the political implications. He had discussed his ideas with his friends and with his seniors. The latter told him to leave politics alone but this did not change his mind. When in August 1960 he was ordered to take part of his battalion through Vientiane and north-wards, to carry out an anti-guerrilla sweep from Vang Vieng, he saw that his chance had come. He decided 'to gain control of the radio station, airfield, power-plant and arsenal'[5]—at night to avoid bloodshed. With this in mind he obtained the agreement of his superiors to begin his move through the capital after dark. All went as planned. The *coup* was smoothly executed shortly after three o'clock in the morning of 9 August.[6]

When dawn came Vientiane found itself in the power of a slight, boyish figure, simple and direct of manner, using the homely speech of the countryside interspersed with images drawn from forest, homestead, and rice field, and attempting, almost it would seem for the first time in Laotian history, to appeal to the people themselves over the heads of their leaders new and old. The cap-tain showed himself abstemious, generous to his men, and full of soldierly good sense—for instance he laid down strict speed limits for his battalion vehicles and was meticulous about observing them himself. His admirers had made him a pennant for his jeep; it carried three stars—three stars, he would say, for a captain. His soldiers were well-disciplined, quiet, and good-mannered as they carried out their duties; it was clear that they adored their commander.

Kong Lae announced his aims as the ending of the civil war, resistance to foreign pressures, the removal of foreign troops from the country, and the suppression of those who were 'making their harvest on the backs of the people'.[7] He proclaimed his loyalty to the king, and respect for the United Nations' charter and for inter-national agreements already made. However, he said, former governments had led the country astray; they had given out that they were fighting Communist invaders, and on the strength of that had drawn large sums in aid from the Americans, very little of which got past their own pockets. This was far worse than the

[5] Zukrowski, op. cit.

[6] Phoumi later claimed that the plan was the one he had made for his own *coup* in December 1959. However, the size of Vientiane is such that any plan for a *coup d'état* there would be much the same. Dommen, op. cit., pp. 139–40 accounts for Kong Lae's action with a story of dissatis-faction over barracks. This has been denied by Kong Lae and is unsup-ported elsewhere.

[7] Kong Lae repeatedly used this traditional phrase for the abuse of power. See p. 115 for an example of its use a century earlier.

traditional squeeze which everyone knew. He and his battalion had been doing the fighting and they knew there was no foreign enemy to fight. On both sides foreigners were promoting the war between Laotians, while other Laotians were making their fortunes. Americans—he liked Americans. There were ten of them attached to his battalion, and he had curbed the initial anti-American exuberance of some of his supporters.[8] But of course they were the foreigners on the one side as the Viet Minh were on the other, and while their wish to help Laos was appreciated, they must not be allowed to fight their own battles in Laotian blood as the price of their aid. The two world power blocs were like two scorpions in a bowl. Both would sting if touched and both were poisonous. Laos must be neutral and practise neutrality and if this cost the country its dollar aid so much the worse; most of it went in military expenses anyway, and doubtless other countries could be persuaded to provide the very much smaller sums really needed for economic projects.

From the first the young rebel showed some understanding of the internal problem, but he saw the external pressures on the country merely as the ambitions of greedy men. To accusations that he and his supporters were opening the door to Communism, he replied impatiently that no Lao could ever be a Communist; it was against the national character and the Buddhist religion.

The West has a somewhat different point of view. Communist ideology, as Richard Harris has pointed out,[9] needs a basic minimum of intellectual sophistication and social injustice in which to flourish. There must be a sprinkling of serious economists and thinkers if there is to be any understanding of its doctrines, and above all a hungry people. The conditions for the spreading of Communism thus do not exist in Laos. The country may be underdeveloped but everybody has enough to eat. There is no land problem: the term 'landowner' is almost meaningless.[10] In spite of less than twenty diehard Communists at its head, in spite of Prince

[8] Anti-American slogans appeared in the early demonstrations in support of Captain Kong Lae, but were stopped after the first day.

[9] 'Communism and Asia, Illusions and Misconceptions' in *International Affairs*, January 1963.

[10] Compare the comment by Phoui Sananikone at Geneva in 1954 on a reference by the Viet Minh to land reform in Laos: '. . . it is almost cruel irony to talk of dividing up the land when there are too few inhabitants to cultivate the immense areas available'; Cmd. 9186, p. 155.

Souphanouvong's commitment to the Viet Minh, the Pathet Lao as a whole are not Communist. Nor is their political indoctrination designed to turn them into ideological converts, for the good reason that their educational standards are not high enough for this to be possible.

Neither for Kong Lae, nor for Laos, was this the point at issue. After his meeting with Mr. Khrushchev at Vienna in 1961, President Kennedy described the Soviet leader as a combination of external jocosity and 'internal rage'.[11] Strangely similar is Kong Lae's description of the Pathet Lao: 'those men are altogether different', he once said, 'they are full of wrath'.[12] Both come near to the heart of the matter. Even if their training does not turn Prince Souphanouvong's followers into Communists, it does convert their tribal discontent into internal rage, so that they become hard, disciplined men of wrath, who identify the interests of Laos with those of North Vietnam and whose efforts can be directed accordingly by the Communist hard core. It was this fact and not what was, to him, the irrelevant question of Communism among the Pathet Lao rank and file, that troubled Kong Lae. The Pathet Lao were serving foreign interests, and so was the government; what matter to the Laotian if one of them was Communist— or even both? Kong Lae's mission was to make Laotian interests predominate and so secure peace and stability.

It is, however, one thing to stage a *coup d'état*, quite another to form and maintain a government. Although Kong Lae now succeeded in bringing Prince Souvannaphouma back to power for a new attempt at national reconciliation, the old Siamese and American fears of the Vietnamese and the Communists eventually took control. The harassed Neutralist régime was driven first to seek support from Russia and then, as it was being ousted by force from Vientiane in December 1960, into alliance with the Pathet Lao. Russian intervention and the new American policy of President Kennedy led away from civil war to the international conference which opened at Geneva in May 1961. But by then the Pathet Lao were incomparably stronger than ever before.

* * *

Whether by accident or design Captain Kong Lae's *coup d'état* had coincided with the absence of the government from Vientiane. The key points were seized and the senior army officers arrested

[11] Arthur M. Schlesinger Jnr., *A Thousand Days* (London, 1965), p.333.
[12] Zukrowski, op. cit., 7 March 1961.

according to plan; but the prime minister and most of his cabinet remained safely in Luang Prabang, where they were in consultation with the king on arrangements for the state cremation of His late Majesty King Sisavang Vong. As soon as news of the *coup* was received in Luang Prabang, General Phoumi was formally authorized as Defence Minister to put down the rebellion and recapture Vientiane. The *coup* had already aroused the gravest anxiety in Siam, and Phoumi called on Marshal Sarit in Bangkok on his way to Savannakhet, the main military base in southern Laos from which any operation against Vientiane would have to be mounted.

Kong Lae's first problem was how to replace the government with one that would conform with his ideas. He consulted Quinim Pholsena, a disaffected, left-inclined former deputy of the Peace Party, who had been defeated in the recent elections. Anxious as he was to influence the rebel leader in the direction of his own opinions, Quinim could take no effective political action from outside the Assembly and advised Kong Lae to approach the chairman of the Assembly, Prince Souvannaphouma; but the prince would have nothing to do with unconstitutional action.

Somehow the government had to be made to resign. For the moment the key to the situation lay in the facts that Kong Lae had control of the Assembly building, that most of the deputies were in Vientiane, and that Luang Prabang could only be reached by air because of the monsoon. After three days of comings and goings between the two towns, and of popular demonstrations in Vientiane strongly flavoured by the enthusiasm of the student left, the government agreed on 13 August to resign on certain conditions. 'As the conditions appeared excessive', says the official account,

Captain Kong Lae, accompanied by a large crowd, went to the Assembly to ask the deputies to overthrow the government. At 6.30 in the evening, after an hour of discussion and amid the shouts of the crowd who remained massed outside the building, the forty-one deputies present voted unanimously a motion of no confidence in the government of Prince Somsanith.[13]

Although the crowd was both less numerous and less menacing than it has since been made to seem,[14] some of the deputies may have believed that their lives were in danger.

[13] *Lao Presse*, 14 August 1960.
[14] See, for example, Sisouk Na Champassak, op. cit., p. 158.

A deputation from the Assembly carried the motion of no confidence to Luang Prabang next morning, together with a request that Prince Souvannaphouma should be appointed prime minister. In spite of arguments that the Assembly was acting under duress and could be ignored, Prince Somsanith insisted on resigning. Phoumi was in Savannakhet. Somsanith could only see bloodshed and civil war as the outcome of further resistance. After receiving the Assembly delegation in person, the king accepted Prince Somsanith's resignation and called on Prince Souvannaphouma to form an administration. The prince now agreed to act. A new government was formed in Vientiane on 15 and 16 August, in which Quinim Pholsena became Minister of the Interior; on 17 August Captain Kong Lae handed over the powers he had seized and declared his *coup d'état* at an end.

For the new government to be fully legal it was necessary that it should receive the formal approval of the king. General Phoumi was able to obstruct this. Refusing to accept defeat, and supported now by the commanders of four out of the country's five military regions, he formed a committee against the *coup d'état* on 15 August and proclaimed martial law. On the grounds that martial law suspended government activity, the documents for the investiture of the new government were withheld from the king when they arrived in Luang Prabang on 17 August. Prince Souvannaphouma's government could not therefore be invested and on a strict reading of the constitution could not take office. Although the ministers had been sworn in at the Wat Sisaket in Vientiane, a traditional ceremony which gave them full authority in Laotian eyes, Phoumi's committee could thus allege claims to legality as well.

Savannakhet is General Phoumi's home. He was born there on 27 January 1920 into a family from Mukdahan across the river in Siam. He called the late Marshal Sarit 'uncle'. After a secondary education at the Lycée Pavie in Vientiane, during which he was known as an amateur boxer, Phoumi became an organizer of youth activities in government service. Recruited into an American-led guerrilla group in north Siam in 1944, he saw no action against the Japanese but in 1945 became involved on his own account in the intrigues of the Lao-Pen-Lao movement, whose aim was to raise resistance to the Japanese among the Lao on both banks of the Mekong, so as to justify a claim for the independence of 'Greater

Laos' when the Allies had won.[15] When Peter Kemp met him in August 1945, remarking his 'very soft voice and an unusually charming smile',[16] Phoumi was on his way to Savannakhet with a Lao-Siamese group to resist the French. He became Chief of Staff of the Lao Independence groups at Savannakhet, saw some action when the French returned in March 1946, and by the end of that year was Chief of Staff to Prince Souphanouvong in exile in Siam.

The next two years were spent at the heart of Lao Independence extremism in close association with the Viet Minh. In 1947 Phoumi went to North Vietnam with a number of Viet Minh leaders and had a narrow escape in an ambush on his way through Laos. After numerous discussions with Ho Chi Minh and General Giap he returned to Siam to help prepare the common Lao-Viet Minh offensive against the French in Laos; this was to include fifteen mixed companies raised in and operating from Siam.

As the Lao Independence Movement lost momentum in 1948, Phoumi was one of those engaged in long drawn out secret negotiations with France for the return home of the rebel forces. When the negotiations were successfully concluded in 1949 he returned to Laos with thirty of his men and in 1950 was made a lieutenant in the army. Thereafter his progress was rapid. Cousin and brother-in-law of Kou Voravong, Minister of Defence from 1951 until his assassination in 1954, Phoumi became Director of National Defence in 1954 and in 1957 was commander of the Second Military Region.

By this time Marshal Sarit was rising to supreme power in Siam. After returning from the École Supérieure de Guerre in 1958 Phoumi also entered politics and from this point his career has already been traced. He became Secretary of State for Defence after Phoui Sananikone had received emergency powers in January 1959, he was widely suspected of promoting the Sam Neua crisis in the following summer as a means to power for himself, and he was the author of the *coup d'état* against Phoui Sananikone at the end of the year. Although this event did not at once carry him to supreme authority, his influence over the C.D.N.I., his dominance in the army, and the powerful Siamese and American support he now possessed, made him indisputably the most significant force in the country.

[15] Caply, op. cit., pp. 222–5. The movement was encouraged and carefully supervised by the Siamese.

[16] P. Kemp, *Alms for Oblivion* (London, 1961), p. 23.

To the Westerner the remarkable thing about Phoumi, apart from the open smile and the persuasive manner, was his apparent ability to get things done. His voice was deceptively soft, his speech disarming. But in fact he was as ruthless as his appearance suggested. When among his own people, there was an air of muted violence about the man, a scarcely hidden enjoyment of power over people, a hint of conscious physical restraint. He was hated and feared, and his orders were obeyed.

At Savannakhet in August 1960 Phoumi's orders were obeyed to the letter. There was immediate help from Marshal Sarit who refused to recognize the new situation in Vientiane, and also, at first quite legitimately, from the United States. On 12 August a new 'Savannakhet Radio' started broadcasting a skilful psychological warfare programme against Vientiane, the transmitter having been supplied by the United States.[17] Leaflets were air-dropped on Vientiane and Luang Prabang. Captain Kong Lae, they said, was a misguided youth who had let in the Communists; Vientiane was now occupied by the Reds. Let all who had their country's interests at heart rally to General Phoumi who would pay the salaries of officials and soldiers who joined him.[18] An operations staff was set up for the liberation of the capital. Troops were moved downriver from Luang Prabang and northwards from Savannakhet. Captain Siho, an intelligence officer in Vientiane, slipped away to Savannakhet and returned to carry out sabotage and terror raids on Vientiane for Phoumi. Kong Lae formed the administrative troops in the capital into defence battalions and issued arms to villagers outside the town. A number of deputies made their way south.[19]

For the moment, however, the peace was saved. Prince Souvannaphouma flew to Savannakhet and agreed with Phoumi that there should be a new meeting of the Assembly in Luang Prabang, away from military pressures, so that a generally acceptable government could be formed. 'This is our last chance,' said the prince. 'If we cannot come to an agreement civil war will certainly follow.'[20]

[17] Dommen, op. cit., p. 161.
[18] Savannakhet Radio, communiqué dated 17 August. This promise was probably decisive in keeping most of the military commanders on Phoumi's side.
[19] New York Times, 29 August 1960.
[20] Radio Phnom Penh, 29 August 1960.

The deputies duly set out in their groups from Savannakhet and Vientiane, the government of Prince Somsanith was momentarily reconstituted in Luang Prabang, and the constitutional procedures of his resignation were repeated. On 31 August the Assembly again unanimously approved a new government headed by Prince Souvannaphouma, this time containing General Phoumi as vice-premier and Minister of the Interior; Quinim Pholsena was moved to the lesser post of Minister of Information.

In Vientiane Captain Kong Lae had carefully followed reports of what was happening in Luang Prabang. He probably realized that for the sake of stability any government would have to include General Phoumi and others ousted by his *coup d'état*, but he and his men were resolutely opposed to Phoumi's return to the Defence Ministry. On 30 and 31 August, however, military head-quarters in Vientiane received messages from Luang Prabang signed by Phoumi as Minister of Defence. It was not altogether realized that this referred to his position in the Somsanith govern-ment and the feelings of the parachute officers ran high. At midday on 31 August, Kong Lae, under pressure from his supporters, broadcast a strong protest, saying that he and his men would resist the inclusion of Phoumi in the new administration in any capacity. This caused some despondency in the royal city. Prince Souvannaphouma flew to Vientiane after the Assembly had approved his government that evening, persuaded Kong Lae to withdraw his opposition—which the captain did with no little psychological skill at a public meeting next day—and returned to Luang Prabang.[21]

As General Phoumi was about to board the aircraft which was to take him to Vientiane with the other ministers later on 1 September, he was handed a message from the capital which said that there would be an attempt on his life during the formal instal-lation of the new government next day. Phoumi stopped, boarded another aircraft and flew to Savannakhet. The message had come through American channels and it was later reliably reported that

[21] The fact that Captain Kong Lae withdrew his opposition, and within twenty-four hours, has escaped Dommen (op. cit., p. 150), Sisouk Na Champassak (op. cit., p. 162), and even Schlesinger (op. cit., p. 297), all of whom regard Kong Lae's attitude as justifying Phoumi's subse-quent action. This may be because the withdrawal speech was not among the transcripts issued to the press in Vientiane.

the general had been 'persuaded to spurn his post in the Government and rebel against it by agents of the C.I.A. and the U.S. military officers stationed in Laos. . . .'[22] However that may be, Phoumi did not return to Vientiane, and on 5 September, after a further consultation with Marshal Sarit, reactivated the committee against the *coup d'état* which he had dissolved in a speech of reconciliation in the Assembly on 31 August.

A new invasion scare followed. The Savannakhet Command Post, which still controlled three out of the five military regions through the allegiance of their commanders to Phoumi, alleged that Viet Minh troops had launched attacks from Dien Bien Phu towards the River Ou valley and that a Viet Minh battalion was marching on Sam Neua from the east.[23]

These stories followed Pathet Lao allegations of attacks by government troops in these areas and were no more true than they had been in 1959, although, as before, some government posts were abandoned. The reports were nevertheless the subject of increasingly strong statements from Siam, Marshal Sarit remarking in a broadcast that the 'Red Lao and Viet Minh'[24] had already taken over in Vientiane. There ensued on 10 September the proclamation of a new revolutionary group under Phoumi's direction. The group claimed to seize power and abrogate the constitution on the grounds that Prince Souvannaphouma's government, which had actually negotiated a cease-fire with the Pathet Lao on 7 September, was responsible for the alleged deterioration in the military position. Presiding over the group was Prince Boun Oum of Champassak, a fact which emphasized the dynastic and regional aspects of a quarrel which Prince Souvannaphouma had already termed a conflict between north and south.[25] The United States specifically refused Phoumi their support, but the general was certain that this attitude would soon change.

The reason for his confidence was soon clear. Crisis reports con-

---

[22] *New York Times*, 10 October 1961.

[23] Savannakhet Radio, 7 September 1960.

[24] Radio Thailand, 8 September 1960. For the extreme Siamese attitude see Nuechterlein, op. cit., pp. 165–74; this author does, however, accept some of the propaganda allegations as fact and his account of events in Laos is unreliable.

[25] Radio Vientiane, 31 August 1960. Prince Boun Oum had shown his association with Phoumi as early as 21 August (Radio Savannakhet, 22 August).

tinued to arrive from Sam Neua. Although precise information as
to the enemy was lacking, the garrison was already running out of
ammunition. It was resupplied from Vientiane and reinforced
from Savannakhet. General Phoumi then reported that the enemy
had been driven back across the frontier, evidently hoping that a
return of American confidence would be his reward.

Meanwhile, on 19 September, after a night in which Vientiane
had been mortared by Captain Siho's raiders, Phoumi had ordered
his two battalions at Paksane to advance on the capital. The force
was routed with ease by two companies of Kong Lae's paratroops
who then took up a position on the Nam Ka Dinh river. Subsequent skirmishing was brought to an end when, on 28 September,
at a meeting called by the king, military representatives of the two
sides agreed upon the Nam Ka Dinh as the effective boundary
between them.

On the same day, however, Kong Lae, who had been dropping
what he called 'confidence teams' of his parachutists in various
parts of the country to explain what had happened and to rally
the population to the government, dropped a party near Sam
Neua. For the defenders of Sam Neua, who had, according to
Phoumi, thrown back the Viet Minh across the frontier less than
a week earlier, the sight of a handful of parachutists floating down
was the final terror. The whole fifteen hundred men abandoned the
town and allowed themselves to be disarmed by Pathet Lao groups
when on their way to the Plain of Jars. They had been intercepted by the same 2nd Pathet Lao Battalion that had escaped
from the Plain of Jars in 1959.[26] It now took possession of Sam
Neua in the name of Prince Souvannaphouma and settled down to
await the arrival of his half-brother, Prince Souphanouvong.

The *coup d'état* of the parachutist captain had confronted the
Americans in Laos with a painful dilemma. Their ambassador was
new to the country. At first, says Dommen,[27] he was told 'to take
such action as would remove Kong Le from the scene as expedi-
tiously as possible'. As the days went by and this could not be
done, his instructions became 'less and less coherent. Conflicting
suggestions would appear in the same telegram.' Eventually the
State Department accepted the recommendation of the united
embassy—including the C.I.A.[28]—that the government should be

[26] W. G. Burchett, *The Furtive War* (New York, 1963), p. 194.
[27] Op. cit., p. 157.   [28] Schlesinger, op. cit., p. 297.

supported, and the ambassador established cordial relations with Prince Souvannaphouma. But behind the sympathetic ambassador was Mr. J. Graham Parsons, now Assistant Secretary of State for Far Eastern Affairs in Washington. Parsons had opposed the Vientiane Agreements as ambassador in 1957 and mistrusted the neutrality of Prince Souvannaphouma as much as ever. The Bureau of Far Eastern Affairs over which he now presided, says Schlesinger,

considered Kong Le a probable Communist and looked with great dubiety on the neutralist solution. Nowhere was the pure Dulles doctrine taken more literally than in this bureau. In 1953 the Republicans had purged it of the Foreign Service officers they held responsible for the 'loss' of China. Then they confided Far Eastern matters to a Virginia gentleman named Walter Robertson. Robertson, like Dulles, judged Chiang Kai-Shek moral and neutralism immoral and established policy on those principles. His successor in 1959 was the J. Graham Parsons who had been applying those principles so faithfully in Laos. As for the Defence Department, it was all for Phoumi . . . the military support convinced Phoumi that, if he only held out, Washington would put him in power.[29]

Nevertheless, on 27 September, the United States joined France and Britain in a statement that they were agreed in supporting the government of Prince Souvannaphouma. Marshal Sarit indicated his disapproval by starting negotiations for economic co-operation with Russia. This was not surprising. 'The tradition of neutral or non-aligned policies', says Dr. Kennedy, will be held up as a threat 'whenever members of S.E.A.T.O. do not act in the manner desired by Bangkok.'[30]

Prince Souvannaphouma had meanwhile begun the new attempt at national reconciliation which had been agreed when his government was formed at Luang Prabang. Prince Souphanouvong, who was still walking through the mountains, had sent back Colonel

[29] Schlesinger, loc. cit.

[30] D. E. Kennedy, *The Security of Southern Asia* (London, 1965), p. 93. D. Insor, *Thailand, a Political, Social and Economic Survey* (London, 1963), pp. 129–30 gives a valuable account of Siamese hostility to neutralism in Laos. Nuechterlein, op. cit., pp. 165–74 is more detailed but less analytical. *Survey of International Affairs 1959–60* (London, R.I.I.A., 1964), p. 278, implies that the accelerated reduction of U.S. aid to Thailand which became known at about this time, also influenced Marshal Sarit's attitude.

Singkapo to make contact with the new government and had promised co-operation.[31] Accordingly, at the beginning of October, the prime minister announced the opening of talks with the Pathet Lao in Vientiane on 11 October, and the establishment of diplomatic relations with the Soviet Union.

These moves, coming so soon after the reoccupation of Sam Neua by the Pathet Lao, albeit in the name of Prince Souvanna-phouma, caused profound disquiet in Washington. On 7 October the United States suspended financial aid to Laos[32] and five days later Mr. Parsons arrived in Vientiane. He made it 'unmistakably clear that the resumption of American cash-grant aid to Souvanna Phouma's government depended on the attitude Souvanna Phouma took towards pending political questions, most urgent of which was the negotiations with the Pathet Lao',[33] already in progress.

Prince Souvannaphouma refused to break off his talks with the Pathet Lao, nor did he accept Mr. Parsons' other suggestion that the government be moved to Luang Prabang. The arrival of the Russian ambassador designate with an offer of Soviet help on 13 October, however, made it impossible for Parsons to apply decisive pressure even if he had wished to do so, and he left unreassured on 14 October. 'I would have liked to meet Mr. Parsons,' said the smiling Russian, 'but he left in such a hurry.'[34]

Three days later the American ambassador was able to persuade

[31] Burchett, *The Furtive War* (New York, 1963), p. 188. The contact point was about twenty miles north of Vientiane. The Pathet Lao had been broadcasting support for Prince Souvannaphouma since 24 August when their station opened.

[32] There was some confusion between various U.S. authorities on the suspension of aid, which was announced by a military spokesman and then at first denied by the American embassy in Vientiane. The immediate reason for the action may have been the belief that some of the arms (from stocks provided by U.S. aid), distributed by Kong Lae for the defence of Vientiane against Phoumi in August, had found their way into Pathet Lao hands and that the U.S. was thus indirectly arming Communists.

[33] Dommen, op. cit., p. 159. R. M. Smith, op. cit., p. 64, states that Parsons threatened the termination of U.S. aid unless the talks were broken off. The State Department denied this. Schlesinger, op. cit., p. 298, says Parsons applied 'intense pressure on Souvanna to forsake neutralism, accept Phoumi and make Laos a bastion of freedom again'.

[34] B. B. Fall, 'Reappraisal in Laos' in *Current History*, XLII (Jan. 1962).

Prince Souvannaphouma, in return for the resumption of cash grants, to permit deliveries of American military aid direct to Phoumi, on the understanding that such aid would not be used against the government but only against the Pathet Lao.[35] It was argued that the Pathet Lao were profiting from the division in the army and that both factions needed maintenance against this threat. In fact, the Americans had decided that Prince Souvanna-phouma must go;[36] they did not inform their allies of this.

The new aid arrangement, whose dangers to himself the prince fully realized, did but legitimize what had already been taking place for two months. U.S. military aid consisted of two elements; Laotian army pay in cash and military stores delivered in kind. There had been 'administrative hitches' in the supply of both elements to Vientiane since August. Kong Lae's men had been paid from the currency reserves, and no stores had arrived because the Siamese had closed the frontier. The frontier with Savan-nakhet was, however, still open because, said Sarit, 'General Phoumi has goodwill towards Siam.'[37] Deliveries intended for Vientiane had therefore been channelled to Savannakhet.

Even this was not the whole story. It is apparent that from the first the American military authorities and C.I.A. had decided to build up General Phoumi's position.[38] From mid-September, at which time, of course, General Phoumi was in open rebellion,

Savannakhet was the scene of an increased number of landings and takeoffs by unmarked C-46 and C-47 transports manned by American crews. These planes belonged to *Air America, Inc.*, a civilian charter company with U.S. Air Force organisational support and under con-tract to the U.S. government. The aircraft, giving the Phoumist forces a badly needed logistical supply system, ferried military supplies from Bangkok to Savannakhet . . . and shuttled between Savannakhet and outlying garrisons loyal to General Phoumi.[39]

The result of Prince Souvannaphouma's agreement with the American ambassador was that all this activity now became legi-

[35] Dommen, op. cit., p. 160.
[36] Schlesinger, loc. cit.: 'In late October, a few days before the American elections, State and Defence agreed that Souvanna must go, though they disagreed on how this should be accomplished.'
[37] Radio Thailand, 8 September 1960.
[38] Dommen, op. cit., p. 158; Schlesinger, op. cit., p. 297.
[39] Dommen, op. cit., p. 154.

timate. It was increased even further: 'American technical aid provided for the operation of clandestine radio stations that were used by the Phoumists to encourage defections from Kong Le's troops and other forces loyal to Prince Souvannaphouma, without attacking the prince by name.'[40] Many of the American military advisers moved to Savannakhet. Two hundred Laotian paratroops who had been training under United States auspices in Siam were handed over to Phoumi in spite of an American promise to Prince Souvannaphouma that this would not be done. On the other hand, although the Siamese declared the border with Vientiane open, there was no resumption of military aid or even normal supplies, and petrol, oil, and even electricity were rationed in the capital.

Within six weeks of the establishment of his revolutionary group, therefore, Phoumi had reason to claim that the Americans were effectively on his side. This enabled him to suborn more and more of the government's supporters. There was a slow trickle of desertions, military and civil, from Vientiane to Savannakhet; on 11 November the Luang Prabang garrison, hitherto loyal to Prince Souvannaphouma, declared for Phoumi; even the force eventually sent as a gesture from Vientiane to Luang Prabang changed sides half-way. The government was once more isolated from the king.

Prince Souvannaphouma was, however, determined not to fire the first shot. He concluded a number of agreements with the Pathet Lao, on aid from Russia for example but not from China, and on a neutral foreign policy, while at the same time making every effort to come to an arrangement with Phoumi. On 18 November, almost in despair at the defection of Luang Prabang which had been a sharp personal blow,[41] he went to Sam Neua and together with Prince Souphanouvong appealed to the king not to lean towards the rebels, to king and people to support the lawful government, and to foreign powers not to interfere.[42]

It was already too late; perhaps it had always been too late. The Mekong had now fallen some twenty feet below its August flood level and the road northwards from Thakhek was beginning to dry out. Phoumi was ready to launch his operation against Vien-

[40] Dommen, op. cit., p. 161.

[41] It had been rumoured for some weeks that a *coup* was in the making n Luang Prabang, and the prince had just visited the garrison to make sure of its loyalty.

[42] *Lao Presse*, 23 November 1960.

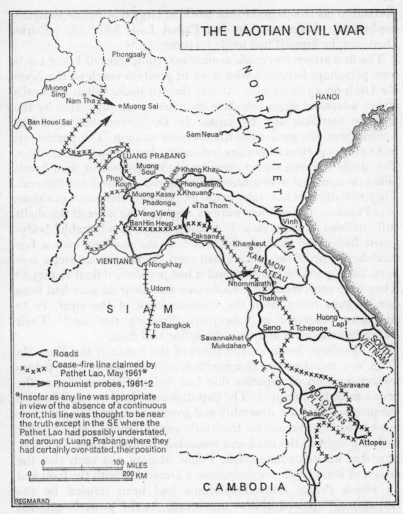

THE LAOTIAN CIVIL WAR

Phongsaly

Muong Sing
Nam Tha
Muong Sai

Ban Houei Sai

HANOI

Sam Neua

LUANG PRABANG
Muong Soul
Phou Koun
Khang Khay
Phongsavan
Muong Kassy
X Khouang
Phadong
Tha Thom
Vang Vieng
Ban Hin Heup
Vinh
Paksane
Khamkeut
VIENTIANE
Nongkhay
KAMMON PLATEAU
Udorn
Nhommarath
S I A M
Thakhek
Huong Lap
to Bangkok
Seno
Tchepone
SOUTH VIETNAM
Savannakhet
Mukdahan

Saravane
BOLOVENS PLATEAU
Pakse
Attopeu

CAMBODIA

~< Roads
×ₓₓₓ Cease-fire line claimed by
      Pathet Lao, May 1961*
➤ Phoumist probes, 1961-2

*Insofar as any line was appropriate
in view of the absence of a continuous
front, this line was thought to be near
the truth except in the SE where the
Pathet Lao had possibly understated,
and around Luang Prabang where they
had certainly over-stated, their position

0   100 MILES
0   200 KM

REGMARAD

tiane. The key to this was the Laotian Army Artillery Battalion, equipped with 105 mm howitzers and heavy mortars, which had been in hard and continuous training under its energetic commander on the ranges near Savannakhet since September. As soon as the road had been repaired Phoumi's forces began to move. The only concession he made to the American undertaking about the use of the equipment with which he had been supplied, was to pretend to his troops and to the world at large that Prince Souvannaphouma's forces were in fact Pathet Lao. After all, remarks Dommen, he himself had made no promises.[43]

The first attack was made against two companies of Kong Lae's own parachute battalion who were in position south of the Nam Ka Dinh on 23 November. It was thrown back. When Phoumi's troops advanced again five days later they were supported by the artillery battalion and by tanks. In the circumstances of the Laotian war, the guns were the ultimate weapon. The paratroops had never experienced gunfire before and had no guns themselves. The shells bursting round them and in the trees over their heads killed or wounded over a hundred men and demoralized the rest. They withdrew as best they could and took up defensive positions near Paksane. The soldiers were on edge and the noise of the shells still rumbled in their ears. But Kong Lae's 'invulnerable' bodyguard had come through the worst of the shelling with a few scratches. One of the officers had seen the monstrous water serpent, the Nguoc, on the river and it had prophesied final victory.[44] They were soon reassuring each other that their disaster had been due to guns firing from the Siamese bank of the river, or to American observers in helicopters directing the fire.[45] Their leadership was good and their discipline still firm.

In Vientiane, however, the effect of the battle of the Nam Ka Dinh was catastrophic. It coincided with the return of a peacemaking mission of deputies that had visited Savannakhet at the prime minister's request. The deputies came back ostensibly with the proposal that the Assembly and government should move once more to Luang Prabang for fresh talks with Phoumi. This, together with the sight of the dead and wounded from the Nam Ka Dinh, provoked an immediate crisis. Public anxiety was such that the arrival of Russian planes daily from 4 December with the food and oil which Prince Souvannaphouma had been refused by the Americans,[46] passed almost unnoticed. As the prince's external

[43] Op. cit., p. 161.

[44] The legendary monster of the Mekong who was supposed to appear in times of crisis.

[45] The U.S. ambassador issued a communiqué on 9 December denying these and other allegations. He also stated that the U.S. had ceased supplying Phoumi on 30 November in response to a request from Prince Souvannaphouma. By that time, of course, the general had all he needed.

[46] Schlesinger, op. cit., p. 298.

position had weakened, so the left-wing influences in Vientiane, secretly sponsored by Quinim Pholsena and encouraged by the presence of the Pathet Lao negotiators, had gained strength. To many it seemed that the Luang Prabang prosposal was a trick to get the Assembly into Phoumi's power.

The real trick was less complicated. With the returning deputies Phoumi had sent orders to Colonel Kouprasith, commander of the Vientiane military region, to carry out a *coup d'état* in Vientiane on the grounds that left-wing pressure on the government was becoming insupportable. The *coup* was to be followed by the arrival of paratroops from Savannakhet. Part of the plan was for the airfield at Paksane to be secured for Phoumi beforehand. Kouprasith agreed to act and named 8 December as the day. On 6 December he sent a message to Kong Lae's commander at Paksane, in the name of Prince Souvannaphouma's Chief of Staff, ordering a withdrawal so as to facilitate 'peace negotiations'. The paratroops exploded with joy and relief. Paksane was willingly abandoned and Phoumi promptly occupied it. At the same time, as anxiety grew in Vientiane, Colonel Kouprasith began to talk of the need to protect Prince Souvannaphouma and his government from left-wing influence so that they could retain freedom to negotiate with Phoumi. A number of Kong Lae's officers, including the ebullient Lieutenant Deuane who was later to throw in his lot with the Pathet Lao, were brought to agree with him.

There had been a small but noisy demonstration outside the Assembly as it was sitting on 1 December. Next morning it was stated that the deputies who had been to Savannakhet had been threatened with arrest by gangs of youths. This turned out to be part of the plot. Prince Somsanith, who had led the delegation, took refuge in the prime minister's office on 3 December. On 7 December, together with eighteen deputies, he fled for safety to Kouprasith's camp at Chinaimo, three miles down-river from Vientiane.

Leaflets had already been printed announcing the *coup* and all was prepared when, at four o'clock on the morning of 8 December, Prince Souvannaphouma received warning of what was afoot. He summoned Kouprasith, who assured him that the action would be in favour of the government and directed against left-wing influence only. His troops were already on the move. They wore white ribbons, white, he said, for true neutrality. The prince accepted this modified revolution, which was still supported by some of Kong Lae's officers. The arrival of two companies of Phoumi's paratroops, however, dropping in full view of Vientiane close to Kouprasith's camp during the afternoon, caused doubts as to the complexion of the new neutrality and in the evening Kong Lae peacefully resumed control.

Kouprasith's action had nevertheless fatally weakened the defence of Vientiane. Bewildered by the swift turn of events and disappointed in their hopes of a rapid peace, many of the soldiers on the government side who had worn his white favours stayed with him. The deputies in Chinaimo Camp went on to Savannakhet. Kong Lae's force was reduced by further desertions. The acquisition of Paksane gave Phoumi an unopposed passage up the Mekong from Savannakhet as far as Nongkhay, to which he had already established a secure line of communication across northeast Siam. From Nongkhay he was in close touch with Kouprasith whom he now designated commander of the assault on Vientiane. The plans made by his American advisers were ready.[47] He sent word that Prince Souvannaphouma was to be 'kept amused' with negotiations while the last preparations were made.

To Phoumi the battle was as good as won. But the parachutists were determined. They now pinned on to their uniforms scraps of red cloth made by tearing up the red scarves which had distinguished them at the Nam Ka Dinh battle and which they often wore on operations. Opposing road blocks were set up a few hundred yards apart between Vientiane and Chinaimo Camp. The soldiers of the two sides agreed to shoot into the air if they were ordered to attack.[48]

Prince Souvannaphouma's position was desperate. He had never ceased in his efforts to come to an agreement with Phoumi. The only response he had received was to be called a Communist and to have his supporters suborned. Nearly all his senior officers had

[47] Schlesinger, op. cit., p. 298.

[48] Observers discovered this on the spot at the time. For corroboration see Prince Boun Oum's letter in *Lao Presse*, 20 January 1961: 'The marks of bullets in the upper parts of the buildings and roofs are clear proof of the wish of the patriot (soldiers) not to cause a single useless death. The small number of our military dead is another.' Official Western sources estimated the casualties as between seven and eight hundred of whom six hundred dead were civilian. Kong Lae's force had 22 dead, Kouprasith's was said to have had 14.

deserted to or been captured by Phoumi. A majority of the deputies was also now in Phoumi's camp; it was only a matter of time before legality passed to the other side. Kong Lae and his men had hitherto accepted the restraints on action which the prince had imposed but they had now sworn to defend themselves. On 9 December, the day on which Phoumist forces began to cross the river in considerable numbers with their artillery from Nongkhay in Siam, Prince Souvannaphouma realized that there was no more that he could do. A fight was inevitable. The prince had never countenanced violence and could not do so now. During the evening he flew to Cambodia together with most of his ministers. Quinim Pholsena, his Minister of Information, remained in Vientiane and next day, 10 December, went to Hanoi to ask for guns.

Russian aircraft delivered three 105 mm howitzers, three heavy mortars, and some ammunition to Vientiane on 11 and 12 December.[49] On 11 December also, thirty-eight deputies met in Savannakhet and passed a motion of no confidence in the government.[50] This time there was no delay or indecision in Luang Prabang. Royal ordinances dismissing Prince Souvannaphouma's government and giving powers provisionally to the Savannakhet Group were signed by the king on 12 December.[51] A further ordinance nominating a provisional government under Prince Boun Oum, with the king's half-brother Prince Khampane as Minister for Foreign Affairs, was signed on 14 December. The new régime was recognized without delay by Siam and the United States.[52]

With legality now on his side, Phoumi launched his forces against Vientiane on 13 December. The attackers were in overwhelming force, infantry, tanks, armed river-craft, artillery. There was never any question of effective resistance, the two sides never

[49] Dommen, op. cit., p. 167, states that six 105 mm howitzers were unloaded in full view of American observers and that North Vietnamese gun crews came with them. In fact no American observer could have been nearer than six or seven hundred yards from the unloading point, and Mr. Dommen's observers could not have seen what was unloaded. They may have seen six pieces of artillery being towed away; this would have included the heavy mortars. As for the North Vietnamese artillerymen, an expert examination of the gun positions afterwards revealed that no experienced gunners could have been present. The guns were manned by volunteers from among Kong Lae's men.

[50] New York Times, 13 December 1960.

[51] Lao Presse, 20 December 1960, has the texts.

[52] New York Times, 16 December 1960.

physically met except by accident and both aimed high. As always in time of trouble the Laotian inhabitants of Vientiane, most of whom had little to lose, fled to the fields and jungles which are nowhere far from the town, or moved across the river. Nevertheless, shelling and mortaring, much of it random, caused hundreds of civilian casualties, particularly among the Vietnamese and Chinese residents who were reluctant to leave their more substantial possessions, and resulted in widespread material damage. Resistance lasted until midday on 16 December, by which time the bulk of Kong Lae's forces, two of his three guns, and about a thousand civilians had withdrawn to the north along the Luang Prabang road. They were confident that they would soon return.

Two hours after the last shells had fallen, Phoumi, Boun Oum, and their principal collaborators entered Vientiane exultant and self-assured, still full of the fiction that they had beaten the 'Communists', a fiction to which the State Department appeared to subscribe.[53] Now that the Neutralists could be safely classed as Communists, now that Prince Souvannaphouma, as Boun Oum put it, could be swept into the same bag as Prince Souphanouvong,[54] the situation was much clearer and very much more comfortable. How could anyone, said Phoumi, expect him to negotiate with 'that sort of person'. An American diplomat, noted for his hospitality, gave a champagne party to celebrate the triumph.[55] The Russian ambassador had watched a group of Phoumi's soldiers pull down and destroy the Soviet flag which had flown outside his hotel in Vientiane. 'No matter,' he was heard to say as he filmed the incident, 'they think they have won the war.'

The Laotian civil war was indeed no longer an internal matter which could be settled in the streets of Vientiane. Only international action could now end it. Prince Sihanouk of Cambodia had always urged the West to support Prince Souvannaphouma. He had called for the neutralization of both Laos and Cambodia in

[53] On 19 December a State Department spokesman said in reference to Laos that the victory over the forces directed by the Communists was a matter of considerable satisfaction; *New York Times*, 20 December 1960.

[54] Policy statement, 20 December. On his arrival in Vientiane, Phoumi told a Western observer that the situation was now much better, it was so much clearer; there were only himself and the Communists.

[55] Michael Field, *The Prevailing Wind* (London, 1965), p. 101.

his speech at the United Nations General Assembly in September. Now he suggested that the Geneva Conference be reconvened with expanded membership.[56] The British Government, a steadfast supporter of Prince Souvannaphouma in the past, pronounced itself in favour of a genuinely unaligned Laos and a broadly based government, as it had always done. Mr. Nehru proposed the re-establishment of the International Control Commission. This idea, to which the State Department was wholly opposed,[57] at first made little progress, for the co-chairmen, Britain and Russia, and India who was chairman of the commission itself, held conflicting views. While deploring, like France, the means by which the new government in Vientiane had been created, Britain accepted it as now fully legal,[58] but India and Russia considered that Prince Souvannaphouma had been overthrown by an Assembly and monarch acting under duress, and that he therefore remained the lawful prime minister.

In the meantime Captain Kong Lae, with the aid of Soviet Russian air supply, and preceded by an engineer detachment re-opening the long, difficult road which had been closed since the rains, made his way on 31 December 1960 to the Plain of Jars. He had abandoned his two guns *en route* and his striking force consisted only of three parachute companies and some heavy mortars. Phoumi, however, announced that seven Viet Minh battalions had crossed the frontier and that two of them were approaching the plain.[59] It was thus hardly surprising that the main garrison there bolted almost as soon as Kong Lae was within mortar range. The men fled to Xieng Khouang and thence south-wards down the Nhiep and Sane river valleys to the Mekong.

The Plain of Jars is at an altitude of some 3,000 feet and is surrounded by mountains covered with jungle. The single road

[56] The prince's suggestion as to the composition of the conference was adopted. It was an important Cambodian initiative: see George Modelski, *International Conference on the Settlement of the Laotian Question 1961–2* (Canberra, 1962), p. 6. For the diplomatic moves leading up to the assembly of the conference in May 1961, see *International Conference on the Settlement of the Laotian Question* (Cmnd. 1828), London, H.M.S.O., 1962.

[57] Dommen, op. cit., p. 175.

[58] It had been remodelled and formally approved by 41 deputies in a session of the Assembly at Vientiane on 4 January 1961; *Lao Presse*, 5 January 1961.

[59] *Lao Presse*, 31 December 1960.

that passes through it from distant Vientiane and Luang Prabang
to the Vietnamese coast, is impassable for much of the year and is
always easily blocked. The small military airstrip built there by the
French in 1953 and 1954 now became for Kong Lae a secure air
base where he could reorganize his troops and receive Russian
material and supplies. Nearby, before the end of January, Quinim
Pholsena had set up in the old Foreign Legion camp at Khang
Khay, what he claimed to be the only legal government of Laos.
In due course Prince Souvannaphouma, bitter at his betrayal by
the United States, resumed his position as prime minister.[60]

Up to this point Kong Lae had received little or no help from
the Pathet Lao. Conditions in the south had not been abnormally
insecure; there had been no attempt to hamper Phoumi's preparations there. The Pathet Lao had stood on the sidelines during
the skirmishing in November and had been conspicuous by their
absence when battle was joined. They had played no part in the
defence of Vientiane, perhaps because they wished to avoid responsibility for the inevitable casualties, and Kong Lae later
attributed his failure to impose greater delay on his pursuers to the
fact that the Pathet Lao were not prepared to fight his sort of
war.[61] They were gaining too much from the situation as it
developed to tarnish their reputation by joining in.

Pathet Lao policy changed after the capture of the Plain of Jars.
There had been a change in Viet Minh policy some months
earlier, when in September 1960 the third Congress of the Lao
Dong Party had decided to step up the rebellion in South Vietnam.[62] The Viet Minh regarded this action as having been forced

---

[60] See *New York Times*, 20 January 1961, for a statement by Prince
Souvannaphouma: 'What I shall never forgive the United States for is
the fact that it betrayed me, that it double-crossed me and my government.' Mr. Graham Parsons . . . 'understood nothing about Asia and
nothing about Laos. The Assistant Secretary of State is the most nefarious
and reprehensible of men. He is the ignominious architect of disastrous
American policy toward Laos. He and others like him are responsible for
the recent shedding of Lao blood.'

[61] Burchett, *The Furtive War* (New York, 1963), pp. 194-5, shows
active Pathet Lao participation in the defence of Vientiane and in the
retreat northwards. However, both at the time and subsequently, Kong
Lae and his officers stated that the Pathet Lao took no part. As Western
observers were able to confirm, the Pathet Lao were not yet fit for conventional operations.

[62] Dommen, op. cit., p. 134.

on them by the rejection by South Vietnam of the general elections scheduled for 1956 in the Geneva Agreement, a rejection which had had the support of the United States. Limited guerrilla action against the South Vietnamese government, begun in 1958–9, had substantially strengthened the American commitment to President Ngo Dinh Diem in a military direction. The Viet Minh had thus lost the two gains they thought they had made at Geneva: the prospect of a unified Vietnam under their control, and the absence of American power from South Vietnam as well as from Laos. The Viet Cong movement accordingly gathered strength in the rural areas of the south, American support of and advice to President Diem in 1958 and 1959 proving as ineffective as French action in the early years of the Indo-China War.

Even in their war with the French, the Viet Minh had used the mountains and jungles of eastern Laos as safe territory through which they could pass agents and cadres undetected between areas they controlled. Since the Geneva Agreement, the partition zone at the seventeenth parallel had made movement from north to south in Vietnam much more difficult. The inauguration of a new phase in the Viet Cong rebellion, marked by the formation of a National Liberation Front of South Vietnam in December 1960, would thus require a substantial increase of the clandestine traffic through Laos, which would be simplified if the Viet Minh could acquire control of the areas in question.

The operations of General Phoumi against Vientiane, and the consequent alliance between Kong Lae and the Pathet Lao in the Plain of Jars could thus not have been more timely from the Viet Minh point of view. Prince Souphanouvong, whose troops had not hitherto been fit for conventional war, could now pass to the offensive in temporary alliance with Captain Kong Lae. Pathet Lao forces were therefore gathered from many parts of the country into the Plain of Jars, formed into regular battalions, encadred with soldiers of a North Vietnamese regiment brought in for the purpose, and sometimes augmented with North Vietnamese mortar detachments. The field and anti-aircraft guns which the Russians at once began to deliver were put into largely Vietnamese hands, while Laotian students Kong Lae had brought with him from Vientiane were trained as gunners. Their air lift to the Plain of Jars became a top priority task for the Soviet Union.[63] The

[63] Schlesinger, op. cit., p. 300.

Neutralists, reinforced by stragglers from the previous Plain of Jars garrison, were reorganized into five battalions and re-equipped with Russian arms. There was intensive recruiting, by the Pathet Lao who continued to draw most of their soldiers from the hill peoples, and by Kong Lae whose forces, still predominantly Lao, jealously preserved their identity although placed under joint command with the Pathet Lao in February.[64]

Around Kong Lae himself the myths began to gather. He would speak often of his battles with the *phis*, the spirits that ranged by night over the Plain of Jars and whom he had vanquished one by one in single combat. For it sometimes seemed to him that his real trials were fought out, as it were, in dreams of which his waking struggles were the mere shadows. The monks were his friends; many of them had accompanied him from Vientiane and some had joined his forces. His wrists were always heavy with strings tied round them in token of blessing. His officers took strange, flam-boyant oaths to be fulfilled on their return to Vientiane. There was the belief in Kong Lae's invulnerability, his modest-seeming refusal to accept promotion even at the insistence of Prince Souvannaphouma. Above all there was the simple gift he had of talking to his own people in terms they understood, which was part of the reason for the devotion of his soldiers and for the firm front they continued to present to the Pathet Lao.

The realities of the military situation were hidden, as had happened in Laos before, by the public campaign of charge and counter-charge between the Soviet Union and the United States, and by the allegations of Viet Minh intervention with which Phoumi once more sought to whip up American support. Confidence in Vientiane went up and down. Most of the people had returned. Their nervousness could be measured by feeling in the market, by the availability of vegetables, and the number of empty stalls. Pavie had noticed the same symptoms in Luang Prabang after Deo-van-Tri's attack on the town in 1887, Henri Deydier at the time of the Viet Minh invasion of 1953.[65] By the time the Government admitted on 26 January 1961 that its stories of massive Viet Minh intervention had been told for reasons of pro-

[64] Roger M. Smith, op. cit., p .65. The continuation of the racial difference in the composition of the two forces would probably have prevented any real integration in any case.

[65] Deydier, *Lokapala* (Paris, 1954), pp. 163 and 170.

paganda,[66] immense damage had been done to military morale. The soldiers who had reluctantly occupied Vientiane in the face of their own countrymen were far from anxious to march against the dreaded Viet Minh. From this point onwards the question as to whether Vietnamese troops were present or not, though often argued, was irrelevant. The soldiers believed that they were there and never waited long enough to find out.

In this unhappy atmosphere government forces, now supported by Harvard training aircraft fitted with rockets for ground strafing, which the United States had recently supplied,[67] advanced slowly northwards through empty villages to Vang Vieng, Muong Kassy, and the road junction 4,500 feet up in the mountains at Phou Koun, where they joined a force which had made its way even more cautiously down the road from Luang Prabang.[68] All attempts to move eastwards in the direction of the Plain of Jars were however checked by a strong defensive position a few kilometres to the east. In the first week of March, when Vientiane too had its moment of panic in a general outbreak of wild firing during an eclipse of the moon,[69] there was a limited counter-attack against the increasingly demoralized soldiers at Phou Koun. The counter-attack succeeded beyond all reasonable expectation. Within a few days government forces had withdrawn in disorder far up the roads to Vientiane and Luang Prabang, and Phoumi's threat to the Plain of Jars had disappeared.

The joint Neutralist-Pathet Lao command then turned its attention to the attempts the government had been making to push up the valleys from Paksane and Tha Thom to Xieng Khouang. These threats were disposed of before the end of March by mortar fire and propaganda, and Tha Thom itself occupied without a fight.

By this time the abandonment by President Kennedy of his

[66] Government Press Conference, 26 January 1961, *New York Times*, 27 January 1961.

[67] *New York Times*, 13 January 1961. See also statement by Brigadier General A. J. Boyle, head of the P.E.O., *The Times*, 24 January 1961.

[68] See articles by C. R. Smith in *The Bangkok World*: 'Scare them Away' (28 Jan. '61), 'Phoumi Moves North' (31 Jan. '61) and 'Laos's Leisurely War' (2 Feb. '61).

[69] *Lao Presse*, 3 March 1961. The panic was ended by an announcement on Radio Vientiane by Colonel Kouprasith, explaining that an old Lao custom was being observed.

predecessor's policy with regard to Laos, and patient negotiations between Britain and Russia, had made the eventual recall of the Geneva Conference a probability. There had been indications of a change of heart at the very end of the Eisenhower administration in January. Kennedy, not yet president, had reserved his position as he had done on other issues. Eisenhower had called Laos the most immediately dangerous of the problems he was passing on: 'You might have to go in there and fight it out,' he said.[70] But the new president had his own views on Indo-China. He had been critical of American policy there as far back as 1951, and in the great debate on United States intervention in 1954 had been 'frankly of the belief that no amount of American assistance in Indo-China can conquer . . . an "enemy of the people", which has the sympathy and covert support of the people'.[71]

So now, Kennedy did not need Lord Harlech to tell him that United States policy in Laos had been unwise and that 'the impression of Washington always rushing about to prop up corrupt dictators in Asia could not have happy consequences'.[72] He realized that the effort to turn Laos into a pro-Western bastion had been ridiculous and that neutralization was the correct policy.[73] American prestige was now so heavily involved, however, that disengagement must be cautious. 'We cannot and will not', he said, 'accept any visible humiliation over Laos.'[74] The Laotian military disasters in March, unforeseen by his military advisers who were predicting a Phoumi victory,[75] compelled him to consider whether to commit American troops, although he already knew that:

if he sent 10,000 men to southeast Asia, he would deplete the strategic reserve and have virtually nothing left for emergencies elsewhere. . . . Equipment was so low that, when Kennedy inspected the 82nd Airborne at Fort Bragg in October, the division had to borrow men and material to bring itself up to complement. The Army could hardly fight longer than a few weeks before running short on ammunition, nor was new production set to remedy the deficiencies. The supply of armoured personnel carriers, self-propelled howitzers and recoilless rifles fell far below the required number. . . . The airlift capacity consisted largely of obsolescent aircraft designed for civilian transportation; it would have

[70] Theodore C. Sorensen, *Kennedy* (London, 1965), p. 640.
[71] Schlesinger, op. cit., p. 293.   [72] Ibid., p. 304.
[73] Ibid., p. 299.   [74] Ibid., p. 301.   [75] Ibid., p. 300.

taken nearly two months to carry an infantry division and its equipment to southeast Asia. And, if such a division had found itself in the jungles of Laos or Vietnam, it would have been like Braddock's army at the Battle of the Wilderness, since counter-insurgency forces hardly existed.[76]

Furthermore, the president's advisers were divided both on what military action should be taken and on the likely consequences of such action. The logistics problem would be complex. 'In the event of large-scale movement of North Vietnamese troops into Laos in response to the commitment of American troops there the enemy supply line would be short, the American line long.'[77]

Military precautions were nevertheless taken, if only to meet the mounting anxiety in Siam,[78] and the clearest warnings conveyed to Moscow and Peking that the United States would intervene to prevent a Communist takeover. The Seventh Fleet was moved to the South China Sea, combat troops were alerted in Okinawa, and five hundred marines with helicopters were moved to Udorn airfield in Siam, thirty-five miles south of Vientiane. But at the same time the new president accepted on 23 March the idea of a ceasefire in Laos followed by an international conference.

The prospect of a new Geneva Conference in 1961 had something of the effect upon the Pathet Lao that it had had on the Viet Minh in 1954. Pathet Lao forces, now operating by companies and sometimes by battalions, set out to gain as much cheap territory as they could, and in particular to occupy the areas of eastern Laos in which the Viet Minh were interested. As a ceasefire became imminent in mid-April, Prince Souphanouvong's men achieved quick and sweeping gains in three areas, government troops making no serious effort to oppose them. North of Luang Prabang they took the important opium trading centre of Muong Sai and approached Nam Tha. East and north-east of Thakhek they took Kamkeut, Nhommarath, and Mahaxay.[79] Further south

---

[76] Schlesinger, op. cit., pp. 286–7.   [77] Dommen, op. cit., p. 188.
[78] Nuechterlein, op. cit., pp. 195–202.
[79] Dommen's accounts of attacks on Kamkeut by Viet Minh assault troops (op. cit., p. 188), and of a conventional attack on Muong Sai accompanied by 'rolling barrages' of shell-fire (op. cit., pp.196–7), reproduce government propaganda, some of which was afterwards denied. They also show this author falling into the error of describing Laotian war in Western terms for which he criticizes others (op. cit., p. 123).

they occupied Tchepone and took into their control the eastern half of the road linking Savannakhet with the frontier of South Vietnam. These latter moves extended the rebels' control from their old fiefs in the north to the unsubdued Kha tribal areas in the south where their influence was already paramount. There was also a sharp attack on the strong government force under Colonel Kouprasith north of Vang Vieng. Vang Vieng returned to Neutralist control.

Western observers who had visited the operational areas were not surprised at Phoumi's continual military disasters, which were partly due to the lack of experienced and worthy leaders. In August 1960 the Laotian Army had still not recovered from the shortage of officers caused by its rapid expansion since 1954. Some battalions were still twenty per cent. below strength in officers. Since the further expansion under Phoumi's aegis, which had raised the strength of the army to some 45,000 men, there were officers trying to command two separated companies in the field at the same time, and battalions with no more than four officers.

Laotian soldiers are tough and devoted when they have leaders who are worthy of them, as many a French officer discovered in the Indo-China War. The defence of Muong Khoua by a Laotian battalion against the Viet Minh in April-May 1953 provided a classic example of fortitude. Ordered to delay the Viet Minh 316th Division for fourteen days, the battalion had held out for five weeks; only four survivors are known.[80] But in the present state of leadership, difficulties were inevitable. Observers saw troops advancing with the greatest reluctance even when unopposed, sentries firing at random on the smallest noise, positions ill-chosen, field works so constructed as to be useless, soldiers sleeping in dug-outs intended for the ammunition they had stacked outside. Phoumi himself was never seen at an active front. Against the dedication of Kong Lae's parachutists, the hard discipline of the Pathet Lao hill-men under their energetic prince, against the Vietnamese cadres and the Viet Minh myth, the soldiers of Phoumi had no chance.

As his military situation deteriorated Phoumi alleged that sixty thousand Viet Minh were operating against him and asked the United States for increased aid. On 19 April the four hundred

[80] B. B. Fall, *The Two Vietnams* (London, 1963), p. 121.

American military advisers in Laos,[81] who had hitherto appeared in civilian clothes, put on their uniforms and assumed a tactical advisory role. But this was also the day of final disaster in the Bay of Pigs, a disaster which subdued the voices urging American intervention in Laos and strengthened President Kennedy in his resistance to them.[82] 'Thank God the Bay of Pigs happened when it did', he said later, 'otherwise we'd be in Laos by now—and that would be a hundred times worse.'[83]

On 24 April 1961, Britain and Russia called for an armistice in Laos which would be followed by the convening of a conference at Geneva. For the moment, the kingdom of Laos had other things to do. The day chosen as auspicious for the cremation of His late Majesty King Sisavang Vong had arrived. The government and diplomatic corps were in Luang Prabang for the magnificent state funeral. Amid the noise of supply aircraft coming and going from the airfield to isolated military posts in the mountains, and the salutes fired with live ammunition by artillery withdrawn from the nearest front, the traditional ceremonies unrolled for three long days. Only when the king's ashes had been deposited with due pomp in the royal pagoda, did attention return to the war.

A cease-fire was eventually proclaimed by the three parties to the conflict between 28 April and 3 May, by which time the Pathet Lao had occupied most of the territory they required. It was confirmed by the newly summoned International Control Commission as being generally effective on 11 May.[84] The Geneva Conference accordingly reassembled; it did so in circumstances which looked disastrous for Western interests.

Only a year had passed since General Phoumi's elections might have been thought to have confirmed the kingdom of Laos on its pro-Western course; the Pathet Lao leaders were in prison and the minor insecurity that existed in the country could have been ascribed to bucolic quarrels about rice, salt, women, and opium—village fights of the sort that recurred year by year. The Phoumist government had at least nominally controlled the whole country;

---

[81] The original three hundred infantrymen of the 'Programs Evaluation Office' had already been replaced by about four hundred Special Forces personnel from the U.S. guerrilla training schools; Dommen, op. cit., p. 184.

[82] Schlesinger, op. cit., pp. 307–8.   [83] Sorensen, op. cit., p. 644.

[84] The Commission met in Delhi on 28 April and the first party reached Vientiane on 8 May 1961.

if roads were impassable it was for lack of maintenance or because of monsoon flooding, not because they were blocked by rebels.

Now, however, at least three-fifths of Laos was in the hands of solid insurgent forces who had convincingly demonstrated their mastery of government troops. In retrospect the *coup d'état* of Captain Kong Lae would be seen as a lost opportunity for the West, perhaps its last real opportunity, to reverse the extreme policies that had been followed since the rejection of Prince Souvannaphouma in 1958, and to return to the neutrality on which the Geneva Agreement of 1954 had rested.

CHAPTER VII

The Geneva Conference 1961–2
and the Renewal of Conflict

THE Geneva Conference on the Laotian question opened on 16 May 1961. It ended on 23 July 1962 with an agreement on Laotian neutrality, endorsed by a Laotian provisional government of national union headed by Prince Souvannaphouma. From the first it had been clear that a confrontation between East and West in Laos was acceptable neither to Russia nor to the United States; had this not been so the conference might never have met. But although the great powers had been able, each from their own side, to induce Siam and North Vietnam to participate, it was less easy to control their divisive influence on the Laotian factions. The internal conflict therefore remained.

Two factors ended it after a year of bitter argument and of some fighting in Laos. In March 1962 the United States persuaded Siam to accept the neutralization of Laos in exchange for additional American guarantees of Siamese security, and in May Phoumi's disastrous military defeats in northern Laos robbed him of what little American confidence he still retained. The necessary pressures were now exerted, a coalition government was formed in Laos, and the conference at Geneva was brought to a conclusion. The hope then was that the substantial Neutralist centre party of Prince Sou vannaphouma would bring together and reconcile the two extremes.

Even by the end of 1962, however, this hope was beginning to disappear. There were two reasons for this. Firstly the ending of the Russian airlift to the Plain of Jars after the Geneva Agreement robbed the Neutralist forces of their independent support; supplies for their Russian weapons now had to be obtained from Hanoi. This enabled not only the Viet Minh but also General Phoumi to exert pressures under which the weakened Neutralist position collapsed. Secondly, even as the Geneva Agreement was signed, Laos was passing into the shadow of the mounting war in Vietnam. The intensification of operations there in 1962 and 1963 made the use of Laotian territory ever more important to the Viet Minh, although their exclusion from it had been a principal condition for American acceptance of the 1962 settlement. Thus were broken both the external and the internal conditions for the neutralization of Laos. The majority of the Neutralists, after outbursts of fighting with the Pathet Lao, lapsed into alliance with the right wing, and the *de facto* partition of 1961 was again a reality by 1964.

*   *   *

The Geneva Conference of 1961–2 had in itself been a success, and the arrangement it achieved was probably the best which the circumstances allowed. There had been misgivings as well as hopes at its inception. Siam, for example, had accepted her invitation with some reluctance and it was not until a week after the conference opened that the Siamese representatives arrived. The position of Siam was much what it had always been. Siamese security required a friendly rather than a neutral Laos to the north and north-east. Siam had watched the change in American policy with anxiety. The failure of the West to understand her point of view, to realize that the source of her anxieties was not some political argument that would wear away with co-existence and *détente*, had been incomprehensible. The crux of the matter for Siam was not that North Vietnam was Communist but that she was pursuing traditional Vietnamese ambitions which conflicted with Siamese interests. It was not against an ideological enemy that Siam needed Western help, but against the traditional one. Hence the threats of a neutralist accommodation with Communist power which the West tended to regard as so much blackmail. They were more than this. To Siam, as to Cambodia, neutralism could be a sane defence policy, because the bogy was not Communism but Vietnam.[1]

---

[1] D. E. Kennedy, *The Security of Southern Asia* (London, 1965), p. 89, says Siam fears a Vietnamese-Lao combination more than she does China. If the Siamese 'cannot obtain what they regard as adequate American support against such a combination, they will try to reinsure with China'. This is what they mean by neutrality. Dr. Kennedy is nearly right. He must know, however, that there is no possibility of a genuine Lao-Viet combination. The Lao are even more apprehensive of the Vietnamese than are the Siamese, for the very good reason that they are closer.

Neutralism in Laos, on the other hand, was dangerous. This was why the Siamese had favoured the restoration of General Phoumi to Vientiane. Washington had once more been under the 'compulsion to take actions disproportionate to the intrinsic strategic value of Laos'.[2] The Russians had intervened, the Americans had changed their minds too late. When danger threatened again, Siam had looked for firm and united action by S.E.A.T.O. Such action had not been taken. Furthermore Siam had still not forgiven the reduction of American economic aid.[3] As lately as 2 May Marshal Sarit had spoken of 'the improvement of friendly relations with the Soviet Union'.[4] Siam accepted the invitation to Geneva with many reservations.

Vice-President Johnson provided some of the reassurance which Siam needed during the tour of the Far East which he was making at this juncture. 'The time for pussy footing around has passed',[5] he said when he arrived in Bangkok on 16 May 1961, the day the conference opened in Geneva. In a joint statement with Marshal Sarit issued two days later, he emphasized that the United States fully understood Siam's concern and was determined to fulfil its treaty commitments to her.[6]

The Siamese Foreign Minister, in critical mood, joined the Geneva Conference for its eighth plenary session early in the following week. The national delegations, assembled, as in 1954, under the joint chairmanship of the Foreign Ministers of Britain and the Soviet Union, had meanwhile commenced the general debate. The nations represented were, firstly, those who had taken part in the conference of 1954: Britain, France, North and South Vietnam, Cambodia, Laos, the United States, Russia, and Communist China; secondly, the members of the International Control Commission: India, Canada, and Poland; thirdly, the remaining two neighbours of Laos: Burma and Siam. The issue was again the neutrality of Laos and its establishment as an effective buffer state. Nor had the Chinese and American objectives changed. China still sought to exclude American military power from Laos, the American aim was once more to end the fighting and to remove the Communist Vietnamese from the country.

[2] Dommen, op. cit., p. 68.   [3] D. E. Kennedy, op. cit., p. 87.
[4] L'année politique, 1961, p. 453. Nuechterlein, op. cit., pp. 212–15 describes but once more does not analyse Siam's attitude.
[5] Guardian, 18 May 1961.   [6] Joint statement, 18 May 1961.

The broadest aspect of the conflict was the first to be settled. Soon after the conference opened, President Kennedy met Mr. Khrushchev in Vienna. They were quite frank with each other. To neither did Laos represent a vital strategic interest; both supported a neutral, independent Laos guaranteed by international agreement.[7] China also was content with Laotion neutrality as she had been in 1954.[8] Correspondingly, in Geneva, procedural difficulties were solved; the months passed; by mid-December patient committee work had evolved a time-table for the withdrawal of foreign troops, and a compromise on methods of supervision of the settlement. 'The degree of real concession made by the Communist powers to achieve these agreements was not great, in fact they did little more than show a mere willingness to negotiate. . . .'[9] Nevertheless it was clear that the outside world was ready to solve the external problem.

The atmosphere was far different in the inner world of Laos, where the three factions were to wrangle for a year. The first disagreement was on the seating of Laotians at the conference. The Vientiane representatives, supported by the Siamese, claimed to be the only legal delegation and refused to take their seats if Pathet Lao and Neutralist representatives were also to be present. The Pathet Lao, backed by the North Vietnamese, and the Neutralists supported by the nations who still recognized Prince Souvannaphouma's government, remained seated in accordance with an agreement between the major powers.[10]

The conference proceeded without any formal representation of Laos and without, at first, any representatives from Vientiane; but it was clearly essential that the three factions should agree on the appointment of a single delegation as soon as possible. This

[7] Schlesinger, op. cit., pp. 333–4. According to Kennedy, op. cit., p. 87, the joint Vienna statement undid some of the good done in Siam by Vice-President Johnson's visit.

[8] 'China's security is better served by the creation of a buffer state in Laos than by the imposition of a Communist one which would tempt the U.S. to intervene': Brian Crozier, 'Peking and the Laotian Crisis' in *China Quarterly*, 1962, p. 116.

[9] E. H. S. Simmonds, 'Independence and Political Rivalry in Laos 1945–61' in *Politics in Southern Asia*, S. Rose (ed.), (London, 1963), p. 195. For a fuller analysis see Modelski, op. cit., pp. 20–38.

[10] '. . . to seat representatives from Laos proposed by individual governments participating in the conference'. Modelski, op. cit. p. 9.

Captain Kong Lae addressing a meeting, August 1960

Captain Kong Lae and General Phoumi at Ban Hin Heup, October 1961

implied the formation of a coalition government, a matter which became unexpectedly difficult. The argument on the allocation of portfolios in such a government raged for over a year, but the real obstacle to agreement was the reluctance of the two extremes to risk their assets in a neutralist settlement. Phoumi, and behind him the Siamese, was not prepared to hand over control of the Mekong valley towns. The Pathet Lao, equally disinclined to surrender the substantial position of power they had now gained, used the delays he caused to build up their forces and improve their organization throughout the country.

The initial difficulty in persuading the three principals, Prince Boun Oum, Prince Souvannaphouma, and Prince Souphanouvong to meet at all, was overcome with remarkable patience by Prince Sihanouk of Cambodia. The princes met under the aegis of the Cambodian leader at Zürich in June, but the apparently cordial agreement they signed proved inconclusive.[11] Months of procrastination and petty intransigence were to pass before the next meeting, which took place early in October on the partly demolished bridge over the Nam Lik, the river separating the military forces fifty miles north of Vientiane.

Ten days later, on 18 October, Prince Souvannaphouma visited Luang Prabang and was invited by the king to form a new administration, the constitution having been amended on 30 July to allow the king to act in this way without an Assembly vote. In accordance with normal procedure, however, Prince Boun Oum was to remain in office until the new government was actually formed.

A series of delaying actions followed. At Phoumi's instance Prince Boun Oum declined six successive invitations by Prince Souvannaphouma to meet for consultations on the Plain of Jars, alleging that his physical safety could not be guaranteed there, and then rejected proposals for joint security measures to permit a meeting to be held in Vientiane. Prince Boun Oum was in fact quite confident of his ability to look after himself and when urgent messages arrived from Geneva he went to the Plain of Jars without hesitation. Here, on 14 December, agreement was achieved on the distribution of portfolios; the two key ministries, Defence and the Interior, were to go to the Neutralists, but there was still no nomination of ministers. The Geneva Conference renewed its appeal to the princes on 18 December: an internal settlement was

[11] Text in Cmnd. 1828, pp. 13-14.

now an immediate necessity if the patiently contrived international agreement was to be concluded.

Prince Souvannaphouma and the Pathet Lao leader visited Vientiane for a further meeting on 27 December. The presence of their security force of three hundred Neutralist and Pathet Lao soldiers, with all the personal and family reunions that this implied, created a kind of joyous and expectant tension in the little town. But Prince Boun Oum, on the excuse of a belligerent speech which Souphanouvong had made on arrival, refused formal discussions and withdrew his agreement to the allocation of the two key ministries to the Neutralists. There followed a third message from the conference, inviting the princes to meet in Geneva so that all possible help could be given them in settling their differences.

The United States had long ago accepted the good faith of Prince Souvannaphouma, with whom the new Assistant Secretary of State for Far Eastern Affairs, Mr. Averill Harriman, had established excellent relations. Realizing that General Phoumi's determination to retain power underlay Boun Oum's obstinacy, the Americans now exerted their considerable influence upon the general. Finding him disinclined to compromise they withheld payment of the four million dollars due to the Laotian government as cash-grant aid for the month of January 1962. Although the Siamese Defence Minister said that the American action 'would expedite the Communist takeover of Laos',[12] Prince Boun Oum now accepted the invitation to Geneva. Before leaving Vientiane, however, he told the National Assembly that he would neither join nor discuss a coalition led by Neutralists, that Prince Souvannaphouma wanted to deliver Laos to the Communists and that if peaceful methods failed his government would 'use other methods to oppose foreign interference'. Even when the United States and Soviet governments announced their own agreement that the two key ministries should be held by the central group, Boun Oum said that he would not accept such an arrangement. While this attitude seems to have been modified in the course of the Geneva meetings, there was still no conclusion.[13]

[12] D. Insor, op. cit., p. 131.

[13] Modelski, op. cit., pp. 133–5. The conference then adjourned until 'the beginning of February' by which time it was assumed that the Laotians would have agreed among themselves on a single delegation. The next plenary session in fact took place on 2 July.

The continued failure to reach a political accord had been accompanied by a military situation far from stable. The cease-fire of May 1961 had left the hills of Laos generally in the hands of the Pathet Lao and Neutralists and the narrow plain on the left bank of the Mekong under the control of General Phoumi.[14] Except on the infrequent roads, however, the two sides were not face to face. Along the jungle valleys of the wide no-man's-land that stretched between river plain, upland plateau, and mountain village, ample opportunity could be found for unopposed infiltration into stronger or more desirable positions.

There was the additional complication of guerrilla organizations behind the lines on each side. The Meo guerrilla groups which Phoumi had built up with American encouragement in Xieng Khouang and Sam Neua provinces, had an estimated strength of more than ten thousand and were entirely dependent on air supply. The Pathet Lao guerrillas were less numerous but perhaps more widely spread through areas which the government claimed to control. As early as 20 May the Control Commission had warned of the possible dangers. The cease-fire was precarious. The two sides had retained the right to use force when provoked or in self-defence: flights over territory in the effective control of a hostile group were always regarded as provocative.[15]

Already one of the Meo mountain bases, the high ridge village of Phadong on the southern fringe of the Plain of Jars, was being harassed at long range by Neutralist guns. Comparable artillery had been flown in to the Meos and their American advisers, while rocket-firing aircraft sought out the hostile guns. For Captain Kong Lae it became essential to remove this centre of resistance which he believed had been built up in his territory since the cease-fire.[16] He increased his pressure and on 6 June, during a

[14] Truce meetings between the two sides began on 11 May 1961 and were suspended in September having achieved very little: see Dommen, op. cit., pp. 206-9. The cease-fire line shown in Quang Minh, *Au pays du million d'éléphants et du parasol blanc* (Hanoi, 1962), which was that claimed by the Pathet Lao in May 1961, was regarded as accurate with small exceptions, by Western observers. As Dr. Kennedy has remarked (op. cit., p. 83) it followed the rough dividing line between the Lao and non-Lao ethnic areas.

[15] Report of the International Control Commission dated 20 May 1961, quoted by Modelski, op. cit., p. 61.

[16] There had apparently been Meo guerrilla groups supplied by the Americans in the Phadong area well before the cease-fire of May 1961.

noisy but innocuous bombardment for which the gunners had saved up their ammunition for days,[17] soldiers under his command approached the ridge from the rear. The Meos and their supporters fled. The incident caused a five-day suspension of the Geneva Conference and an appeal from the co-chairmen for the observance of the cease-fire.[18]

The issue of Vietnamese participation in Neutralist and Pathet Lao operations after the conference began, became obscure. Each side was monitoring the wireless links of the other, and some messages certainly had a propaganda content. Claims of 'orders on the wireless in Vietnamese', used to substantiate allegations of Viet Minh presence, were thus suspect. At one stage Kong Lae made a speech boasting that he had fifteen Viet Minh battalions on his side; but he later admitted to a Western observer that this had been said for the benefit of Phoumi's troops. Vietnamese units were, however, probably present and held in reserve in case of a Phoumist break-through. If they fought, there was never any possibility of proof because the Lao troops never waited for them. On balance, participation by Viet Minh infantry, as opposed to cadres and support detachments, in the skirmishes of 1961–2 is unlikely.[19]

The onset of the rains in June stopped further active operations but the three factions continued to recruit and build up their strength with supplies and armaments. Captain Kong Lae received from the Russians anti-aircraft artillery, armoured cars, and, towards the end of the year, some forty tanks. The Pathet Lao battalions were trained with their Vietnamese cadres into respectable infantry. Chinese influence increased in the province of Phongsaly, where, at the request of Prince Souvannaphouma to whom Phongsaly had remained loyal, Chinese labour was building

Dommen, op. cit., p. 208, states that correspondents had visited them in March. There is less certainty, however, about exact locations, and Kong Lae may have been right about the ridge position attacked.

[17] Ammunition was being brought from the Plain of Jars by porter and pony and supplies were limited. The guns, manned by Kong Lae's men trained by the Vietnamese, were firing at extreme range. The shells nearly all burst in front of the ridge or passed over it into the valley behind. Dommen, op. cit., pp. 207–8, takes a more dramatic view.

[18] Modelski, op. cit., p. 65.

[19] There were equally substantial reports of Siamese units on Pheumi's side; these could have engaged in battle with far less risk of discovery than the Vietnamese but there is no evidence that they did so.

the province's first road. The Vientiane government reorganized its forces and raised their strength progressively to about sixty thousand men, trained and advised down to company level by excellent groups from the American Special Forces, with teams of interpreters provided by Siam. The Meo guerrilla effort was developed and extended under the Meo Colonel Vang Pao, until it involved numerous bases around the Plain of Jars and in Sam Neua, many with their own airstrips and American advisory teams, and a reputed armed strength of eighteen thousand.[20]

Up to the end of the rains in October 1961, only minor incidents took place. Nevertheless, as early as the end of August both General Phoumi and the Pathet Lao were openly speculating about a resumption of hostilities after the rains, and troop movements to improve Phoumi's military position were being reported. In view of the bad faith of the other side, Phoumi would say, such action was imposed on him. However, it soon began to appear that '. . . the course followed by Boun Oum and Phoumi Nosavan indicated an attempt to scuttle the negotiated settlement, presumably in the expectation that if general hostilities were renewed, the United States would have no choice except to throw its full support behind their faction.'[21] In October Phoumi began to undertake what he described as 'probing actions' deep into hostile territory, the most important being into the Kam Mon Plateau east of Thakhek, and from two directions towards Muong Sai north-west of Luang Prabang. Both were areas where his opponents could be expected to be sensitive and where probes would provoke military reactions which could be used as excuses for delay on the political front. There followed precipitate retreats by Phoumi's forces towards the Mekong and new alarmist cries of 'Viet Minh!'

When, in December 1961, the progress in the negotiations at Geneva made agreement in Laos urgent, and when the United States began to apply financial pressure upon Phoumi in order to hasten it, the general issued a new series of communiqués.[22]

[20] See additional note 1 at end of chapter.

[21] Oliver E. Clubb, *The United States and the Sino-Soviet Bloc in Southeast Asia* (Washington, 1962), p. 67.

[22] See *Lao Presse* for January 1962. These communiqués naïvely reveal in their detail the extent to which Phoumi was operating behind the cease-fire line.

Not only the Viet Minh, he said, but Chinese and even Russian troops were now active in the country. A whole Viet Minh division was crossing southern Laos into South Vietnam and government positions were being attacked everywhere. These false stories were aimed, as so often before, at the nervousness of neighbours whose influence with the Americans Phoumi hoped would revive his own. He also used them as an excuse for the despatch of four battalions supported by artillery and aircraft, on a 'probing action' some twenty-five miles through the hills north of Thakhek where Laos is narrowest and the Siamese most sensitive. The force reached a village on the enemy's line of communication with North Vietnam.[23] Here it ran into predictable opposition and, in spite of the presence of United States' advisory teams, dissolved in panic. The Mekong boatmen charged a pound per head to ferry the fleeing rabble into Siam, instead of the customary shilling.

At the end of January 1962 attention moved towards the north-west where, after throwing back Phoumi's thrust towards Muong Sai, the Pathet Lao were mortaring the airfield of Nam Tha, apparently to close it to government offensive aircraft and to prevent the arrival of ground reinforcements for further probes to the east.

The village of Nam Tha, capital of Nam Tha province, lies about fifteen miles from the Chinese border, at the head of a wide upland valley through which the Tha river flows south-westwards for over a hundred miles to the Mekong. The place was in government hands at the time of the cease-fire, being at least seven miles outside the territory claimed by the Pathet Lao.[24] Mortaring of the Nam Tha airfield by weapons with a range of very much less than seven miles, was thus an admitted breach of the cease-fire. Prince Souphanouvong defended it by referring to the use of Nam Tha by Phoumi as a base for deep probing into Pathet Lao territory, and to the air attacks on Pathet Lao villages which had been going on for months.[25] However, it now enabled Boun Oum to refuse to attend a meeting on 2 February, called by the king to decide on membership of the new government.

[23] Commanders on the spot told Western journalists that their aim was to cut the Pathet Lao/Neutralist communications with North Vietnam. See *Bangkok World*, 23 January 1962.

[24] See additional note 2.

[25] Letter to the co-chairmen of the Geneva Conference, 29 January 1962.

The efforts of British and Russian diplomats in the Plain of Jars eventually persuaded the Pathet Lao to stop their mortaring. Prince Souvannaphouma visited Luang Prabang, was received by the king and had discussions with Phoumi and other right-wing leaders from 16 to 19 February. The United States meanwhile expressed its view of the situation by suspending cash-grant aid to the Vientiane government. Phoumi simply released more bank-notes;[26] even now there was no settlement. When Prince Souvanna-phouma produced a list of ministers based on his negotiations, Vientiane replied with completely new ideas for a government headed by the king, and then rejected suggestions for new talks in March.

The Neutralist leader began to lose patience. The United States, he said, was playing a double game by talking in terms of a coalition while sabotaging the project by supplying Phoumi with military aid and allowing the Siamese government to go on helping him. He gave warning that he could not hold back the Pathet Lao very much longer and that, unless the Americans forced Phoumi to agree to the Neutralist formula for a coalition, he would abandon his mission of conciliation and leave the two extremes to fight it out.

The Americans were in fact doing their best. They had greatly reassured the Siamese—who were moving troops towards their frontier on the upper Mekong—by in effect giving them at last the unilateral defence guarantee for which they had hankered ever since 1954.[27] This had smoothed the way for a more constructive Siamese policy towards Laos, and when, 'alarmed by the increasingly suicidal character of General Phoumi's stubbornness',[28] Mr. Harriman went to Bangkok in March, Marshal Sarit was persuaded to help. At Nongkhay on 24 March, Sarit confronted Phoumi in Mr. Harriman's presence:

Amid considerable diplomatic trepidation, Marshal Sarit talked in low tones in Thai for about twenty minutes, explaining patiently why it was advisable for General Phoumi to accede to the coalition. He did not look at Phoumi. When he had finished, the General replied in French, enumerating the reasons for his reluctance. After several minutes of this, Harriman, apparently not realizing that the General's speech was the necessary prelude to his acceptance without loss of face of Marshal

[26] Dommen, op. cit., pp. 219 and 228.
[27] See additional note 3.   [28] Dommen, op. cit., p. 216.

Sarit's advice, lost patience and interrupted him. He said flatly that the General was wrong and intimated that the Phoumist forces were finished in Laos if they did not agree to the coalition.

Back in Vientiane, Harriman had further conversations with General Phoumi in what one of the General's aides termed an 'animated and occasionally venomous' atmosphere. Shortly after this, a State Department official who had accompanied Harriman to Laos, William H. Sullivan, showed up at Khang Khay, Souvanna Phouma's 'capital'. There, he gave reassurances to Souvanna Phouma that the United States was doing everything possible to expedite the formation of a coalition.[29]

Meanwhile Phoumi was preparing to play his last card. Against United States' military advice and without their military assistance the general had built up the garrison of Nam Tha to a strength of five thousand, through an air strip at Muong Sing, twenty-five miles to the north-west. He was once more using the town as a base for probes into hostile territory. American warnings that these tactics might provoke Pathet Lao retaliation went unheeded.[30] In fact the Pathet Lao, aware from the consequences of their mortaring in February of the international sensitivity of Nam Tha, proved remarkably unresponsive. It was not until further provocative sallies from Nam Tha had resulted in an actual clash that they resumed their mortaring.

On 3 May, when skirmishing had been going on for ten days, the outpost and air strip at Muong Sing changed hands, possibly as the result of a mutiny fomented by the Pathet Lao.[31] Whatever the means adopted, the Pathet Lao object was clearly to stop the reinforcement of Nam Tha. Phoumi claimed that Muong Sing had been attacked by Chinese troops. This, and an intensification of the desultory mortaring, proved enough for the garrison of Nam Tha, now commanded by Phoumi's commander-in-chief, General Boun Leut. After a flurry of firefights but no Pathet Lao attack, Nam Tha was abandoned. This time there could be no doubt about it; General Boun Leut is no poltroon; he had obeyed Phoumi's orders.[32]

The allegation that the Pathet Lao had been supported by Chinese troops was dismissed by the American advisers in the area.

[29] Dommen, op. cit.; see additional note 4.
[30] *New York Times*, 7 May 1962.
[31] See additional note 5.   [32] See additional note 6.

It was generally believed that there was at least a battalion of Viet Minh in Muong Sai, but many observers were satisfied that the Pathet Lao no longer needed even Viet Minh advice in order to deal effectively with their opponents.

Government forces retreated without resistance down the valleys to Ban Houei Sai on the Mekong and on 11 May crossed the river into Siam. By 15 May about three thousand men, including General Boun Leut himself, were being air-lifted back to Vientiane, and two thousand more had surrendered to the Pathet Lao. Fresh troops reoccupied Ban Houei Sai a few days after it was abandoned and found no enemy near it. An American patrol 'back up the trail to Nam Tha found only scattered bands of Pathet Lao guerrillas and no North Vietnamese'.[33] On 27 May, however, the Pathet Lao were said to have captured an outpost nine miles from the place. American helicopters rushed more reinforcements to the scene next day, but after alleged Pathet Lao mortaring the majority of the garrison again crossed the Mekong on 31 May, their military advisers being obliged to follow. As before, the Pathet Lao made no attempt to move up to the Mekong and no further incidents were reported from the area.

It had always been clear that, if ever the Pathet Lao seriously menaced one of the Mekong towns, Siam could reasonably consider this a threat to herself and demand action by her allies in the South East Asia Treaty Organization. The Neutralists and the Pathet Lao had been well aware of this. Their last-minute grabs of territory before the cease-fire in 1961 had stopped well away from the Mekong, and their reaction to Phoumi's earlier probes east of Thakhek and towards Muong Sai had been no more than local. Phoumi had worked for the Nam Tha and Ban Houei Sai fiasco, bizarre even by Laotian standards, because after the suspension of American aid, his only hope had been to lose a Mekong town and thus involve the West militarily on his side.

The West was not unaware of these factors. However, it was obliged to consider the effects in Siam of the abandonment of Ban Houei Sai, which is immediately across the Mekong from Siamese territory, and of the dramatically revealed worthlessness of Phoumi as a bulwark against Siam's enemies. It was known that France did not favour action by S.E.A.T.O., which in accordance

[33] Dommen, op. cit., p. 218.

with the treaty would have had to be unanimous. The United States therefore acted under the joint U.S.–Siamese statement of 6 March, and other powers responded individually to Siamese appeals for support. A battle group of a thousand American marines already in Siam for a S.E.A.T.O. exercise was moved towards the Mekong, and on 16 May the leading elements of a further four thousand American troops began to arrive in Bangkok. Token detachments from Australia, New Zealand, and Great Britain followed.

Nevertheless, Phoumi had lost. The S.E.A.T.O. troops did not cross the Mekong into Laos. The Siamese, now doubly reassured as to the reality of American protection,[34] did not encourage Phoumi further. A message was sent from Vientiane to Prince Souvannaphouma in Paris,[35] agreeing to the proposed composition of his new administration.

As General Phoumi's long and obstinate resistance to American pressure was ending, *The Times* published two substantial despatches from its Washington correspondent who stated that the United States government held the C.I.A. partly responsible for the situation in Laos.[36] C.I.A. agents had deliberately opposed the official American objective of trying to establish a neutral government, had encouraged Phoumi in his reinforcement of Nam Tha, and had negatived the heavy financial pressure brought by the Kennedy administration upon Phoumi by subventions from its own budget.

The American State Department promptly denied these allegations,[37] saying that the C.I.A. and other government agencies were carrying out the policy decided by the president. *The Times* then further reported that although the United States embassy in Vientiane had asserted that there was no evidence of the C.I.A. disregarding official policy, Washington had received information to the contrary from other foreign missions in Vientiane, including the embassies of Britain and France. Contrary evidence of a kind was also provided by General Phoumi himself: 'the General apparently was quite outspoken, and made it known that he could disregard the American embassy and the military advisory

---

[34] By the Dean Rusk–Thanat Khoman statement of 6 March, and by the arrival of U.S. troops.

[35] The Prince had gone to Paris for the wedding of his daughter.

[36] *The Times*, 24 and 31 May 1962.

[37] *The Times*, 25 May 1962.

group because he was in communication with other American agencies'.[38]

Money may not in fact have been the most critical element in the delicate position of the United States *vis-à-vis* the stubborn general. From the beginning of his action against Captain Kong Lae in August 1960, Phoumi had been firmly supported both by Marshal Sarit and to a lesser extent by President Diem of South Vietnam, whose joint resources dwarfed American subventions to Laos.[39] The principal American difficulty had perhaps been to persuade these two rulers that a neutral Laos was in the best interests of their countries. Phoumi had constantly played on their fears and had been able to count on them if there was any question of his abandonment by the United States.

An equal difficulty was the dilemma within the policy itself. Phoumi was to be encouraged to negotiate and yet his forces had to be restored to a condition in which they would be effective if negotiation failed. The question was mainly one of military morale, and it was therefore necessary to insist on United States' readiness in the last resort to intervene with United States' forces. Such insistence did however operate against sincere negotiation by Phoumi, for it assured him that he would be supported by force in the end even if it were his own intransigence that was the occasion for it.[40]

An example of the sort of thing that became unavoidable can be found in the speech of the United States' Commander-in-Chief, Pacific, Admiral Felt, when he visited Vientiane in October 1961. A conference of the three princes was imminent and the admiral recommended that the Vientiane government do its best to negotiate a peaceful solution. But he went on to say that if, in spite of the government's efforts, a peaceful solution were not achieved, 'American forces in the Pacific and the forces of S.E.A.T.O. were always ready to come to the aid of Laos. . . .'[41] Small wonder if

[38] *The Times*, 31 May 1962.

[39] The personal resources amassed by Sarit were estimated after his death at thirty million pounds sterling. *The Times*, 8 July 1964.

[40] Compare the British dilemma over support for Siam against France in 1893; *supra*, pp. 40–42.

[41] *Lao Presse*, 6 October 1961. Dommen, op. cit., p. 211, comments similarly. President Eisenhower, *Mandate for Change* (London, 1963), p. 355, in dealing with military statements on possible U.S. intervention in Indo-China in 1954 which caused political embarrassment, writes:

the American advisory officers who had followed Phoumi from
Savannakhet, and who had developed an understandable measure
of personal loyalty to him, were unable to adjust themselves. Some
of them wore his ring, the ring of the Savannakhet Group;[42] even
if they spoke of the necessity of negotiation, their very continued
presence with Phoumi belied their words. The general's con-
viction that the United States were bound to support him whatever
he did and whatever they said, was thus impossible to break.

Hence, in spite of the pressure that the American government
was now determined to exert, it was not until 24 June 1962 that
Prince Souvannaphouma took office as head of a coalition in
Vientiane, and even then General Phoumi's position was little
weakened. This was to prejudice from the first the chances that the
neutralist solution would work.

After talks on the Plain of Jars from 7 to 12 June, the three
princes signed a formal agreement. The provisional government of
national union was to consist of seven of Prince Souvannaphouma's
Neutralists, four from General Phoumi's group, four Pathet Lao,
and four so-called Right-wing Neutralists, men who had remained
in Vientiane without political commitment to Phoumi. General
Phoumi and Prince Souphanouvong were both to be Vice-
Premiers, while Phoumi as Finance Minister would continue to
control American aid and all other funds, including those which
Souphanouvong would need to carry out his work as Minister of
the Plan. At its first meeting the government ordered the cessation
of all military activities, and a week later it decided on other
practical measures to restore communications between the zones
controlled by the factions, and to begin anew the process of reconciliation. In the general euphoria Prince Souphanouvong himself was the Minister to propose the health of President Kennedy
at the United States embassy in Vientiane on the Fourth of July.

'State says "We are for peace" while Defence underscores "we are ready
to fight".' The right of a Defence department to make what are in such circumstances foreign policy statements is, of course, the root of the matter.

    [42] A heavy gold ring with a red enamel ornament, bestowed as a
personal distinction by Phoumi. Warner, op. cit., p. 283, describes a
similar ring worn by the trusties of the Siamese Police General Phao,
contender for supreme power in Siam until outmanoeuvred by Sarit in
1957. Phoumi's own C.I.A. adviser, Mr. Jack Hazey, a strong personal
adherent, was only withdrawn in February 1962: Wise and Ross, *The
Invisible Government* (London, 1965), p. 153.

When the Geneva Conference reassembled on 2 July, a Laotian government delegation was at last present. Three weeks later the new agreement was signed. It was comprehensive, embodying a formal statement of intent by Laos herself and solemn undertakings to respect the neutrality of the country by all the nations represented.[43] If the agreement was carried out in the spirit and letter it would solve the Laotian international problem, leaving the internal social and economic problems to be solved peacefully with appropriate foreign aid.

Britain had played a major part in the Geneva achievement. As co-chairman, with his Russian counterpart, of the 1954 conference, the British Foreign Secretary and his special deputy Mr. Malcolm MacDonald, had assumed perhaps the main burden of negotiations on behalf of the West. The main issue, the essential role of Laos as a buffer between Siam and the Communist world, had been clear to Lord Home as it had been to Mr. Anthony Eden in 1954. The world had owed much to the fair-minded firmness, the moderation and coolness displayed by British diplomacy in the systematic ironing out of disagreements with the Russians. But what might have been achieved in the autumn of 1960 if Prince Souvannaphouma had been given from the first the undivided support and encouragement of the West, a policy which Britain and France had urged in vain on the Eisenhower administration, was less easy in the embittered atmosphere of June 1962.

The Breakdown of the Geneva Agreement of 1962

At first some progress was made. S.E.A.T.O. troops were withdrawn from the Mekong, a development which was greeted with displeasure by the Siamese whose Foreign Minister shortly afterwards publicly stated his country's desire to go its own way.[44] The prisoners taken by both sides were released, the Neutralist officers accepted their promotion, Captain Kong Lae became a major-general. The continuation of United States aid was formally accepted by the coalition government. American forces, already reduced, were meticulously counted out of the country by the International Control Commission—666 Americans and 403 Filipino technicians. On 28 November the government decided to form a single army of 30,000 men, drawn equally from the forces of the three factions. General Phoumi, who still had 60,000 men

---

[43] Texts in Cmnd. 1828.   [44] See additional note 7.

under arms, began to demobilize. Kong Lae with about 11,000, and the Pathet Lao with some 14,000, had lesser problems.

As the winter of 1962 passed, however, the hope that the Laotian dilemma was indeed solved began to fade. In his excellent analysis,[45] George Modelski criticizes the assumption, which the Geneva Conference made, that only the external aspects of neutralization were within its competence. If neutralization involves elements of internal policy, as it nearly always must do, the international regulation of some internal matters may be an advantage. The assumption was, however, probably the only one on which a settlement could have been negotiated at all. There is less doubt about the definition of the essentials of the settlement with which he concludes:

The Laotian settlement may be defined as the maintenance of neutrality by a régime presided over by Prince Souvanna Phouma's neutralists, but strongly influenced by both the Pathet Lao and the Vientiane group. Its stability must depend, in the final analysis, not only on internal, but also on external factors. The continued viability of all three factions in the internal political situation is a precondition of neutrality.[46]

In short, not only had the external bargain between the Communist powers and the United States to be kept, but the factions had to be maintained as independent entities until the process of reconciliation could persuade them to coalesce.

The essentials of the external bargain were, on the one hand the removal of American forces from Laos, and on the other the departure of the Viet Minh. Part of this latter requirement was that the North Vietnamese should be prevented from using the Pathet Lao territory in eastern Laos as a safe route for the reinforcement of the insurgents in South Vietnam. In December 1961 the United States had satisfied themselves from the interrogation of rebel prisoners in South Vietnam that substantial reinforcements were coming from the north through the Pathet Lao areas,[47] thereby avoiding the demilitarized zone along the 17th parallel. The Americans were now more than ever committed to the support of the South Vietnamese government. It was basic to their

[45] Op. cit., pp. 20–38.   [46] Ibid., p. 37.
[47] See *A Threat to the Peace* (Washington, Dept. of State, December 1961).

acceptance of the Geneva Agreement of 1962 that this traffic should be stopped.[48]

The war in South Vietnam had, however, by now entered upon another new phase. Following the formation of the National Liberation Front for the south at the end of 1960, the rebel effort had been sharply increased in 1961. Alarmed by the consequent deterioration in the government position, the Americans had in 1962 further expanded their military effort. Helicopters and amphibious vehicles were provided in quantity, the number of United States advisers was augmented, and the emphasis of the training they carried out was shifted to counter-insurgency operations, the importance of which was a personal preoccupation of President Kennedy.[49]

These developments were bound to reduce the ability of the new Laotian government to stop the movement of insurgents through eastern Laos as it had promised at Geneva.[50] The Viet Minh required their reinforcement route more than ever. They had also reacted to the appearance of American troops in Siam by stationing battalions—no less than eleven, it was alleged—on the main passes between Vietnam and Laos.[51] Furthermore, although the Laotian government professed itself satisfied that all the Viet Minh advisers and cadres had left the country, only forty Vietnamese had been seen to depart and there was widespread suspicion that many hundreds remained integrated into the Pathet Lao forces. From the Viet Minh point of view, indeed, as Schlesinger says, the settlement never went into effect.[52]

The internal situation in Laos was just as unsatisfactory. Before the Geneva settlement, as we have seen, each of the three factions had had its own source of military supplies; the Pathet Lao deriving its support from the North Vietnamese and the Russians, the Neutralists depending entirely on the Russians, and General Phoumi on the Americans. Once the settlement was achieved, the Russians, probably under Chinese and Viet Minh pressure,[53] ended their air-lift to the Plain of Jars. This left the Neutralists to obtain their supplies, including the ammunition for their Russian weapons, through Hanoi, which enabled the Viet Minh and Pathet

---

[48] Schlesinger, op. cit., p. 451.
[49] Schlesinger, op. cit., pp. 309–10.   [50] Cmnd. 1828, p. 16.
[51] Dommen, op. cit., p. 253.   [52] Op. cit., p. 453.
[53] See additional note 8.

Lao to exert leverage on them. It was not the only pressure to which they were subject, as Jean Lacouture made clear in April 1963:

If until November 1962 the Americans on the one hand and the Chinese and Vietnamese on the other appeared to respect the spirit and letter of the Geneva Agreements, since then a double operation of whittling away the strength of the centre for the benefit of the two extremes has been going on. While the United States military mission seems to have as its sole objective to ensure the complicity of the greatest possible number of supposedly neutralist officers, the Pathet Lao, assisted and probably financed by its eastern friends, has been organizing the penetration of the forces of the centre.[54]

These stresses proved too much for the sorely tried parachutists. Quinim Pholsena, whose early association with them in their *coup d'état* of August 1960 had won him more respect than, as a politician, he perhaps deserved, was involved in the Pathet Lao intrigues.[55] Open quarrelling between factions within the Neutralist camp had begun in November 1962. Deuane, always one of the more ambitious of the parachutist officers, accused Colonel Ketsana, whose courage and level-headed political awareness had been the strength of his friend Kong Lae, of selling out to the Americans. There was an unsuccessful attempt on Ketsana's life.[56] Then on 28 November an Air America plane carrying supplies for which Kong Lae had finally been constrained to ask Vientiane, was shot down by Deuane's men.

The military split soon spread to the Neutralist group inside the government, Kong Lae being supported by Prince Souvannaphouma and Deuane by Quinim Pholsena. On 12 February 1963, the able and devoted Ketsana was killed by a left-wing Neutralist assassin of Deuane's group, a tragedy as sad and in its way as significant as the murder of Kou Voravong in 1954.

Kong Lae arrested five dissident Neutralists on suspicion but the assassin had sought sanctuary with the Pathet Lao. Tension

[54] 'Vers la rupture d'un équilibre?', in *Le Monde*, 16 April 1963; translation from *Keesing's Contemporary Archives*, p. 19593.

[55] Simmonds, 'The Evolution of Foreign Policy in Laos' in *Modern Asian Studies*, II, 1 (1968), p. 21.

[56] Dommen, op. cit., p. 245, says that Ketsana's statements urging the International Control Commission to investigate reports of North Vietnamese troops in the border areas were the immediate cause.

Crown Copyright, British Army Public Relations Service GHQ FARELF

The King and Queen of Laos at the That Luang Festival in Vientiane, November 1961

Prince Boun Oum, Prince Souvannaphouma, and Prince Souphanouvong, after reaching agreement, 11 June, 1962 (behind at right Mr. Avtar Singh, Indian chairman of the International Control Commission)

sharply increased. After a brawl in Xieng Khouang market place on 31 March, fighting broke out between the two Neutralist factions. For the Pathet Lao, Deuane was the genuine Neutralist as opposed to the 'deviationists' under Kong Lae. Further skirmishing and fire-fights followed, in which, by a combination of mortaring and propaganda, Deuane and the Pathet Lao ousted Kong Lae from the joint headquarters of Khang Khay, from Xieng Khouang town, and also from the important village and air-strip of Phongsavan, where Ketsana had been based. On 18 April, after more shooting, Kong Lae withdrew from the Plain of Jars airfield which was now within easy mortar range of Pathet Lao positions, to Muong Phanh, six miles to the north-west. Here he was joined by Phoumist reinforcements and eventually set up a joint headquarters with them. His troops were necessarily re-equipped with American weapons now that there was no ammunition for those given them by the Russians, a fact which confirmed their alliance with Phoumi.

Attempts by the International Control Commission, by the British and Russian ambassadors, and by Prince Souvannaphouma to halt the renewed outbreaks of skirmishing failed or were frustrated. Artillery and mortar duels became frequent and there appeared in the Plain of Jars, for the first time in Laos, what might almost be called a battle front. There were repercussions elsewhere. The Pathet Lao were able to dispose of the Neutralists' position at Nhommarath, east of Thakhek, which had always been relatively weak, and to create a crisis of panic in the perennially insecure Phoumist garrison of Attopeu surrounded by Kha territory in the south.[57] Away from the towns, southern Laos was more than ever penetrated by the Pathet Lao.

Meanwhile, on 1 April 1963, the day after his return from a foreign tour with the king and Prince Souvannaphouma, Quinim was assassinated, apparently in revenge for the murder of Ketsana. The murder of a second left-wing Neutralist in Vientiane on 12 April led to a near panic and six days later the Pathet Lao ministers

[57] Ever since French explorers first reached Attopeu in 1867, it has been known as a nervous place. In Garnier's day it was a centre for gold and slaves. Slave-raiders made life precarious in the tribal areas and bandits preyed on the road and river trade. This is one of the reasons why the French found the area difficult to penetrate and why the Lao finds it impossible to control now. The population of the province is overwhelmingly Kha; the Lao ventures into the hills at his peril.

began to leave for Pathet Lao headquarters at Khang Khay whither Prince Souphanouvong had already retired. Some Neutralist ministers followed. Within ten months of the Geneva Agreement on the neutralization of Laos, the coalition government on which that agreement depended had effectively broken up.

As the military situation worsened Britain was eventually forced to admit failure in her attempts to concert a course of action with Russia, in spite of success by the staunch and indefatigable Mr. Harriman in talks with Mr. Khrushchev in April. In any case it began to be doubted if the Russian had any influence left in the Plain of Jars now that he was in open conflict with China. Prince Souvannaphouma resumed perforce his old task of trying to arrange meetings, but meetings now between the elements of his own cabinet, his efforts endlessly frustrated by military provocation and reaction on one side or the other. In December 1963 the murder of a Neutralist officer in Vientiane led to new departures for Khang Khay. In January 1964, when some chance of success for the prince began to appear, Phoumi's troops made another foray into the Kam Mon Plateau and were thrown back in such disorder that large numbers crossed the Mekong into Siam. The usual cries of alarm[58] were heard with diminished concern in Bangkok, for towards the end of 1963 Marshal Sarit had died and with him much of the continued Siamese interest in the fate of Phoumi.[59]

The position of the Neutralists was now rapidly crumbling. However, political talks between the three factions had already started again on the Plain of Jars when, on 19 April 1964, a group of younger right-wing officers in Vientiane, led by the chief of Phoumi's secret police, the half-Vietnamese Siho, in uneasy alliance with General Kouprasith, arrested Prince Souvannaphouma and took control of Vientiane. They said they wanted a 'truly neutralist' government, but the real object may have been to break the power of Phoumi. Phoumi escaped arrest but was powerless to intervene against his former protégé. Protests by the Western powers, at first ignored by the military junta, eventually secured the prince's release, but control of the Mekong towns

[58] That four Viet Minh and six Pathet Lao battalions had attacked: *Christian Science Monitor*, 31 January 1964.

[59] The end of the Diem régime in South Vietnam in November 1963 also meant a reduction in the external support for Phoumi.

remained in the hands of Siho and 'his thuggish-looking guards'.[60]

Phoumi was quickly deprived of the commercial interests which had been the real basis of his power. Speaking of military dictatorships in Siam, Mr. D. A. Wilson[61] has pointed out that a rising politician needs money to cement to himself followers 'who are not obligated by more personal ties of loyalty'. Phoumi had been a strong man somewhat on the Siamese pattern; the loss of his commercial assets removed the last props.

The Pathet Lao had not been slow to exploit the military situation in the Plain of Jars where three battalions of right-wing troops had for some time been stationed alongside the Neutralists at Muong Phanh. Disputes broke out among the Neutralist officers as to their attitude to the new *coup d'état*, and between the Neutralists and the right wing. When the ferment was at its height the Pathet Lao began to shell the right wing positions. As the troops withdrew the Neutralists' disputes grew hotter. Were they to help the Phoumist units by using their artillery against the Pathet Lao or not? Emissaries from the Pathet Lao pointed up the dilemma: well, they said, what about the affair in Vientiane? Did the Neutralists support a government controlled by Siho? Who was harvesting on the backs of the people now?[62] Was the agile Kouprasith to be trusted once more? If not the Neutralists had no choice but to make common cause with the Pathet Lao as they had done in 1961.

Under these agonizing pressures the Neutralist position disintegrated. Some, comparatively few, Neutralist officers and men joined Deuane and the Pathet Lao. Kong Lae and the rest were quickly pushed off the Plain of Jars, together with their right-wing allies, by the familiar mixture of Pathet Lao mortar shells and their own propaganda. They lost all their guns and most of their tanks.

Control over Phongsaly, where the attitude of the local Neutralist commander had always been ambivalent, passed to the Pathet Lao. In the meantime Prince Souvannaphouma had acquiesced in a remodelling of his government unacceptable to the Pathet Lao.

---

[60] *The Sunday Times*, 27 April 1964. The story of this *coup* and of its effects on a French adviser in Laos has been told in a somewhat romanticized form by Jean Lartéguy, *Les tambours de bronze* (Paris, 1965).

[61] D. A. Wilson, *Politics in Thailand* (New York, 1962), p. 135.

[62] See p. 115 above.

Some doubted whether he was any longer his own master. He asked the United States to carry out air reconnaissance of the Plain of Jars[63] and, when two aircraft were shot down, permitted jet fighter escorts from the American Seventh Fleet. There followed a series of air strikes in which the Pathet Lao headquarters at Khang Khay and other targets in and around the Plain of Jars were attacked.[64] Neutralist and right wing troops merged under the command of General Ouane, who had been Commander-in-Chief of the Laotian army before the *coup d'état* of Kong Lae. Kong Lae himself, furious at his betrayal by the 'spiritually foreign' Pathet Lao,[65] accepted whatever aid he could get and cleared his communications rearwards to Luang Prabang and Vientiane. The bamboo curtain had descended once more between the hills and valleys of Laos, much along the lines of ethnic division.

The Chinese threatened to intervene but did not do so. The North Vietnamese and Pathet Lao took up the new suggestion of Prince Sihanouk that there should be another international conference. The Russians, having said they wished to end their involvement in the Laotian problem, sent limited assistance to the North Vietnamese. The British, on whose patient diplomacy the issue of peace and war in Laos had turned twice in a decade, renewed their search for ways to peace. The French, having established relations with Communist China, favoured the calling of a conference to deal with the Indo-Chinese problem as a whole.

For by the beginning of 1965 the situation in Vietnam had begun to overshadow the continuing crisis in Laos, where another *coup d'état* in January 1965 had driven Phoumi and Siho into exile in Siam, leaving Prince Souvannaphouma free from their irresponsible pressures. In February 1965 the United States carried out a series of sharp air raids on North Vietnam, in retaliation for

[63] Dommen, op. cit., p. 238, and Grant Wolfkill, *Reported to be Alive* (London, 1966), pp. 273–4, show that this had been going on since 1962.

[64] 'The United States disclaimed responsibility for the attack (on Khang Khay), but the *New York Times* revealed that some of the pilots were nationals of Thailand, the first time that military personnel of Thailand had been publicly, and without an official denial, implicated in the Laos conflict.' Dommen, op. cit., p. 259.

[65] Field, op. cit., p. 372, quoting Kong Lae. In October 1966 Kong Lae himself was forced into exile, the internal political differences in his country, which he had once tried to solve, having finally proved too much for his simplicity.

rebel attacks on American bases and advisory staffs in the south. It was soon evident that the Americans had decided to take the guerrilla war in South Vietnam, which they were convinced depended on North Vietnamese direction and supplies, into their own hands. American and South Vietnamese aircraft carried the war further and further into the north. More and more United States troops were moved into South Vietnam. The American President was determined to finish the task he had undertaken. The Lao watched, content perhaps for a solution of his own problem to be delayed, so long as the war was waged over his head rather than across his territory.

ADDITIONAL NOTES TO CHAPTER VII

1. The Americans tended to criticize the French for having made no attempt to enlist the hill peoples in the Laotian army. See, for example, Dommen, op. cit., pp. 272–3. The criticism is only partly valid. There were several hill Thai battalions in the French army at Dien Bien Phu; under good leaders some of them had done well; some had done very badly indeed. There had also been Meos in the Laotian army; for example Colonel Vang Pao's own original 10th Infantry Battalion. But in general the French had found the Meos too self-centred to be useful. A Meo, they said, will fight for himself, his hilltops, his family, but for very little else. He would therefore accept arms and whatever else the Americans chose to give him, but in the long run he would use them against his own enemies and for his own purposes. He was not a reliable ally in the present war.

2. Dommen, op. cit., p. 214, refers to the reoccupation of Ban Nam Mo by Vietnamese and Pathet Lao as signs of a forthcoming attack. This operation was in fact the end of the action to clear a Phoumist probe towards Muong Sai. Ban Nam Mo is 24 miles from Muong Sai and about 16 from Nam Tha, and it was captured by the Pathet Lao at the end of April 1961. In December 1961 Phoumist forces moved towards Muong Sai from Nam Tha via Ban Nam Mo, as well as up the Nam Beng valley from the south. These forces were driven back by the Pathet Lao in January and Ban Nam Mo was reoccupied. Dommen gives only one half of this tale. If Phoumi's build-up at Nam Tha was due to danger of a Pathet Lao attack, it was a danger he had deliberately courted for political reasons.

3. See Chapter IV. On 6 March 1962 Mr. Dean Rusk and Mr. Thanat Khoman, the Siamese Foreign Minister, issued a joint statement in Washington. They agreed that 'S.E.A.T.O. provides the basis' for collective assistance to Siam in case of Communist armed attack. The U.S. intended to give full effect to its obligation under the treaty, but this did not depend upon the prior agreement of all other parties . . . 'since this treaty obligation is individual as well as collective'. *Department of State*

Bulletin, 26 March 1962. Nuechterlein, op. cit., pp. 228–36 deals extensively with Siamese expressions of nervousness at this time. Once more one of the motives appears to have been to secure more aid for Siam, this time because of the increase in aid to South Vietnam which had followed General Taylor's visit to Saigon at the end of 1961.

4. Dommen's account is confirmed in general by Schlesinger, op. cit., p. 451: 'Speaking with brutal frankness, Harriman informed Phoumi that he could not expect American troops to come to Laos and die for him and that the only alternative to a neutral Laos was a communist victory. Phoumi was still unyielding until April when the Thai Government, which had hitherto backed him, accepted the Harriman logic and urged him to join a government under Souvanna.' Mr. Harriman appears also to have threatened Phoumi with a suspension of U.S. military aid which had not been affected by previous cuts: Nuechterlein, op. cit., p. 234.

5. Warner, *The Last Confucian* (London, Penguin, 1964), p. 266, states that there was a Pathet Lao attack, although there was no fighting: 'An army Dakota, unaware that anything was amiss, attempted to land, and was promptly shot down. Its crew members were the only known casualties of this battle.' Neutralist sources said that there had been a mutiny. It may be that the truth lies between the two, in some variety of peaceful persuasion. The Pathet Lao aim was however clearly to stop the use of Muong Sing air-strip to reinforce Nam Tha; whatever means were required to achieve this would have been used.

6. Dommen, op. cit., pp. 213–17, and Warner, op. cit., p. 267, give contrasting views of the Nam Tha affair. Dommen regards it as a Viet Minh initiative to force the pace of political negotiations. Warner thinks it improbable that Phoumi planned the crisis in order to involve the West militarily but continues: 'What Phoumi wanted and desperately needed was a major break in the cease-fire and a chance to cause a last-minute upset at Geneva.'

It is possible to agree that both sides needed an incident. However, Prince Souphanouvong would have prevented the occupation of Nam Tha if he could, because he was aware of the international sensitivity about the place which had developed. Phoumi's plan succeeded in spite of this because the local Pathet Lao commander could not resist the temptation to occupy Nam Tha after it had been abandoned.

7. Speech to the United Nations General Assembly, 27 Sept. '62. See Paul Sithi-Amnuai, 'Thailand and Neutralism' in *Far East Economic Review* (Hong Kong, 10 Jan. '63). Insor, op. cit., p. 132, says that 'responsible circles' began to talk of neutrality 'if the West forsook Thailand'. The cooling of U.S.–Siamese relations at this time was, however, partly due to the decision of the International Court in Cambodia's favour on the Preah Vihear case, to Cambodia's requests for more U.S. military aid, and to deliveries to Cambodia of U.S. military equipment already due which happened to be made at about this time: Nuechterlein, op. cit., pp. 249–57.

8. See E. H. S. Simmonds: 'The Evolution of Foreign Policy in Laos' in *Modern Asian Studies*, II, 1 (1968), p. 21.

Despite the growth of Sino-Soviet differences generally, a degree of Communist solidarity was displayed during the Geneva negotiations of 1961–2. However, while the People's Republic of China and the D.R.V. saw Geneva as a small step forward in a continuing struggle, the Soviet Union appears to have hoped that a genuine slackening of tension would be achieved. Once it became clear that the civil war was being resumed, the Soviet Union found itself in an embarrassing position in relation both to Peking and Hanoi . . . . Moscow could not afford to be seen as applying a brake without losing further influence in Hanoi, which by now had little room for manoeuvre, and least of all could it appear to be giving independent support to the neutralists.

CHAPTER VIII

Conclusion

FOR over a thousand years the Indo-Chinese peninsula has been the scene of a conflict between the Indian-influenced kingdoms to the south and west of the Annamitic Chain, and the sinicized Vietnamese, pressing southwards with their colonists from the over-crowded delta of Tongking. It is not so much a matter of cultural differences, manners, or ways of thought, although after a millennium the yawning gulf that lies between the austere and self-contained civilization of China and the tolerant earthiness of Hindu cultures, adds an inevitable measure of mutual dislike to the antique fears and ambitions of thirty generations. It is a matter of land; the need for living space on the one hand, and the fear of conquest and extermination on the other.

At the end of the seventeenth century the encroaching Vietnamese, having established themselves in Saigon, were pushing their colonies westwards into Cambodia and extending their influence through Laos to the borders of Siam. A century later Siam, in her own defence, had asserted her control over Laos and was competing with Vietnam for power in Cambodia. When the French arrived in the middle of the nineteenth century, the two great Indo-Chinese peoples faced each other across what might have been called a neutral zone, which comprised much of the territory that is now Laos and Cambodia. In the north were mountain states such as Xieng Khouang and the Sipsong Chau Thai, that had traditionally paid tribute to their neighbours on both sides of the mountains, while in the south Cambodia acknowledged Siamese and Vietnamese suzerainty at the same time. In between lay the belt of territory east of the Mekong and west of the Annamitic Chain, which was part depopulated as a defensive measure by Siam, and part inhabited by sturdy hill peoples whom neither side had ever been able to bring under control.

Over Vietnam and over the whole of this neutral zone France

extended her empire. She based its prosperity upon the vigour of the Vietnamese who were seven times as numerous as her Laotian and Cambodian subjects, and it was naturally in the Vietnamese areas that the main economic development took place. Hence France came to see her imperial problems much as a Vietnamese emperor might have seen them; the logic of geography and of the massive population of Vietnam drove her to rule as a Vietnamese might have done. The problem of over-population she adopted as her own, she encouraged Vietnamese migration from Tongking into the empty lands, subordinated the interests of Cambodian and Lao, and took what France and Vietnam wanted from the Siamese.

In consequence the traditional fears, hatreds, enmities, and ambitions of the peninsula were immeasurably increased. While the French peace endured indeed—and it was intended to endure—Cambodia, Laos, and even Siam knew that they had little to fear. But all the populations doubled, and when French power cracked the Vietnamese was more vigorous, more ambitious than ever, and his neighbours more conscious than ever of the danger he represented.

The end of the Second World War and the establishment of Mao Tse-Tung as master of China soon led to a new crisis. In 1946 the Vietnamese had begun their nationalist war against the French. The fact that they fought it under Communist leadership and with Chinese help brought the Americans to the aid of France. The defeat of France in 1954 brought them, with their allies in S.E.A.T.O., on to the side of the Siamese, whose anxieties about the reviving power of Vietnam, backed by the resurgence of their even older Chinese enemy, were by this time beginning to be realized, if not understood. It was thought that if the Siamese position could be sufficiently strengthened, a neutralized Laos would serve as a protective pad to the north and north-east of Siam—the part played by the whole zone from Dien Bien Phu south to Cambodia in the nineteenth century—and so avert the larger clash that was threatened between East and West. The essence of the settlement at Geneva in 1954 was, in the words of Mr. Anthony Eden, who saw the problem in its larger framework: 'that Laos should remain as an independent and neutral buffer between China and Siam. It was therefore essential that the United States should not attempt to establish any military influence. Any attempt to do so was bound to provoke some counter move by China.'

Between the United States, for whom the conflict was ideological,

and China, for whom the prize was the security of her southern
borders, there lay a hidden difficulty. Modern Laos was no longer
partly depopulated, partly neutral, as the buffer zone had been a
hundred years earlier. Against the actual or potential hostility of
over half its mixed peoples, Laos was dominated by a Lao majority. Most of its non-Lao elements had strong kinship links across
the border with North Vietnam. The Lao community, on the other
hand, which was not without its own quarrels, was in effect an extension across the Mekong of one of the largest ethnic groups in Siam.
The peoples of Laos were thus much more likely to take the part
of one or other of their two neighbours than to unite against them.
Unless this tendency to division could be overcome—and it had
already been exploited by the Viet Minh in the formation of the
Pathet Lao, which profited from the Lao fear of the Vietnamese—
Laos could not function satisfactorily as a buffer state.

The situation was only too well understood by the Siamese,
who had not been parties to the Geneva Agreement, and by the
North Vietnamese who had accepted the removal of their forces
from Laos with reluctance. Neither of the two neighbours of Laos
was prepared to see hostile bases in the Laotian hills.

Up to a point the formation of S.E.A.T.O. in 1954 reassured
Siam. In spite of S.E.A.T.O. the North Vietnamese had felt their
long-term interests in Laos safeguarded by the promised integration of their Pathet Lao allies into the national structure of the
country. The United States took over from the French the duty
of backing the Laotian economy. Prince Souvannaphouma began
the thorny task of building national unity and, in spite of outbursts of nervousness or intransigence on the part of his neighbours,
came to a reasonable agreement with the Pathet Lao in 1957.
When, however, it appeared in 1958 that the process of integration
had given the Pathet Lao undue political influence, Siamese and
American apprehensions took charge. Prince Souvannaphouma was
forced from the scene. The Pathet Lao were deprived of their
positions in the government and subjected to increasing harass-
ment. In 1959 measures were taken to end the independence of
their two remaining military units; when one of these decamped the
Pathet Lao leaders were arrested. With the aid of the North
Vietnamese the rebellion was revived. By the end of 1959 the conflict was no longer a purely Laotian affair. The United States was
now hardly less committed on the one side than was North Viet-

nam on the other; Laos had become a theatre of the Cold War.

As the issue was joined, Siam needed strong friends in Laos, the United States needed anti-Communist ones. Now that Marshal Sarit was master of Siam, who could be more suitable for both roles than Sarit's kinsman Phoumi Nosavan? With General Phoumi rising to power, Siamese interests seemed secure against Vietnam and China, as well as those of the United States in the continuing battle against Communism. In the spring of 1960 the general organized the elections and emerged as virtual dictator of Laos.

The consequences of the abandonment of neutralism were to prove disastrous. Pathet Lao propaganda, the indoctrination of potential village leaders in North Vietnam or China, not so much with Communist ideas as with anti-government ones, and a very few armed men, had already enlarged the areas all over the country which were out of government control. It had become impossible for the administration to pass on the benefits of foreign economic aid to the rural mass of the population even if it wished to do so. Such benefits as were not frustrated by corruption remained concentrated in the Mekong valley centres and in a few relatively accessible areas. All the Pathet Lao had to do was to send a handful of villagers to a valley town, in order to prove conclusively to peasant minds the accusations of government chicanery and indifference on which their propaganda rested. When they were forced back into insurgency, therefore, by the political swing to the right, the Pathet Lao had a much stronger rural base.

In order to cope with the renewed insecurity, the Laotian army was re-equipped, strengthened, and retrained, but while there was always something of fantasy in its efforts to crush the Pathet Lao, its sojourns in the countryside, even in areas which had not always been hostile, tended further to alienate the population from the government. This was what the French had found in the Indo-China war. The attempt to solve the essentially political and social problem by military force simply drove people who would not otherwise have been attracted by Communism into the Pathet Lao camp.

It was against this situation of intense national discomfort that Captain Kong Lae rebelled in August 1960. In the following month Prince Souvannaphouma began his second major attempt to create national unity. This time it was not merely a matter of reconciling a splinter group with a nationalist-minded majority as it had been in 1954, but of bringing into his own central, neutralist position, two powerful extremes each supporting and supported by foreign interests. If the Siamese had been nervous in 1958, they were now alarmed. Phoumi overthrew the prince's government by force with Siamese and United States help. This brought Russia to the aid of the Neutralists. The Viet Minh, newly committed to a 'war of liberation' in South Vietnam, made the most of the opportunity. In the ensuing civil war Kong Lae, together with the assembled Pathet Lao forces encadred by Viet Minh, occupied most of the Laotian hill country, as well as the areas of eastern Laos which were of interest to the Vietnamese. The Geneva Conference was reconvened in May 1961. President Kennedy and Mr. Khrushchev agreed at their Vienna meeting in the following month that the kingdom of Laos should be neutral ground between them. It was indeed evident that none of the great powers wished to fight a war, hot or cold, in Laos.

The acceptance of Laotian neutralism by her American ally, however, redoubled the fears of Siam. To Marshal Sarit in Bangkok it seemed that the power of Siam's enemies had now reached the edge of the Mekong valley; it was the more important that control of the river plain from his side should be quite firm. Thus in spite of all the Americans could do, it was not until June 1962, when General Phoumi's headlong rush into fresh military disasters had obtained the emergency deployment of S.E.A.T.O. forces on the Mekong as the ultimate in reassurance to Siam, that his right-wing faction agreed to the formation of a coalition government under the Neutralist prince. By this time the development of the Sino-Soviet dispute and of the war in South Vietnam had gravely prejudiced the prospects of the Laotian international settlement, which for months had only awaited formal and unanimous Laotian assent.

The essentials of the Geneva bargain of July 1962 were not dissimilar to those of the 1954 agreement in so far as it had concerned Laos. Externally, the condition was that American and North Vietnamese troops should be removed from the country. Internally, the three factions needed to be kept in careful balance as they progressed towards integration. Neither of these conditions could be met. On the one hand, North Vietnamese involvement in the South Vietnamese insurgency had now reached a point where Laotian territory held by the Pathet Lao was assuming importance in the passage of reinforcements into South Vietnam. This traffic was specifically excluded by the 1962 settlement and it was quite unacceptable to the United States. On the other hand, the Russians, in the stress of their dispute with the Chinese, terminated their airlift to the Plain of Jars which had enabled the Neutralist forces to remain independent of the two extremes. Under the competitive pressures of right and left the Neutralist position crumbled. In March 1963 fighting broke out between factions within the Neutralist camp. At the same time, following a series of assassinations, the Pathet Lao leaders left Vientiane. The coalition government had broken up.

Field Marshal Sarit died in December 1963. There were *coups* within the right-wing faction in April 1964 and January 1965. These removed Phoumi from the scene and led eventually to the integration of most of the Neutralists and the right wing under Prince Souvannaphouma. All efforts to revive the coalition proved vain. Partition by altitude, along much the same contour line between valley and hill peoples that had limited direct Siamese authority in Laos before the arrival of the French, was an accomplished fact. The highlanders, who had once, in traditional neutrality, served and guarded the interests of both sides, were almost entirely controlled by the Pathet Lao in the interests of North Vietnam and China.

*   *   *

It may even now be over-pessimistic to say that the longest and most heroic of Prince Souvannaphouma's three attempts to achieve unity in Laos has failed, although the domestic problem he set out to solve does not at present admit of a domestic solution. Further progress in Laos seems indeed to depend on a settlement of the war that is being fought out by the United States in Vietnam, where—so it may sometimes seem to historically minded Siamese—the tables are being turned on the Vietnamese for the damage done to Siam on their behalf by France.

It is, however, perhaps inevitable that a further attempt will eventually be made to settle the Laotian question internationally, and this study cannot be concluded without an attempt to enumerate the factors which would then be relevant. If agreement between China and the United States on the neutrality of Laos can be assumed in the future as in the past, the problem will be the reconciliation of the interests and requirements of Siam, North

Vietnam, and Laos. It may be useful to attempt to define what these might be.

Siam's basic requirement would appear to be the exclusion of Vietnamese and Chinese power from the Mekong valley. She might be content for there to be a neutral zone in the mountains, but, if only because of her large Lao population, her vital interest in a Laos which includes part of the river plain is clear. She is therefore bound to demand special guarantees against damage to her interests in a neutralist settlement. A relationship of the traditional suzerain-vassal character between Laos and her neighbours would be difficult to translate into acceptable modern terms. The essential for Siam, however, is that Laos should acknowledge the special Siamese interest and that satisfactory guarantees should be provided.

For North Vietnam the permanent issue is not one of land and routes in Laos, but that of her own security. The Vietnamese do not need to colonize Laos. The problem of food and population in Tongking must be solved by peace and the restoration of trade with the South, and eventually by industrialization. Lao control of the traditionally neutral hills was, however, already risk enough for the northerners, who view Siamese and Lao with the same jaundiced eye, even before the United States became involved. Now it is more than ever necessary for North Vietnam that Siam should not be allowed to obtain a foothold there. Laotian neutrality is thus only acceptable to the North Vietnamese if their interests in the hills can be safeguarded, through Pathet Lao control, through the grant of semi-independence to the tribal areas, or by some special acknowledgement of the Laotian government which could be internationally and effectively guaranteed.

Between the two the Laotian has his own views. 'If we sit in a boat we must sit in the middle,' said Captain Kong Lae. But is the Laotian, in his ethnic diversity, still free to choose neutrality? Does the possibility still exist for him? Is it reasonable to expect that the Lao people of Laos will ever be neutral as between the mass of their kinsmen across the great river and the Vietnamese whom they fear and dislike; or that the mountain folk from north to south will ever prefer their traditional Lao enemies to their tribal fellows across the border in Vietnam?

If not there is little hope of stability within the frontiers of Laos.

APPENDIX I

REPORT OF M. FRANÇOIS DELONCLE, 19 JULY 1889

Made to the French Ministry of Foreign Affairs on the policy to be pursued *vis-à-vis* Siam in regard to Laos.

Translated from *Le Laos*, by L. de Reinach, ii, 19–29.

Fifteen years ago France established her first protectorate over Annam and Tongking. The object was to put an end to coastal piracy, to avenge the murder of Francis Garnier and his comrades, and to save the honour of the name of France in the Far East. At that time England only occupied lower Burma. Siam was confined within its natural limits and ruled by a wise regent. In 1882, when M. Harmand was successful in carrying French influence into Siam and M. Le Myre de Vilers was preparing to make our protectorate over Annam and Tongking effective, the British frontiers in Burma and those of Siam in Indo-China had not changed. Then Commandant Rivière was murdered, M. Harmand sent to Tongking, the old regent of Siam died, and a new, ambitious king came to the throne. France captured Hué and conquered the Red River and its delta.

At this point the English woke up, showered advice upon the king of Siam and encouraged him to profit by our wars with China to take over the hinterland of the empire of Annam. Meanwhile they themselves went up the Irrawaddy, took Mandalay, and with a stroke of the pen annexed the empire of Ava together with the tributary Shan states as far as the borders of China in the north, and across the Salween in the east. Since 1885 England and Siam have continued their forward march in parallel. The English have encountered difficulty after difficulty in confirming their annexations; they have not yet been able to go beyond the Salween and can hardly be said to have reduced the Shan states on the Chinese border. The Siamese, however, have been somewhat protected by the anarchy in which Annam and Tongking have been thanks to the continual disorganization of our colonial administration. They have insinuated themselves regardless into one after another of the territories which everybody knows belong to our protectorate. Not content with reviving their pretensions to central Laos between the

Mekong and the Menam, they want to make the kingdom of Luang Prabang, our tributary state, into one of their own provinces. With an audacity unheard of on the part of a small state, Siam has sent in a handful of men to occupy the Annamite districts of Tran Ninh, Cammon, Camkeut, Lakhone, etc., on the other side of the Mekong. She has even dared to set up posts on the Black River. These are only a few days' march from the sea, from Lai Chau and from Hanoi. She has at the same time been raising embarrassments for us in Cambodia, where she has been supporting the rebellion of Si Votha in territories which fall within our sphere of influence under the Treaty of 1867. In order to leave us nothing but a desert, if one day our indignation against her many outrages should bring us to take back these usurped territories, she has carried off their meagre population of Cambodians, Laotians, and Annamites into slavery on the banks of the Menam: *'solitudines faciunt pacem'*. The cries of these unhappy people long went unheard. Annam, a prey to palace revolutions and civil war, did not resist the Siamese invasions, and our troops were too occupied with the pirates to be able to watch out for frontier incursions. However, the Annamite coast and the delta area were pacified some months ago; the government of Annam now fully understands that we are friends and allies and that we have a treaty obligation to preserve the integrity of the empire. Its reaction has been to load us with complaints against Siam and to call for all the help we can give. The latest despatches show a regular panic.

It is perhaps fortunate that if our army in Tongking and Annam has been incapable over recent years of dealing with Siamese aggression, at least our Foreign Office has been preparing for the day when we would have to take over the external rights of Annam. As early as 21 May 1884, M. F. Deloncle (the author), then on a secret mission to Mandalay, obtained from the Burmese Foreign Ministry written confirmation of certain passages in the credentials of the Burmese ambassadors in Paris, which stated among other things that 'the western bank of the Mekong is the limit of Burma; the eastern bank, from the point where the river leaves Chinese territory, to the frontier of Xieng Sen, is the boundary of French Tongking'. At this time M. F. Deloncle (Political Despatch from Rangoon No. 11, 27 May 1884) accurately predicted future Siamese encroachments and forcefully recommended that the Siamese should be brought to order by a *démarche* at Bangkok. He also provided France with a first class diplomatic argument which she could use to stop the English and the Siamese on the Mekong. However, a few months later the English took Mandalay and M. Deloncle was disgraced for having dared to outface England and to ask the king of Burma to recognize French rights.

The policy of anti-colonial reaction and the denigration of our efforts in Tongking which followed the events of 1885, encouraged the Siamese and the English in their forward policy. It took the mission of M. Pavie to Luang Prabang to enlighten the department on the progress of their audacity. M. Pavie's first reports raised no echo in Paris, Bangkok, or Saigon. Nevertheless orders were quickly sent to Hué and Bangkok; the colonial administration charged General Bégin to give vigorous support to M. Pavie and ordered Captain Luce to look into Annamite rights in Laos by examining the archives in Hué. The result of this new policy has been that in less than six months all the Chinese bands which were disturbing the north-west frontier of Tongking have been pacified, the Sipsong Chau Thai—a Tongkingese province which had been occupied by the Siamese—has been completely evacuated; it has been possible to make a topographical report on the whole of north Laos; the essentials of a map of Indo-China have at last been assembled, and advanced posts have been established at the places most threatened by the Siamese invasion. All this has been done without bloodshed, thanks to the policy followed by M. Pavie which M. F. Deloncle, in his political despatch no. 11 from Rangoon on 27 May 1884 had seen as the only one capable of regaining our lost frontiers.

The reports and maps of the Pavie Mission, the official documents gathered by Captain Luce in the archives of Hué—which enabled General Bégin, C-in-C in Indo-China, to send to the department a definitive report on the indisputable territorial rights of Annam and Cambodia—the journey notes which M. Deloncle brought back from Cambodia, the interpretation of the old Annamite and Chinese maps done by Captain Luce, and lastly a new and profound study of the map attached to the Treaty of Peking showing the boundaries of Tongking: these are the elements which have made it possible to draw up the enclosed map, which sets out for the first time our precise claims in Indo-China. It also shows the smallest area which our empire should cover if we are to take advantage of the conquests of Cochin-China, Cambodia, Annam, and Tongking, which have cost us so much money and so many men.

The essential points can be seen on the map. They are:

(1) The frontiers of the empire of Annam should be moved forward at least as far as the east bank of the Mekong. The hinterland is mostly inhabited by aboriginal tribes. It should be attached to the coastal provinces as was the case before the Siamese occupation.

(2) Among these territories some, such as those which neighbour Cochin-China in the area of the Se-Bang-Hien, should be returned to Cambodia. They belong to her just as much as did the provinces of old Cambodia which were to have been demarcated after the treaty of 1867 with Siam. This abominable treaty unreasonably agreed to the abandonment to Siam, without com-

pensation, of the two Cambodian provinces of Battambang and Angkor. However, it stipulated a demarcation of the other provinces of ancient Cambodia which might have given some of these provinces back to the modern kingdom. Siam has been clever enough hitherto to avoid any demarcation and continues her unjustified usurpation of these essentially Cambodian territories which are indispensable to French plans.

(3) To the north of ancient Cambodia and running up to the west bank of the Mekong are small, more or less independent, Laotian states which used to pay or still pay tribute, some to Bangkok, others to Hué. Some, more particularly in the areas of Bassac, Oubon, Lakhon, and Xieng-Kane have sometimes even been integral parts of Annam. These states should remain open to our influence and we cannot allow Siam to annex or dominate them. Their political relations with us are analogous to those of the Shan States (Xieng-Mai and others) with England. England will never allow the Shan States, above all Xieng-Mai, to become openly Siamese. She has already taken precautions to this effect. We must take measures of our own, following the English example which we can use as an argument.

(4) The strategic and commercial position of Luang Prabang is all-important. The kingdom used to pay tribute to Annam and Siam every three years. Now, however, under the pretext of clearing out of the kingdom the Hos (Chinese bands which invaded it when we were conquering Tongking), the Siamese have established a Royal Commissioner there with full powers, and Bangkok considers Luang Prabang a Siamese province. It would be a good thing to put everybody back in their places. Certainly those extremely competent Englishmen, McLeod, Yule, and Colquhoun, did recognize our rights over Luang Prabang in their reports. However they recommended to their government that this extremely important position on the Mekong should one day be seized.

(5) The English are less categorical regarding the provinces of Muong Lu between Luang Prabang and China. Their Press thinks that England should possess all that is not definitely part of Tongking and Annam, but considers that the difficulties of occupation make it perhaps not worth trying. The forward British columns are still fighting on the west bank of the Salween. The warlike Burmese Shan states of Xieng Tong and Xieng Hong on the west bank of the Mekong are preparing to resist them vigorously. There has been much talk lately of missions which the Rangoon government is supposed to have sent in the direction of Xieng

Hong, to study ways of taking the country! So far none of these
missions has appeared and in fact unrest in Upper Burma is
hampering British progress towards the Mekong. We French on
the other hand, thanks to M. Pavie, already possess posts commanding the Nam Hou, a few days' journey from Xieng Hong
which is the nexus of all Laotian routes to China. We should not
therefore at any price admit that Xieng Hong has for some time
been subjected to Burma and China as well as to Tongking. The
princes who administer it send mules as tribute to Mandalay and
tea to Peking. Before the conquest of Mandalay by the English
the Burmese government gave M. Deloncle a declaration re-
nouncing its own rights over these territories in favour of French
Tongking. Moreover M. Deloncle found during his stay at
Semao in 1884 that China had on her side given up her protectorate, causing thereby much embarrassment to government
officials in Yunnan. In Garnier's day and also in McLeod's these
officials were grumbling about having to maintain order which
was continually being disturbed by the comings and goings of
bands from north and south, successively looting the country
like the Grandes Compagnies aux Marches in the Middle Ages.
When M. Constans signed an agreement in Peking for the demarcation of Tongking, which made the Black River the frontier
from Lai Chau, the Marquis Tseng stated that Muong Lu had
deliberately been left to France by China, and that China was
happy to have on her borders a serious, peaceful neighbour,
capable of maintaining law and order. It would not be difficult
to get this declaration in our favour confirmed and to obtain a
very clear demarcation of the frontier line which, under the
terms of the Treaty of Peking, should run from the Black River
to the Mekong along the line indicated on the attached map. We
shan't even have to insist on the rights of Annam on this point,
although these are incontestable, Captain Luce having given us
proof that in 1841 a Muong Lu embassy came to Hué with the
traditional tribute of gold and silver flowers for the Emperor of
Annam. In any case these territories belong geographically to
Annam. To stop at the Nam Hou would be to commit an outright scientific heresy. It might have been proposed when no map
existed, but it is impossible to sustain the theory now that the
attached map, drawn up by M. Deloncle with the aid of the old
official maps of Annam, shows that the territory between the
Nam Hou and the Mekong to the west has always been a natural
dependency of the Annamite Empire, and that the trough of the
Nam Hou is indispensable to our empire unless we want it
constantly invaded by Chinese bands from Yunnan. At the same

time we should remember that it is through this trough that Colquhoun and Hallet intend to push the railway from Moulmein or Bangkok into China, so as to drain towards Siam and Burma the trade of the Chinese Empire. The Siamese have willingly joined in the railway project. They put a million at the disposal of Sir Andrew Clark to make studies for it in the hope that the contribution will give them the right to push forward into this territory themselves. They were trying at the same time to establish a postal service up the Nam Hou to Semao. The arrival of our troops at Dien Bien Phu and the reconnaissance of the Pavie Mission north of the Nam Hou have stopped the implementation of these fine projects for the moment, and there is no doubt that if we follow the lines laid down by the Pavie Mission, Sir Andrew Clark and the Siamese will soon leave us a clear field. There it is; the attached map gives us, *a priori*, the right to a broad zone about twice as large as France.

We must take action as soon as possible to establish our possession of this area. The fact that M. Étienne is at the head of the Colonial Office will guarantee the rapid execution of the orders given. We propose the following action:

(1) Confirm the general instructions to the authorities at Hué, Saigon and Hanoi that the frontier areas should be pacified without bloodshed and that benevolent and energetic action by our diplomats should everywhere replace the provocative policy of certain military agents.

(2) Send M. Harmand to Bangkok on a special mission. His task should be not to prepare for a demarcation—this, we should at all costs avoid until we are in occupation of the territory that belongs to us—but to put an end to Siamese insolence by his presence and prestige, and to resume the vigorous policy in regard to these people by which, in 1882, he kept them within their frontiers and prevented their resisting our local action in Cambodia and Laos.

(3) Instruct our residents in Cambodia to encourage the Cambodians to remember their own authority over the frontier areas of ancient Cambodia. Maintain the national Cambodian character of our administration in Cambodia. Refrain as far as possible from introducing Annamites into the administration, as Cambodians have a natural dislike for Annamites and would side with the Siamese rather than put up with them. Encourage natural separatist tendencies in the ex-Cambodian provinces of Siam. Refrain from fixing the boundaries between Siam and Cambodia—as with those between Laos and Siam—but take

advantage of the lack of demarcation to infiltrate into these provinces Cambodian agents or commissioners taking their orders from Phnom Penh. Negotiate with Si-Votha, not to give him a pension and intern him in Saigon, but so that he will turn to our profit in old Cambodia the policy which he has hitherto used on Siam's behalf against us. France, Cochin-China and Cambodia should never ask Siamese permission to accredit or establish any commercial agent or official vice-consul in old Cambodia. We should take care that we do not recognize the legitimacy of Siamese encroachments in old Cambodia in some indirect way.

(4) Follow the same policy in central Laos, notably in the kingdoms of Oubon, Bassac, etc. Never recognize Siamese sovereignty over these states in writing. Enumerate the large number of kidnappings of Annamites and Cambodians by the Siamese authorities in these areas. Show that these crimes have no other object than to provide slaves for the Siamese officials in Bangkok; and, by a solemn decree, extend to old Cambodia and Laos the ordinance for the suppression of slavery which King Norodom issued at the instance of M. Thomson. On the passing of this decree we should hold a great public demonstration so as to prove to the English that we are pursuing an energetic anti-slavery policy in Indo-China. Then, at the appropriate moment, we should place with the various chiefs or kings of old Cambodia and Laos, commissioners for the suppression of slavery who are intended in fact to become virtual French residents.

(5) Nominate M. Pavie as non-resident consul and French commissioner in Laos. As consul accredited to the Siamese government, he would continue to take his orders from the Foreign Office, which would furnish him with the emoluments of his existing post of vice-consul at Luang Prabang. He would report to the Foreign Office and at the same time would maintain contact with M. Harmand at Bangkok. As commissioner he would be appointed and paid by the Colonial Office, or rather by the Protectorate. In his double capacity his orders would be:

(a) To continue to watch the Siamese at Luang Prabang, to check their influence with the king, to get the ancient tribute of Luang Prabang to Annam re-established, and to await a favourable moment to have the king sign a convention which, under one form or other, for some such object as the suppression of slavery, would put Luang Prabang under our protectorate.

(b) To administer the so-called 'pacification territories'; i.e.

the territories of Attopeu, Saravane and the phus of Cam-Lo, Lac-Bien, Tran-Tinh, Sipsong-Chau-Thai and Muong Lu, would be administered by M. Pavie as long as they are traversed or occupied by Chinese or Siamese bands. As and when they are evacuated by the bands they would be returned to the direct administration of the coastal residents, i.e. those of Quang-Ngai, Quang-Nam, Quang-Duc (Hué), Quang-Tri, Quang-Binh, Ha-Tinh, Nghe-An (Vinh), Than-Hoa and Hong-Hoa. M. Pavie would arrange for the evacuation of these territories as he has already done for the Sipsong-Chau-Thai—without bloodshed. Officers, devoted as he is to the true colonial policy, men such as Colonel Pernot and MM. Pennequin, Pelletier, Laffitte, Degrasse, Nicolon, Cupet, Micheles, etc., should be put at his entire disposal for the establishment of the necessary posts, in agreement with the authorities of Annam and Tongking.

M. Pavie should moreover have the right to appoint such of his agents as he considers most suitable to exercise the powers of vice-consul in Luang Prabang.

M. Pavie should be furnished with a written commission from the king of Cambodia and the Emperor of Annam and should act throughout in their names so as to obtain the complete cooperation of the Cambodians and Annamites. It would be very helpful if he could equally be supplied with a special Chinese passport issued by the Tsung-Li-Yamen. Nothing would contribute more to the negotiations which are to be conducted with the Chinese bands, whom M. Pavie could if necessary turn into auxiliaries against the Siamese.

The detailed arrangements should be made direct by MM. Pavie and Luce at Saigon in agreement with the Governor General of Indo-China.

(6) M. Pavie should be given a special mission to assist him here and now in topographical, industrial and commercial exploration and in the provisional administration of the Laotian regions. The team should consist of one or two young officers or vice-residents from the Protectorate, who are acquainted with the Annamite or Cambodian languages, topographical officers such as Captain Cupet with experience of work in Indo-China, and finally traders and industrial engineers from private firms. The expenses of the team would be paid by the Protectorate except for those of the industrial and commercial agents, which would be borne by a

private syndicate such as that which MM. Leon Tharel and Lapierre propose to form. The topographical work under M. Pavie's orders should be directed by Captain Cupet, whose capacity in this respect is acknowledged. He should copy the successful methods of the English and Siamese, forming as it were native topographical groups composed mostly of young Cambodians trained at the Colonial School in Paris. These groups would be able to cover the country with operators who are used to the climate, who know the local languages, who would travel light and who would be able to make the initial penetration of peoples who often refuse to admit Europeans. The special mission would work quietly just as the Pavie Mission has always done, and would be at the disposal of the government when required for the demarcation of our frontiers with China. It would meanwhile complete the survey of upper Laos, giving priority to the exploration of Muong-Lu where, if circumstances permit, it would leave our commercial agents in a position to open the country peacefully to our civilization. The past achievements of these explorers assures us of the future. What they have already done is truly admirable. When they feel themselves encouraged and supported from home, nothing will stop them. They will lift the veil from these regions for us, regions where tea and opium are cultivated, where salt, coal and teak are already being extracted and where there are to be found musk, benzoin, lacquer, cinnamon, iron, copper, gold and precious stones; where the summits of the high plateaux rise to 4000 metres, where the climate is temperate and where Europeans could easily settle. They will show us that hitherto we have only possessed those parts of Tongking which are unsuitable to our colonial genius and our health. These deltas which we have acquired are certainly rich, but they are also wet, unhealthy and difficult for French labour to cultivate. To the north there await us salubrious and easy regions, accessible to our settlers, and full of produce which will repay five times over our expenses in getting them.

(7) The question of communications is fundamental. The Pavie Mission has reported the possibility of opening a speedy route to upper Laos via the Song-Ma and an even more rapid route via Vinh and Houten on the Mekong. But it is clear that if river craft can go up the Mekong as far as Luang Prabang and from there ascend the Nam Hou, this would be an excellent route of penetration from the point of view of time, cheapness and commercial facilities. M. Rueff, Director of Inland Waterways in Indo-China, has for some years been studying the problem of creating

a river service on the upper Mekong from above the rapids as far as Luang Prabang. He proposes to attach to the Pavie Mission at his own expense, an hydrographer who, in agreement with M. Pavie and the Protectorate authorities, would carry out complete soundings and make a report on which definite plans could be based. We should congratulate ourselves on this initiative for it must be remembered that Siam is also eager to see her flag flying on the Mekong and that there is talk in Bangkok of transporting a steam-boat overland to Luang Prabang. We must certainly not let ourselves be forestalled by the Siamese who are only the forerunners of the English and Germans.

This is the general outline of the policy which we envisage for Indo-China; it is in complete conformity with that which M. François Deloncle proposed in his despatch No. 11 from Rangoon on 27 May 1884; we can borrow our conclusions from that despatch:

Regarding the frontier with Burma the statements of the Mandalay government are completely satisfactory and also give us the right to a new series of extensions of our territory. The other territories between Annam, Tongking and Siam can be attached to us merely by a proclamation of the Emperor of Annam, supported of course by the despatch of a well escorted delegation in the direction of the Chinese bands with whom it will be necessary to negotiate (compare the 'summunds' of the Government of India with the Akas, Duphla, Abors, Mishmis, Khamptes, Singphos, etc.). See also Despatch No. 8 from Penang, 22 March 1884.

The Annamite, Laotian and Cambodian territories on the eastern bank of the Mekong farther south, where the encroachments of the Siamese have never been recognised by Annam and Cambodia—and particularly the basin of the Se-Bang-Hien, the Plateau des Bolovens, the Sieng-Pang and the eastern part of Stung-Treng (which still figures on the official list of Cambodian provinces) can be filched one by one without any difficulty from the hateful influence of Siam. Simple treaties with the local chiefs—in the Anglo-Indian manner—will make us masters of these areas. Siam will not be able to protest and our action will deliver this unhappy country from the odious slave-trade which the Siamese commissioners openly favour.

Our object should be to abolish slave-trading, commercial monopolies and the forced exactions which are crushing these poor people, and to substitute individual liberty, the right to private property, the spirit of initiative, enterprise and trade which characterise the Annamite democracy (sic); to use the strong expansionist qualities of the natives of Annam and Cambodia, furthering their penetration as our pioneer colonists, in the Siamese territories where they are often in a considerable majority (Lakhone, Bassac, Melu-Prey, Chanta-boun). Areas put under our flag by simple articles of alliance should not be treated as conquered territory, but should be given a simple and patriarchal form of government. Our policy should be to speak the truth, administer justice, be tactful, patient, firm and above all polite. We should respect the people's own pride, keep our promises and make them keep theirs, and, as a general rule govern with and through the native chiefs; this should be the programme, this would be the secret of our expansion in the Mekong and Menam valleys. With it, borrowed as it is from the English colonisation of the Straits and Sarawak and from the Dutch administration in Java, nothing would be easier for us than to establish, next, our protectorate over Luang Prabang. The nearest French resident would obtain it without a shot fired. But we must face the fact that this policy will involve us in difficulties with the Siamese government who will use it as an excuse to demand that the frontiers of Siam and Annam should now be demarcated. It would be a great mistake to agree to this even in principle. It should be perfectly plain to all that if France wants her empire in Indo-China to last, she should from now onwards refuse to make with Siam any arrangements whatever which would have the direct or indirect effect of affirming or reviving the independent character of the kingdom. Our diplomats should rather seize every opportunity of intervening in Siam's internal and external affairs, should assume every day more authority there and, without provoca-tion, dominate the palace by a firm and resolute surveillance. If this is done the Siamese officials will quickly lose any remaining will to resist French pressure, their temperament will become more ac-commodating and they will gradually get used to submitting to us.

Today, as in 1884, there is no other possible policy. It should be adopted without hesitation, for if we delay further Siam's audacity will increase by the measure of our indecision. Before long she will have gone so far that it will be too late to fight her on the Mekong; then we shall have to go to the heart of the matter and, willy nilly, occupy Bangkok to save our empire.

The moment favours us. The Colonial Office is under the direction of an eminent, active and energetic man. M. Étienne should be entrusted with the task of organizing Laos and of protecting our frontiers in accordance with the practical and prudent programme that we have just outlined.

APPENDIX II

EXTRACT FROM A REPORT BY M. AUGUSTE PAVIE TO THE FRENCH COMMANDER-IN-CHIEF IN INDO-CHINA, dated: 5 July 1888

(Mission Pavie, géographie et voyages, vol. VII, pp. 130–2)

The mountainous region between the Black River and Laos proper is divided politically into three parts which in Laos are called:

Muong Sip-song Chau thais (the country of the twelve Thai cantons),

Muong Hua panh ha tang hoc (the country of the five or six thousand springs) [now Sam Neua],

Muong Pou Eun (the country of the Pou Euns: called Tran Ninh by the Vietnamese) [now Xieng Khouang].

It is inhabited by peoples differing in customs and language, who originated in China or in the eastern borders of Tibet. We cannot say at present how long they have been established in their present homes or give their order of arrival. Of necessity they live side by side in neighbourly fashion under the authority more apparent than real of two among them, the Pou Thais and the Pou Euns. These two peoples are numerous and prefer to live in the valleys and on the plateaux, while the rest dwell in the forests or on the mountain tops.

The Pou Thais are spread across the Sipsong Chau Thai and . . . [Sam Neua], and are also generally in the majority in the region between the Tongking delta and China. The Pou Euns inhabit . . . [Xieng Khouang], which is the only place where they are to be found. . . .

The Pou Thais . . . are of the race which has peopled Laos and Siam, as the similarity of their languages proves and as the Laotian annals assert. The Pou Euns differ little from them and doubtless have the same origin, though closer contact with the Vietnamese is perhaps responsible for small differences in their manners and customs.

All three parts of the region have a feudal system under hereditary chiefs. They have paid tribute to the Vietnamese from early times. Nevertheless they retain a certain autonomy and are completely inde-

pendent of each other. This is probably due to the difficulties of assimilation with Vietnam which arise from the unhealthy climate and from
geographical factors. Confined as they are between Vietnam and Laos,
from whom they obtain salt and basic necessities by barter, their way of
life makes them fearless neighbours and, even as vassals, only relatively
respectful of their suzerains with whom good relations are almost
obligatory. Their chiefs do not ever appear to have tried to weld them
into a nation. They are unwarlike, peaceable and extremely obedient.
Their docility may nevertheless make it possible to use them extensively for defence purposes.

The Thais keep their distance from the Vietnamese who haven't a
very high idea of them. The marked gap between them is comparable
with, but less than, that which exists between the Cambodians and
Vietnamese in the south of Indo-China. One might explain it by the
difference of character which their different education gives to the two
races.

The Pou Thais and the Pou Euns observe what must be called pure
Buddhism, which came to them from Cambodia and Ceylon. It is to the
precepts of Buddhism that they owe the softness of character and the
honesty which you notice as soon as you are in contact with them. The
Buddhist religion, as much as the difference of race, has divided Indo-
China into two great blocs; on the one hand, Chinese Buddhism, on
the other the pure Buddhism of Thai and Khmer. The Khmers or
Cambodians introduced the dogmas of Ceylon into the peninsula and
they are still first as far as purity of religious observation and instruction are concerned. The Pou Thais received Buddhism last, that is to
say after the Siamese and Laotians. There are pagodas in their villages.
Chinese and Vietnamese influences, while curiously modifying its
practices, do not seem to have stopped the spread of this Buddhism.

APPENDIX III

THE ROYAL FAMILY OF LUANG PRABANG

ANOUROUT
King of Luang Prabang 1791-1817

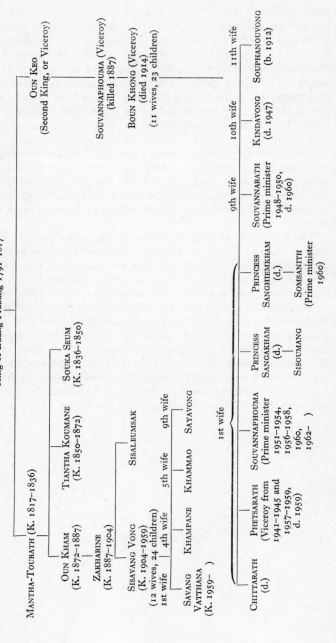

BIBLIOGRAPHY

BRITISH PARLIAMENTARY PAPERS:

Miscellaneous No. 16 (1954), *Documents relating to the Discussion of Korea and Indo-China at the Geneva Conference, April 27–June 15, 1954* (Cmd. 9186).

Miscellaneous No. 20 (1954), *Further Documents relating to the Discussion of Indo-China at the Geneva Conference, June 16–July 21, 1954* (Cmd. 9239).

South-East Asia Collective Defence Treaty, Manila, September 8, 1954 (Cmd. 9282).

Laos No. 1 (1955), *First Interim Report of the International Commission for Supervision and Control in Laos, August 11–December 31, 1954* (Cmd. 9445).

Laos No. 2 (1955), *Second Interim Report of the International Commission for Supervision and Control in Laos, January 1–June 30, 1955* (Cmd. 9630).

Laos No. 1 (1957), *Third Interim Report of the International Commission for Supervision and Control in Laos, July 1, 1955–May 16, 1957* (Cmnd. 314).

Laos No. 1 (1958), *Fourth Interim Report of the International Commission for Supervision and Control in Laos, May 17, 1957–May 31, 1958* (Cmnd. 541).

Laos No. 1 (1962), *International Conference on the Settlement of the Laotian Question, May 12, 1961–July 23, 1962* (Cmnd. 1828).

Treaty Series No. 27 (1963), *Declaration and Protocol on the Neutrality of Laos, July 23, 1962* (Cmnd. 2025).

Miscellaneous No. 25 (1965), *Documents relating to British Involvement in the Indo-China Conflict 1945–1965* (Cmnd. 2834).

OTHER OFFICIAL PAPERS:

Accord sur la cessation de tous actes hostiles dans les provinces de Sam Neua et Phongsaly, Royal Lao Government, Vientiane, 1955.

American Foreign Policy 1950–55, Department of State publication No. 6446, Washington, December 1957.

Annuaire statistique du Laos, Vientiane, yearly from 1950.

L'Année Politique, Presses Universitaires de France, Paris, annual volumes for 1953–1961.

L'Assemblée constituante Laotienne, 15 Mars–10 Mai 1947, Royaume du Laos, Saigon, 1949.

Briefing Notes on the Royal Kingdom of Laos, Vientiane, U.S. Information Agency, 1959.

Bulletin officiel du Royaume du Laos, Vientiane, quarterly from 1952.

Bulletin statistique du Laos, Vientiane, quarterly from 1950.

Comments by the Department of State and I.C.A. on the Report of the House Committee on Government Operations, Washington, 1959.

Constitution du Royaume du Laos, 11 Mai, 1947. Texte revisé et adopté par le Congrés National en sa séance du 29 Septembre, 1956, Vientiane, Royal Lao Government, 1957.

Economic Cooperation Agreement and Notes between the United States of America and Laos, Washington, Government Printing Office, 1952.

Lao Presse, Vientiane, daily from 1953.

Laos, Central Office of Information, London, February 1958, pamphlet No. R.3706.

Laos, Political Developments 1958–60, Central Office of Information, London, January 1960, supplement to above.

Laos, Central Office of Information, London, January 1961, pamphlet No. R.4935.

Laos, Political Developments, 1961, Central Office of Information, London, 1961.

Report of the Security Council Sub-Committee under Resolution of 7 September, 1959, New York, U.N. Security Council, 5 November 1959.

Statement of His Excellency the Prime Minister on the Situation in the Kingdom of Laos, 21 September, 1960, Thailand, Ministry of Foreign Affairs.

A Threat to the Peace: North Vietnam's effort to Conquer South Vietnam, United States State Department Publication No. 7308, in two parts, Washington, December 1961.

Thailand: *How Thailand Lost her Territories to France*, Bangkok, 1940.

United States Aid Operations in Laos: Hearings before a Subcommittee of the Committee on Government Operations, House of Representatives, Eighty-Sixth Congress, First Session, Washington, 1959.

United States Aid Operations in Laos: Seventh Report by the Committee on Government Operations, June 15, 1959, Washington, 1959.

United States Information Service, Vientiane, broadcast and other transcripts issued 14 August–29 October 1960.

United States: *Public Papers of the Presidents of the United States, John F. Kennedy, 1961*, Washington, 1962.

ACCOUNTS OF TRAVEL AND EXPLORATION:

AYMONIER, ÉTIENNE, *Voyage dans le Laos*, two vols., Paris, 1895-7.

BOWRING, SIR JOHN, *The Kingdom and People of Siam, with a narrative of the mission to that country in 1855*, London, 1857.

CAPLY, MICHEL, *Guérilla au Laos*, Paris, 1966.

CARNÉ, L. DE, *Voyage en l'Indochine et dans l'empire chinois*, Paris, 1872.

Carte de l'Indochine, Capitaines Cupet, Friquegnon, et de Malglaive, Paris, 1895. (See also below, *Mission Pavie*.)

Carte ethnolinguistique de l'Indochine, École Française d'extrême orient, 1949.

COUSSOT, A., and RUEL, H., *Douze mois chez les sauvages du Laos*, Paris, 1898.

DARTIGE DU FOURNET, LOUIS, *Journal d'un commandant de la Comête*, Paris, 1896.

FRANCK, H. A., *East of Siam, Ramblings in the five divisions of French Indo-China*, New York, 1926.

GARNIER, F., *Voyage d'exploration en Indochine*, Paris, 1885.

GENTIL, PIERRE, *Remous du Mekong*, Paris, 1950.

GUTZLAFF, 'The Country of the Free Laos' in *Journal of the Royal Geographical Society*, XIX (1849), pp. 33-41.

HERVEY, H., *Travels in French Indo-China*, London, 1928.

LAJONQUIÈRE, E. LUNET DE, *Le Siam et les Siamois*, Paris, 1906.

LEFÈVRE, E., *Un voyage au Laos*, Paris, 1898.

LEGENDRE, S. J., *Land of the White Parasol and the Million Elephants*, London, 1937.

LEVY, P., 'Two Accounts of Travels in Laos in the 17th Century' in *Kingdom of Laos*, R. de Berval (ed.), Saigon, 1959.

LEWIS, N., *A Dragon Apparent*, London, 1951.

LYAUTEY, L.-H., *Lettres du Tonkin et de Madagascar*, Paris, 1921.

McCARTHY, J., *Surveying and Exploring in Siam*, London, 1900.

McLEOD, W. C., 'Abstract Journal of an expedition to Kiang Hung on the Chinese frontier, starting from Moulmein on 13 December, 1836' in *Journal of the Asiatic Society of Bengal*, VI, part 2 (1837).

Mission Pavie, eleven volumes, Paris, 1898-1919.

Études Diverses:

Volume I: 'Recherches sur la littérature du Cambodge, du Laos et du Siam', A. Pavie, 1898.

Volume II: 'Recherches sur l'histoire du Cambodge, du Laos et du Siam', A. Pavie, 1898.

Volume III: 'Recherches sur l'histoire naturelle de l'Indochine orientale', A. Pavie, 1904.

Géographie et Voyages:

Volume I: 'Exposé des travaux de la mission, 1879–1889', A. Pavie, 1901.

Volume II: 'Exposé des travaux de la mission, 1889–1895', A. Pavie, 1906.

Volume III: 'Voyages au Laos et chez les sauvages du sud-est de l'Indochine', Capitaine Cupet, 1900.

Volume IV: 'Voyages au centre de l'Annam et du Laos et dans les régions sauvages de l'est de l'Indochine', Capitaine de Malglaive et Capitaine Rivière, 1902.

Volume V: 'Voyages dans le Haut-Laos et sur les frontières de Chine et de Birmanie', P. Lefèvre-Pontalis, 1902.

Volume VI: 'Passage du Mekong au Tonkin, 1887–1888', A. Pavie, 1911.

Volume VII: 'Journal de marche (1888–1889), Événements du Siam (1891–1893)', A. Pavie, 1919.

Volume VIII: 'Atlas, notices et cartes', 1903.

MOUHOT, HENRI, *Voyages dans les royaumes de Siam, de Cambodge, de Laos et autres parties centrales de l'Indochine*, F. de Lanoye (ed.), Paris, 4th edn., 1883.

NEALE, F. A., *Narrative of a Residence in Siam*, London, 1852.

NGO VAN CHIEN, *Journal d'un combattant Vietminh*, Paris, 1955.

NORDEN, H., *A Wanderer in Indo-China*, London, 1931.

NORMAN, H., *Peoples and Politics of the Far East*, London, 1907.

ORLÉANS, PRINCE HENRI D', *Around Tonkin and Siam*, London, 1894.

PAVIE, A., *À la conquête des coeurs*, Paris, 1921.

RAQUEZ, A., *Pages Laotiennes*, Hanoi, 1902.

ROCHET, C., *Pays Lao, le Laos dans la tourmente*, Paris, 1946.

SMYTH, H. WARRINGTON, *Five Years in Siam*, London, two vols., 1898.

WOODTHORPE, COLONEL R. G., 'The Country of the Shans', in *Journal of the Royal Geographical Society*, Vol. VII, No. 6, July, 1896.

ZUKROWSKI, WOJCECH, 'I was Konglé's shadow', a series of articles in *Literaturnaya Gazeta*, Moscow, 28 February and 2, 4, and 7 March, 1961.

UNPUBLISHED THESES:

MURTI, B. S. N., *Anglo-French Relations with Siam, 1880–1904*. Unpublished Ph.D. thesis, London University, 1952.

NGO-BA-TAY, *Les difficultés Franco-Anglaises à propos du Siam durant la période 1887–1904*. Unpublished master's thesis, Institut d'études politiques, University of Paris, 1951–2.

BIBLIOGRAPHIES:

HAY, S. N., and CASE, M. H., *Southeast Asian History, A Bibliographic Guide*, New York, 1962.

KÈNE, THAO, *Bibliographie du Laos*, Vientiane, 1958.

LAFONT, P. B., *Bibliographie du Laos*, École Française d'extrême orient, Paris, 1964.

MCKINSTRY, JOHN, *Bibliography of Laos and Ethnically Related Areas*, Berkeley, 1962.

GENERAL WORKS:

ANDERSON, LADY FLAVIA, *The Rebel Emperor*, London, 1960.

AYROLLES, L.-H., *Indochine ne répond plus*, Paris, 1948.

BARNETT, A. D. (ed.), *Communist Strategies in Asia*, London, 1963.

BATOR, VICTOR, *Vietnam, a Diplomatic Tragedy: origins of U.S. involvement*, London, 1967.

BEAUVAIS, R. DE, *Louis Delaporte, explorateur 1842–1925*, Paris, 1929.

BERTHELOT, A., *L'Asie ancienne centrale et sud-orientale, d'après Ptolémée*, Paris, 1930.

BERVAL, R. DE (ed.), *Kingdom of Laos*, Saigon, 1959: originally appeared in French as three special numbers of *France-Asie*, March, April, and May 1956.

BLANCHARD, WENDELL (*et al.*), *Thailand, its People, its Society, its Culture*, New Haven, Conn., 1957.

BODARD, L., *La guerre d'Indochine—l'enlisement*, Paris, 1963.

—— *La guerre d'Indochine—l'humiliation*, Paris, 1965.

BRIGGS, L. P., *The Ancient Khmer Empire*, Philadelphia, 1951.

BRIMMELL, J. H., *Communism in South East Asia*, London, 1959.

BRUK, S. I., *The Peoples of Indochina*, translation from Russian, U.S. Joint Publications Research Service, 1964.

BURCHETT, W. G., *Mekong Upstream*, Berlin, 1959.

—— *The Furtive War*, New York, 1963.

BUTTINGER, J., *The Smaller Dragon, a Political History of Vietnam*, New York, 1958.

CADY, J. F., *The Roots of French Imperialism in Eastern Asia*, Cornell, 1954.

CATROUX, GÉNÉRAL, *Deux actes du drame Indochinois*, Paris, 1959.

CHAKRABONGSE, PRINCE CHULA, *Lords of Life*, with introduction by Professor H. Trevor Roper, London, 1960.

CHALERMNIT PRESS CORRESPONDENT, *The Battle of Vientiane of 1960*, Bangkok, 1961.

CHENNAULT, C. D., *The Way of a Fighter*, New York, 1949.

CHURCHILL, W. S., *The Second World War*, vol. VI, London, 1954.

CLUBB, OLIVER E., Jr., *The United States and the Sino-Soviet Bloc in Southeast Asia*, Washington, D.C., 1962.

COAST, J., *Some Aspects of Siamese Politics*, New York, 1953.

COEDÈS, G., *Les états hindouisés d'Indochine et d'Indonésie*, Paris, new edn., 1964.

COLE, A. B. (*et al.*), *Conflict in Indo-China and International Repercussions, a Documentary History 1945–1955*, Ithaca, N.Y., 1956.

COLANI, M., *Mégalithes du Haut-Laos* (*Hua Pan, Tran Ninh*), Paris, two volumes, 1935.

Collective Defence in South-East Asia, Royal Institute of International Affairs, London, 1956.

CONDOMINAS, G., *Nous avons mangé la forêt*, Paris, 1957.

COWAN, C. D. (ed.), *The Economic Development of South-East Asia*, London, 1964.

CRIPPS, F., *The Far Province*, London, 1965.

CROSBY, SIR JOSIAH, *Siam: The Crossroads*, London, 1945.

CROZIER, B., *South East Asia in Turmoil*, London, 1964.

DARLING, FRANK C., *Thailand and the United States*, Washington, 1965.

DECOUX, AMIRAL, *À la barre de l'Indochine*, Paris, 1949.

DEVILLERS, P., *Histoire du Viet-Nam de 1940 à 1952*, Paris, 1952.

—— with J. LACOUTURE, *La fin d'une guerre*, Paris, 1960.

DEYDIER, H., *Introduction à la connaissance du Laos*, Saigon, 1952.

—— *Lokapala: génies, totems et sorciers du nord Laos*, Paris, 1954.

DOBBY, E. H. G., *Southeast Asia*, London, 1950.

DOMMEN, A. J., *Conflict in Laos*, London, 1964.

DOUMER, P., *L'Indochine Française*, Paris, 1905.

DRUMMOND, R., and COBLENTZ, G., *Duel at the Summit*, New York, 1960.

DUCOROY, MAURICE, *Ma trahison en Indochine*, Paris, 1949.

DUKE, PROFESSOR PENSRI (SUVANICH), *Les relations entre la France et la Thailande* (*Siam*) *au XIX siècle d'après les archives des Affaires Étrangères*, Bangkok, 1962.

EDEN, SIR ANTHONY, *Memoirs: Full Circle*, London, 1960.

—— as LORD AVON, *The Eden Memoirs—The Reckoning*, London, 1965.

EISENHOWER, D. D., *Mandate for Change, the White House Years 1953–56*, London, 1963.

ELSBREE, W. M., *Japan's Role in South East Asian Nationalist Movements*, Harvard, 1953.

ÉLY, GÉNÉRAL P., *Indochine dans la tourmente*, Paris, 1963.

EMERSON, R., MILLS, L. A., and THOMPSON, V., *Government and Nationalism in Southeast Asia*, New York, 1942.

FALL, B. B., *Le Viet-Minh 1945–60*, Paris, 1960.

—— *Street without Joy*, Harrisburg, Pennsylvania, 1961 (London, 3rd edn., 1963).

—— *The Two Vietnams: a Political and Military Analysis*, London, 1963.

—— *Viet-Nam Witness, 1953–1966*, London, 1966.

—— *Hell in a Very Small Place*, London, 1967.

FERRY, J., *Le Tonkin et la mère-patrie*, Paris, 1890.

FIELD, M., *The Prevailing Wind*, London, 1965.

FIFIELD, R. H., *The Diplomacy of Southeast Asia: 1945–1958*, New York, 1958.

—— *Southeast Asia in United States Diplomacy*, New York, 1963.

FIRTH, R., and YAMEY, B. S. (eds.), *Capital, Saving and Credit in Peasant Societies*, London, 1964.

FISTIÉ, P., *La Thailande*, Paris, 1963.

GAUDEL, A., *L'Indochine française en face du Japon*, Paris, 1947.

GAULLE, CHARLES DE, *Mémoires de guerre, l'unité, 1942–1944*, Paris, 1956.

—— *Mémoires de guerre, le salut, 1944–1946*, Paris, 1959.

GIAP, VO NGUYEN, *People's War, People's Army*, Hanoi, 1961.

—— *Dien Bien Phu*, Hanoi, 1962.

GOSSELIN, CAPITAINE, *Le Laos et le protectorat français*, Paris, 1900.

GOUROU, P., *L'utilisation du sol en Indochine française*, Paris, 1940.

GREY OF FALLODON, VISCOUNT, *Twenty-five Years*, London, two volumes, 1925.

GROSLIER, B. P., *Angkor, hommes et pierres*, Paris, 1956.

—— *Angkor et le Cambodge au XVIème siècle*, Paris, 1958.

HALL, PROFESSOR D. G. E., *A History of South-East Asia*, London, 2nd edn., 1964.

HALPERN, J. M., *Economy and Society of Laos, a Brief Survey*, Southeast Asia Studies, Yale University, 1964.

—— *Government, Politics and Social Structure in Laos, a Study of Tradition and Innovation*, Southeast Asia Studies, Yale University, 1964.

HAMMER, E. J., *The Struggle for Indochina*, Stanford, 1954.

—— *The Struggle for Indochina Continues*, Stanford, 1955.

HARVEY, G. E., *History of Burma*, London, 1925.

HONEY, P. J., *Communism in North Vietnam*, London, 1965.

HUDSON, G. F., *The Far East in World Politics*, London, 1937.

HULL, CORDELL, *Memoirs of Cordell Hull*, New York, two vols., 1950.

Indo-China, Geographical Handbook Series, Naval Intelligence Division, London, 1943.

INGRAM, J. C., *Economic Change in Thailand since 1830*, Stanford, 1955.

INSOR, D., *Thailand, a Political, Social and Economic Analysis*, London, 1963.

JAMES, R. R., *Rosebery*, London, 1961.

KAHIN, G. McT. (ed.), *Governments and Politics of Southeast Asia*, Cornell, 2nd edn., 1964.

—— *The Asian-African Conference*, Cornell, 1956.

KATAY DON SASORITH, *Contribution a l'histoire du mouvement d'indépendance national Lao*, Bangkok, 1948.

KATAY DON SASORITH, *Le Laos: son évolution politique, sa place dans l'union française*, Paris, 1953.

Keesing's Contemporary Archives, Bristol, annual volumes 1953 to 1965.

KEMP, P., *Alms for Oblivion*, London, 1961.

KENNEDY, D. E., *The Security of Southern Asia*, London, 1965.

LACOUTURE, J., and DEVILLERS, P., *La fin d'une guerre*, Paris, 1960.

LANCASTER, D., *The Emancipation of French Indo-China*, London, 1961.

LANDON, K. P., *Thailand in Transition*, Chicago, 1939.

LANGER, W. L., and GLEASON, S. E., *The Undeclared War 1940–41*, New York, 1953.

LANIEL, J., *Le drame indochinois*, Paris, 1957.

LARTÉGUY, J., *Les tambours de bronze*, Paris, 1965.

LeBAR, F. M., and HICKEY, G. C., *Ethnic Groups in Mainland Southeast Asia*, H.R.A.F. Press, New Haven, 1964.

—— and SUDDARD, A. (eds.), *Laos, its People, its Society, its Culture*, New Haven, Conn., 1960.

LE BOULANGER, P., *Histoire du Laos français*, Paris, 1931.

LECLÈRE, A., *Histoire du Cambodge*, Paris, 1914.

LEDERER, W. J., *A Nation of Sheep*, London, 1961.

LEHAUT, P., *La France et l'Angleterre en Asie*, vol. I, 'L'Indochine', Paris, 1892.

LE MAY, R. S., *An Asian Arcady, the Land and Peoples of Northern Siam*, Cambridge, 1926.

MANICH, M. L., *History of Laos*, Bangkok, 1967.

MASPÉRO, G. (ed.), *Un empire colonial français: l'Indochine*, two vols, Paris, 1929.

—— *Le royaume de Champa*, Paris, 1928.

MAYBON, C., *Histoire moderne du pays d'Annam*, Paris, 1920.

MAGNABAL, CAPITAINE, *L'Indochine française*, Paris, 1910.

MAHASILA VIRAVONG, *History of Laos*, U.S. Joint Publications Research Service, Washington, 1958 (mimeographed).

MEEKER, O., *The Little World of Laos*, New York, 1959.

MEIRING, D., *The Brinkman*, London, 1964.

MILLS, L. A., *British Malaya 1824–1867*, Journal of the Malayan Branch, Royal Asiatic Society, vol. III, Part II, Singapore, November 1925.

MITTON, G. E. (LADY SCOTT), *Scott of the Shan Hills*, London, 1936.

MODELSKI, G. A., *S.E.A.T.O., Six Studies*, Melbourne, 1962.

—— *International Conference on the Settlement of the Laotian Question 1961–62*, Australian National University, Canberra, 1962 (mimeographed).

MORDANT, GÉNÉRAL, *Au service de la France en Indochine*, Saigon, 1950.

MOUNTBATTEN OF BURMA, the EARL, *Report by S.A.C.S.E.A.*, London, H.M.S.O., 1951.

MURPHY, AGNES, *The Ideology of French Imperialism*, Washington, 1948.

NAVARRE, GÉNÉRAL H., *Agonie de l'Indochine*, Paris, 1956.

NORMAN, H., *The Far East*, London, 1895.

NUECHTERLEIN, D. E., *Thailand and the Struggle for Southeast Asia*, Cornell, 1965.

PATHAMMAVONG, SOMLITH, 'Compulsory Education in Laos' in *Compulsory Education in Cambodia, Laos and Vietnam*, U.N.E.S.C.O., Paris, 1955.

PELLIOT, P., *Mémoires sur les coutumes du Cambodge de Tcheou Ta-Kouan*, Paris, 1951.

PHANUPHANTUVONGSWARDJA, PRINCE, *Répression de la révolte de Vientiane*, Bangkok, 1926.

POUVOURVILLE, A. DE, *Études coloniales, l'affaire de Siam 1886–1896*, Paris, 1897.

—— *Francis Garnier*, Paris, 1946.

PURCELL, V., *The Revolution in South East Asia*, London, 1962.

REINACH, L. DE, *Le Laos*, Paris, two vols, 1901.

RENOUVIN, P., *La question d'extrême orient 1840–1940*, Paris, 1946.

ROBEQUAIN, C., *The Economic Development of French Indochina*, translated by Isabel A. Ward, London, 1944.

ROBERTS, S. H., *History of French Colonial Policy 1870–1925*, London, 2nd edn., 1963.

ROSE, SAUL, *Britain and South-East Asia*, London, 1962.

—— (ed.), *Politics in Southern Asia*, London, 1963.

ROSENMAN, S. I. (ed.), *The Public Papers and Addresses of Franklin D. Roosevelt: Victory and the Threshold of Peace*, New York, 1950.

ROY, JULES, *La bataille de Dien Bien Phu*, Paris, 1963.

Royal Institute of International Affairs:
Survey of International Affairs 1954, London, 1957.
Survey of International Affairs 1955–56, London, 1960.
Survey of International Affairs 1956–58, London, 1962.
Survey of International Affairs 1959–60, London, 1964.
Survey of International Affairs 1961, London, 1965.

SABATTIER, GÉNÉRAL G., *Le destin de l'Indochine. Souvenirs et documents, 1941–1951*, Paris, 1952.

SAINTENY, J., *Histoire d'une paix manquée*, Paris, 1953.

SASORITH, *see* Katay.

SCHLESINGER, ARTHUR J., Jr., *A Thousand Days*, London, 1965.

SCOTT, SIR J. G., *France and Tongking*, London, 1885.

—— *Burma, from the Earliest Times to the Present Day*, London, 1924.

—— (as Shway Yoe), *The Burman, his Life and Notions*, London, 1882.

SHERWOOD, R. E., *The White House Papers of Harry L. Hopkins*, two vols, London, 1948–9.

SIMMONDS, E. H. S., 'Independence and Political Rivalry in Laos 1945–61' in *Politics in Southern Asia*, S. Rose (ed.), London, 1963.

SISOUK NA CHAMPASSAK, *Storm Over Laos*, New York, 1961.

SIVARAM, M., *Mekong Clash and Far East Crisis*, Bangkok, 1941.

SMITH, NICOL, and BLAKE, CLARK, *Into Siam*, New York, 1945.

SMITH, ROGER M., 'Laos' in *Government and Politics of Southeast Asia*, G. McT. Kahin (ed.,) Cornell, 2nd edn., 1964.

SORENSEN, THEODORE C., *Kennedy*, London, 1965.

STEBBINS, R. P., *The United States in World Affairs 1954*, New York, 1956.

STETTINIUS, E. R., Jr., *Roosevelt and the Russians*, London, 1950.

STRONG, A. L., *Cash and Violence in Laos*, Peking, 1962.

TANHAM, G. K., *Communist Revolutionary Warfare*, New York, 1961.

THOMPSON, VIRGINIA, *French Indo-China*, London, 1937.

—— and ADLOFF, R., *Minority Problems in Southeast Asia*, Stanford, 1955.

—— also with R. EMERSON and L. A. MILLS: *Government and Nationalism in Southeast Asia*, New York, 1942.

TRUONG CHINH, *La Révolution d'août*, Hanoi, 1962.

VELLA, WALTER F., *Siam under Rama III*, New York, 1957.

VERCEL, R., *Francis Garnier à l'assaut des fleuves*, Paris, 1952.

WARNER, D., *The Last Confucian*, London (Penguin), 1964.

WEDERMEYER, GENERAL ALBERT C., *Wedermeyer Reports!*, New York, 1958.

WILSON, D. A., *Politics in Thailand*, Cornell, 1962.

WINT, GUY, *The British in Asia*, London, 1947 (new edn., 1954).

WISE, DAVID, and ROSS, THOMAS B., *The Invisible Government*, London, 1965.

WOLFKILL, G. (with JERRY A. ROSE), *Reported to be Alive*, London, 1966.

WOOD, W. A. R., *A History of Siam*, London, 1926.

X., *Le Laos*, Paris, 1948.

YOUNG, G., *The Hill Tribes of Northern Thailand*, Bangkok, 1962.

ARTICLES

BLOODWORTH, D., 'The General and the Gold Trade' in *Observer*, 15 December 1963.

BRIGGS, L. P., 'The Appearance and Historical Usage of the Terms Tai, Thai, Siamese and Lao' in *Journal of the American Oriental Society*, 1949, pp. 60–73.

BRITSCH, J., 'Après un an de neutralité au Laos' in *L'Afrique et l'Asie*, No. 63, 3ème trimestre, 1963.

BUI QUANG TUNG, 'Chao Anou, roi de Vientiane' in *Bulletin de la société des études indochinoises*, XXXIII (1958), pp. 401–6.

COEDÈS, G., 'À propos des anciens noms de Luang Prabang' in *Bulletin de l'école française d'extrême orient*, XVIII (1918), pp. 9–11.

CROZIER, B., 'Peking and the Laotian Crisis: an Interim Appraisal' in *China Quarterly*, No. 7 (July–Sept. 1961), pp. 128–37.

—— 'Peking and the Laotian Crisis: a Further Appraisal' in *China Quarterly*, No. 11 (July–Sept. 1962), pp. 116–23.

DUPARC, C. H., 'Le problème politique laotien' in *Politique Étrangère*, XII (November 1947), pp. 529–56.

FALL, B. B., 'International Relations of Laos' in *Kingdom of Laos*, R. de Berval (ed.), Saigon, 1959.

—— 'The Laos Tangle' in *International Journal*, 16 February 1961.

—— 'Reappraisal in Laos' in *Current History*, XLII (January 1962).

—— 'Problèmes des états poly-ethniques en Indochine' in *France-Asie*, No. 172 (Mar.–Apr. 1962).

—— 'A "Straight Zigzag": The Road to Socialism in North Vietnam' in *Communist Strategies in Asia*, A. D. Barnett (ed.), London, 1963.

FISHER, C. A., 'Some Comments on Population Growth in South-East Asia, with Special Reference to the Period since 1830' in *The Economic Development of South-East Asia*, C. D. Cowan (ed.), London, 1964.

HALPERN, J. M., 'Trade Patterns in Northern Laos' in *Proceedings of the Ninth Pacific Science Congress, 1957*, vol. 3, 1963.

—— 'Economic Development and American Aid in Laos' in *Practical Anthropology*, vol. 6, No. 4 (July–Aug. 1959).

—— 'American Policy in Laos' in *Michigan Alumnus Quarterly Review*, vol. LXVII, No. 18 (20 May 1961).

—— 'Traditional Medicine and the Role of the Phi in Laos' in *The Eastern Anthropologist*, vol. XVI, no. 3 (Sept.–Dec. 1963).

—— (with BARBARA HALPERN), 'Laos and America—A Retrospective View' in *The South Atlantic Quarterly*, vol. LXIII, No. 2, 1964.

HARRIS, R., 'Communism and Asia, Illusions and Misconceptions' in *International Affairs*, London, Royal Institute of International Affairs, January, 1963.

HICKEY, G. C., and SUDDARD, A., 'Laos: Pawn in Power Politics?' in *Current History*, XLI (December 1961), pp. 350–4.

LACOUTURE, J., 'Vers la rupture d'un équilibre?' in *Le Monde*, 16 April 1963.

LANDON, K. P., 'Thailand's Quarrel with France in Perspective' in *Far Eastern Quarterly*, I, No. 1 (November 1941), pp. 25–42.

Neak Chest Nyum, Phnom Penh, Cambodia, 'Avec le Prince Souvannaphouma; coup d'oeil neutre sur le Laos', special correspondent's despatch from Xieng Khouang, 23 Feb. 1961.

NHOUY ABHAY, 'People's names' in *Kingdom of Laos*, R. de Berval (ed.), Saigon, 1959.

PARET, P., 'The French Army and La Guerre Révolutionnaire' in *Journal of the Royal United Service Institution*, Feb. 1959.

PHOUVONG PHIMMASONE, 'The That Luang of Vientiane' in *France-Asie*, No. 82 (March 1953).

PIETRANTONI, E., 'La population du Laos de 1912 à 1945' in *Bulletin de la société des études indochinoises*, XXVIII, i (1953), pp. 25–38.

—— 'La population du Laos en 1943 dans son milieu géographique' in *Bulletin de la société des études indochinoises*, XXXII, iii (1957), pp. 223–43.

ROBERTS, CHALMERS M., 'The Day We Didn't Go to War' in *The Reporter*, XI (14 September 1954), pp. 31–35.

ROUX, H., 'Quelques minorités ethniques du nord Indochine' in *France–Asie*, 92, 93 (Jan.–Feb. 1954), pp. 143–413.

SIMMONDS, E. H. S., 'The Independent State of Laos' in *The World Today*, October 1957.

—— 'A Cycle of Political Events in Laos' in *The World Today*, February 1961.

—— 'Power Politics in Laos' in *The World Today*, December 1962.

—— 'Breakdown in Laos' in *The World Today*, July 1964.

—— 'The Evolution of Foreign Policy in Laos since Independence', *Modern Asian Studies*, II, 1 (1968).

SITHI-AMNUAI, P., 'Thailand and Neutralism' in *Far East Economic Review*, Hong Kong, 10 Jan. 1963.

SMITH, C. R., articles in *The Bangkok World*:
'Scare Them Away', 28 January 1961.
'Phoumi Moves North', 31 January 1961.
'Laos's Leisurely War', 2 February 1961.

SMITH, R. M., 'Laos in Perspective' in *Asian Survey*, vol. III, No. 1, January 1963.

SOUVANNAPHOUMA, PRINCE, 'Le Laos, avant-garde du monde libre' in *France–Asie*, No. 164 (Nov.–Dec. 1960), pp. 1427–34.

—— 'Le Laos: le fond du problème', in *France–Asie*, No. 166 (Mar.–Apr. 1961), pp. 1824–6.

—— Speech to the Geneva Conference, 14 June 1961, in *Pour un Laos pacifique, indépendant et neutre*, 'Royal Government of Laos', 1961.

STIRLING, J., 'On With the Puppet Show' in *Sunday Times*, 27 April 1964.

THOMPSON, VIRGINIA, 'Undeclared War along the Mekong' in *Far Eastern Survey*, XXII, vi (May 1953), pp. 62–66.

TRÈVE, CAPITAINE DE VAISSEAU, 'Notice sur Francis Garnier' in *Revue maritime et coloniale*, 1874.

WARNER, G., 'Escalation in Vietnam, the Precedents of 1954' in *International Affairs*, R.I.I.A., April 1965, pp. 267–77.

WYATT, D. K., 'Siam and Laos 1767–1827' in *Journal of South East Asian History*, IV, No. 2, September 1963, pp. 13–32.

INDEX

DATE DUE
